BON APPÉTIT

THE
CHRISTMAS
SEASON

BON APPÉTIT

THE CHRISTMAS SEASON

FROM THE EDITORS OF BON APPÉTIT

Condé Nast Books

Clarkson Potter/Publishers

NEW YORK

For *Bon Appétit* Magazine

William Garry, Editor-in-Chief
Laurie Glenn Buckle, Editor, Bon Appétit Books
Marcy MacDonald, Editorial Business Manager
Carri Marks, Editorial Production Director
Sybil Shimazu Neubauer, Editorial Administrator
Laura Samuel Meyn, Assistant Editor
Marcia Hartmann Lewis, Editorial Support
James Badham, Text
Sarah Belk King, Supplemental Text
H. Abigail Bok, Copy Editor
Gaylen Ducker Grody, Research
Elizabeth A. Matlin, Index
Jeanne Thiel Kelley, Food Research

For *Condé Nast* Books

Lisa Faith Phillips, Vice President and
    General Manager
Tom Downing, Direct Marketing Director
Deborah Williams, Operations Manager
Colleen P. Shire, Direct Marketing Manager
Jennifer Zalewski, Direct Marketing Assistant
Barbara Giordano, Direct Marketing Assistant

Produced in association with Patrick Filley Associates, Inc.

Designed by Vertigo Design, NYC

Front Jacket: Individual Frozen Cake "Presents"
    with Strawberry Sauce (page 58).

Published by Clarkson Potter/Publishers,
New York, New York.
Member of the Crown Publishing Group.

Random House, Inc. New York, Toronto, London,
Sydney, Auckland

CLARKSON N. POTTER, POTTER, and colophon
are trademarks of Random House, Inc.

Manufactured in Hong Kong

Library of Congress Cataloging-in-Publication Data
is available upon request.

ISBN 0-609-60725-1

10 9 8 7 6 5 4 3 2 1

FIRST EDITION

Condé Nast Web Address: www.bonappetit.com
Random House Web Address: www.randomhouse.com

Introduction 7

The Parties 11

Holiday Tea Party 12

Christmas Cocktail Party 20

Yuletide Dessert Party 28

Tree-Trimming Buffet 36

Family Christmas Eve Dinner 44

Elegant Christmas Eve Dinner 52

Christmas Breakfast 60

New Year's Eve Dinner à Deux 64

New Year's Day Brunch 70

New Year's Day Open House 76

The Menu 85

Christmas Dinners 86

The Main Course 88

The Starters 102

The Soups & Salads 110

The Side Dishes 118

The Breads & Rolls 126

The Desserts 134

The Guide 149

Gifts from the Kitchen 150

Christmas Cookies 160

Christmas Candies 168

Christmas Projects 176

Index 186

Acknowledgments 192

Shopping Directory 192

Contents

Introduction

Is there another word that conjures as many shared images
as *Christmas* does?

To say "Christmas" is to unlock a storehouse of favorite memories and evoke a
world of best-loved tastes, smells, sounds and scenes: candy canes and gingerbread, Christmas trees and simmering cider, carols and the quiet of a snowy
night, stockings and beribboned gifts, crowded streets and gathered family.

But Christmas is so much more than a word or day or date. It is a season
and a feeling, a spirit as infectious as laughter. We anticipate its arrival all year
long, and when it finally gets here, we celebrate it for almost a month, moving
from one party to the next, shopping, wrapping, decorating and cooking. This
is the time—that fast, furious, fabulously exciting stretch between Thanks-
giving and New Year's—when we want to (and try to) do it all: bake cookies,
hang lights, make a gingerbread house, craft a centerpiece, trim the tree,
throw parties and see all of our friends.

But in fact, no one can do it all.

What you *can* do is make December special by making it personal, editing
your to-do list down to those things that mean the most to you and the ones
you love. Maybe it includes a trip to a distant Christmas tree farm to chop

down one of your own, or a late-night drive through a neighborhood festooned with lights. It's likely that list also includes a festive party, at least one afternoon in the kitchen spent baking and a special meal or two with family or friends—or both.

The memorable parties, the big-deal meals and the kitchen projects are where this book comes in. In fact, that's how we've organized this versatile guide to the season, with three sections designed to simplify all of your entertaining and cooking and crafting options: The Parties, The Menu and The Guide. The first lays out ten different parties, with a menu, recipes and serving ideas for each. The second section is devoted entirely to the big Christmas Day meal, with best-of-the-best recipes for every course, appetizers through desserts. The Guide is full of decorating tips, as well as the kinds of kitchen-oriented holiday projects that make Christmas fun.

For many Christmas devotees, taking the annual plunge into the fast lane of holiday cheer leads immediately to an overwhelming urge to throw a party. That's understandable: how better to spread the spirit and share the feeling? In The Parties, you'll find game plans for a variety of occasions, from a post-shopping tea you might stage one afternoon early in December to a casual

tree-trimming buffet with a Mexican-themed mix of dishes. There are menus for Christmas Eve, both family-style and extravagantly elegant; for Christmas morning; and for New Year's Eve (à deux) and New Year's Day (with brunch and open-house options). Every menu comes with entertaining tips and hints, from how to bring the smells of Christmas into your home to ideas for simple seasonal centerpieces. And every recipe includes detailed do-ahead advice, which makes entertaining of any kind—but especially holiday entertaining—all the more possible.

In The Menu, it's all about the perfect-in-every-way Christmas lunch or dinner. This versatile section offers tempting recipes within every menu category so that you can mix and match to create the meal that most says "Christmas" to you. Start with the main course: Whether you had in mind roast beef, turkey, duck or goose, it's all here, plus seven other options. Add an appetizer, then a sit-down first course, if you like. There are side dishes of all kinds, including some wonderful breads (with do-ahead steps included). For those who choose to plan their big meal backwards, turn to desserts first, where you'll find the traditional (an elegant *croquembouche*) and the contemporary (a creamy, chestnut-flavored cheesecake).

Many favorite Christmas traditions get their start in the kitchen, where families gather to bake Santa-shaped cookies, stir up a holiday specialty (fruitcake, perhaps, or toffee) or decorate a gingerbread house. The Guide is just that: a guide to kitchen adventures of all kinds, including cookie baking, candy making and other gifts of food, plus projects ranging from place cards to a topiary tree of pears and kumquats. Spend an afternoon in the kitchen to fill your house with Christmas smells and yourself with Christmas spirit.

In addition to the menus and recipes that fill the pages of this book, we've also included gorgeous photographs packed with ideas for decorating your house and your table; sidebars that cover the bases, from the right way to carve a turkey to unusual ideas for wrapping presents; and recipe introductions that clarify and simplify, along with do-ahead notes and tips on where to buy some of the harder-to-find ingredients.

It's all here: the perfectly wonderful, perfectly possible Christmas.

T H E
Parties

Anyone who likes to entertain may fantasize about hosting a holiday tea, a cocktail party, a big Christmas Eve feast

and a New Year's Day bash. The reality is that at this especially busy time of the year—with all the shopping, the wrapping, the cooking and the routine everyday things that don't go away just because it's December—it's hard to find the time to get dinner on the table, let alone entertain in high style. But what about planning one special gathering? Now, that *is* possible, and in this section of the book you'll find ten party ideas, all eminently do-able.

There are menus here for small gatherings and large ones, elegant occasions and casual get-togethers. There are two approaches to Christmas Eve and three suggestions for ringing in the New Year (for the big Christmas meal itself, turn to the book's center section). In other words, there's something for everyone, a menu for every party. And they all come complete with lots of do-ahead tips and advice on everything from setting up the bar to decking the halls. So pick a party and start your planning.

Holiday Tea Party

MENU FOR EIGHT

SPARKLING WATER AND WHITE WINE

SMOKED-TURKEY SANDWICHES
WITH ARUGULA MAYONNAISE

SMOKED-SALMON SANDWICHES
WITH RED ONION RELISH

FRESH FRUIT PLATTER

MINI MINCEMEAT PIES

ORANGE-CURRANT SCONES

CLOTTED CREAM, BUTTER AND
FRUIT PRESERVES

DOUBLE-LEMON BARS

CHOCOLATE-WALNUT RUM BALLS

HOT TEA

12

Sitting down to afternoon tea with friends, especially if it's after a busy couple of hours at the mall, can be a relaxing way to close a hectic day. The sparkling china, the lustrous preserves on scones as fluffy as fresh snow, the delicate sandwiches and sweets in shapes and colors that would be right at home with the other gifts under the tree—it's all perfectly in step with the look and feel of Christmas. And the invitation itself makes for a perfect excuse to slow down and enjoy the day and the season.

If you're wondering how exactly you might spend the morning at the mall and the afternoon entertaining a party of eight, the answers are right here in this easy, do-ahead menu. It's really just sandwiches, scones and sweets, but each recipe comes with a flavor or a twist that makes it unique. The scones are accented with dried currants, for example; the lemon bars get a double dose of lemon (peel and juice).

So brew up a pot of tea (see the sidebar on page 16 for tips), put on some Christmas carols and set out this spread. Your friends will appreciate the break from mall madness.

SMOKED-TURKEY SANDWICHES WITH ARUGULA
MAYONNAISE, AND SMOKED-SALMON SANDWICHES WITH
RED ONION RELISH (ON TIERED PLATES); ORANGE-
CURRANT SCONES; CHOCOLATE-WALNUT RUM BALLS;
AND DOUBLE-LEMON BARS.

Smoked-Turkey Sandwiches with Arugula Mayonnaise

TRIMMING THE CRUSTS FROM THE BREAD AND
ADDING CHOPPED ARUGULA AND LEMON PEEL TO
THE MAYONNAISE MAKE THESE SIMPLE SANDWICHES
ELEGANT ENOUGH FOR TEA. INCLUDE A PLATTER OF
SEASONAL FRESH FRUIT IN THE MENU.

8 servings

⅔ cup mayonnaise
½ cup (packed) coarsely chopped arugula
  leaves plus 40 whole arugula leaves
  (about 5 large bunches total)
4 teaspoons minced shallots
4 teaspoons chopped fresh parsley
½ teaspoon (generous) grated lemon peel

16 thin slices firm white sandwich bread,
  crusts trimmed
14 ounces thinly sliced smoked turkey

Mix mayonnaise, chopped arugula, shallots,
parsley and lemon peel in small bowl. Season
with salt and pepper.

Place bread slices on work surface. Spread
mayonnaise mixture over each slice, dividing
equally. Top 8 bread slices with turkey, dividing equally. Place 5 arugula leaves atop turkey
on each. Top with remaining 8 bread slices,
mayonnaise side down, pressing gently to
adhere. Cut each sandwich diagonally into
quarters. *(Can be prepared up to 1 hour ahead.
Cover with clean, damp cloth and refrigerate.)*

Smoked-Salmon Sandwiches with Red Onion Relish

GARNISH THE PLATTER WITH CUCUMBER SLICES,
WATERCRESS SPRIGS AND RADISHES.

8 servings

8 ounces cream cheese, room temperature
6 tablespoons chopped chives
¼ cup crème fraîche or sour cream
2 tablespoons chopped fresh dill or 2 teaspoons
  dried dillweed

2 cups finely chopped red onions
2 tablespoons sugar
2 tablespoons rice vinegar

24 slices thin Danish-style pumpernickel bread*
12 ounces thinly sliced smoked salmon

Mix cream cheese, chives, crème fraîche and
dill in medium bowl. *(Can be prepared 1 day
ahead. Cover and refrigerate.)*

Mix red onions, sugar and vinegar in another
medium bowl. Let stand 10 minutes.

Spread each bread slice with about 1 tablespoon
cheese mixture to cover. Divide salmon among
16 bread slices. Sprinkle about 1 tablespoon red
onion mixture atop salmon on each bread slice.
Top each of 8 salmon-topped bread slices with
another salmon-topped bread slice, salmon side
up. Top each stack with 1 cheese-covered bread
slice, cheese side down, forming a total of
8 three-layer sandwiches. Cut each sandwich
diagonally into quarters. *(Can be made 1 hour
ahead. Cover with clean, damp cloth and chill.)*

**Danish-style pumpernickel bread is available in
the refrigerated deli section of many supermarkets.*

Mini Mincemeat Pies

MADE IN MINI MUFFIN CUPS, THESE LITTLE PIES ARE
A NOD TO THE BRITISH SIDE OF AFTERNOON TEA.
THE ENGLISH WOULD TOP THESE WITH A DAB OF
HARD SAUCE, MADE BY MIXING SOFTENED BUTTER
WITH POWDERED SUGAR AND A LITTLE BRANDY.

makes 18

1¾ cups all purpose flour
10 tablespoons powdered sugar
3¼ teaspoons grated orange peel
¼ teaspoon salt
½ cup (1 stick) chilled unsalted butter,
    cut into ½-inch pieces
1 large egg yolk
2 tablespoons (or more) orange juice

¾ cup purchased mincemeat from jar
3 tablespoons minced crystallized ginger
¼ teaspoon ground cinnamon
1 egg, beaten to blend (for glaze)

Mix flour, 6 tablespoons powdered sugar,
2½ teaspoons orange peel and salt in processor.
Add butter; process until mixture resembles
coarse meal. Whisk egg yolk and 2 tablespoons
orange juice in small bowl. Add to processor;
blend until moist clumps form, adding more
juice by teaspoonfuls if dry. Gather dough into
ball; flatten into disk. Chill at least 30 minutes.
*(Can be prepared up to 2 days ahead. Wrap in
plastic and keep chilled. Let stand at room
temperature 30 minutes before continuing.)*

Butter eighteen 1¾-inch-diameter mini muffin
cups. Mix mincemeat, crystallized ginger, cinnamon, remaining 4 tablespoons powdered
sugar and ¾ teaspoon peel in small bowl. Roll
out dough on floured surface to 17-inch round.

Using 2½-inch-diameter cookie cutter, cut out
18 dough rounds. Press 1 round into bottom
and up sides of each muffin cup. Using 1¾- to
2-inch-diameter cookie cutter, cut out 18 more
dough rounds (reroll dough if necessary). Fill
crust in each muffin cup with 1 heaping teaspoon mincemeat filling. Brush edges of smaller dough rounds with some of egg glaze. Place
1 round atop filling in each muffin cup, glazed
side down, pressing dough edges to seal. Cut
small X in center of each pie. *(Can be prepared
4 hours ahead. Cover pies and remaining egg glaze
separately and then refrigerate.)*

Preheat oven to 375°F. Brush pies with remaining egg glaze. Bake until crusts are golden,
about 20 minutes. Using small knife, cut
around pies to loosen; turn out onto rack. Serve
warm or at room temperature.

Teatime

A PROPER POT OF TEA

Fill the kettle with cold tap water and bring to a boil. Pour a little bit of hot water into the teapot to warm it. Swirl the water around inside the pot, then discard the water. Put in one teaspoon of loose tea per cup. Pour the water onto the tea leaves and brew three to five minutes. Pour the tea through a strainer into cups.

WHAT TO SERVE WITH TEA

A pitcher of milk, a plate of lemon slices and a bowl of granulated or lump sugar are musts. You can also offer honey and low-fat milk.

HELPFUL HINTS

❋ Arrange the goodies on a variety of serving pieces, including tiered trays, plates and platters, lining them with doilies if you like.

❋ Garnish platters with small bunches of red grapes or dried apricots for color.

❋ When serving bar-type sweets, cut them into manageable sizes; two fingers wide is the guideline most caterers suggest. (The same goes for cake: Cut slices in half; guests can always go back for seconds.)

❋ Keep scones warm by wrapping them in a fresh linen or cotton napkin.

❋ Use ramekins, small crocks or little silver dishes for serving sweet butter, jam and clotted cream (available at specialty foods stores).

❋ For each guest, set out the following: knife, fork and spoon; cup and saucer or mug; napkin; and luncheon-size plate.

❋ To keep a pot of tea warm, cover with a tea cozy or wrap with a linen napkin (leaving the top and spout exposed) and tie in a knot.

Orange-Currant Scones

WHAT'S AFTERNOON TEA WITHOUT SCONES? THESE (OPPOSITE) ARE TERRIFIC WITH BUTTER, CLOTTED CREAM AND FRUIT PRESERVES.

makes 16

  3 cups all purpose flour
$\frac{1}{3}$ cup sugar
$2\frac{1}{2}$ teaspoons baking powder
$\frac{3}{4}$ teaspoon salt
$\frac{1}{2}$ teaspoon baking soda
$\frac{1}{2}$ cup (1 stick) chilled unsalted butter, cut into pieces
$\frac{1}{2}$ cup chilled solid vegetable shortening, cut into pieces
  1 cup plus 2 tablespoons chilled buttermilk
$\frac{3}{4}$ cup dried currants, dried cranberries or dried cherries
  1 tablespoon grated orange peel
    Additional sugar

Preheat oven to 425°F. Line large baking sheet with foil. Stir flour, $\frac{1}{3}$ cup sugar, baking powder, salt and baking soda in large bowl to blend. Add butter and shortening; using fingertips, rub in until coarse meal forms. Add 1 cup buttermilk, currants and orange peel. Stir gently until dough comes together in large moist clumps. Gather dough into ball. Transfer dough to lightly floured work surface. Gently knead 3 or 4 turns to combine well. Divide into 2 pieces; flatten into $\frac{3}{4}$-inch-thick rounds. Using floured knife, cut each round into 8 wedges. Transfer wedges to prepared baking sheet. Brush with remaining 2 tablespoons buttermilk and sprinkle with additional sugar.

Bake scones until light golden brown, about 15 minutes. *(Can be prepared up to 4 hours ahead. Cover loosely and keep at room temperature.)* Serve warm or at room temperature.

Double-Lemon Bars

WITH BOTH FRESH LEMON JUICE AND LEMON PEEL IN THE CURD, THESE BITE-SIZE SWEETS (OPPOSITE) ARE EXTRA-DELICIOUS. CANDIED VIOLETS WOULD MAKE A PRETTY GARNISH.

makes 24

1½ cups all purpose flour
½ cup powdered sugar
¾ cup (1½ sticks) butter, cut into pieces, room temperature

4 eggs
1½ cups sugar
½ cup fresh lemon juice
1 tablespoon plus 1 teaspoon all purpose flour
1 tablespoon grated lemon peel

Powdered sugar

Preheat oven to 350°F. Combine 1½ cups flour and ½ cup powdered sugar in processor. Add butter and cut in, using on/off turns, until mixture resembles coarse meal. Press into bottom of 9 x 13 x 2-inch baking dish. Bake until crust is golden, about 20 minutes. Remove from oven. Maintain oven temperature.

Beat eggs, 1½ cups sugar, lemon juice, 1 tablespoon plus 1 teaspoon flour and lemon peel in medium bowl to blend. Pour into crust. Bake until mixture is set, about 20 minutes. Cool.

Cut into 24 bars. *(Can be prepared 1 day ahead. Refrigerate in airtight container.)* Sift powdered sugar over top before serving.

Chocolate-Walnut Rum Balls

THESE DENSE, MOIST TREATS ARE IRRESISTIBLE. IF YOU HAVE TIME TO MAKE AN EXTRA BATCH, THEY ARE AN IDEAL PARTY FAVOR, ENCLOSED IN A FESTIVE GIFT BAG AND TIED WITH GROSGRAIN RIBBON. (THEY'LL KEEP IN THE REFRIGERATOR FOR DAYS.)

makes about 45

1 cup semisweet chocolate chips (about 6 ounces)
1 cup sugar
3 tablespoons light corn syrup
½ cup dark rum
2½ cups finely crushed vanilla wafer cookies (about 10 ounces)
1 cup finely chopped walnuts (about 4 ounces)

Stir chocolate in top of double boiler set over simmering water until melted and smooth. Remove from over water. Whisk in ½ cup sugar and corn syrup, then rum. Mix vanilla wafers and walnuts in medium bowl to blend; add chocolate mixture and stir to blend well.

Place remaining ½ cup sugar in shallow bowl. For each rum ball, roll 1 scant tablespoon chocolate mixture into generous 1-inch ball. Roll balls in sugar to coat evenly. Cover and refrigerate at least overnight and up to 5 days.

Christmas Cocktail Party

MENU FOR SIXTEEN

CHAMPAGNE AND COCKTAILS

SWEET AND SPICY OLIVES

FRENCH BREAD AND BREADSTICKS

CAVIAR STARS

PROSCIUTTO-WRAPPED ASPARAGUS

CHICKEN, WILD RICE AND PECAN
SALAD IN ROMAINE SPEARS

WILD MUSHROOM AND CRAB
CHEESECAKE

SMOKED BLUEFISH DIP

HOLIDAY EGGNOG

The holidays are often the time when we catch up with old friends in far-away places. We send cards, letters and photographs; make those annual phone calls; or pack up the car and take to the road. But Christmas is also an opportunity to remember all those people who live in the same city with us, people we love to spend time with but don't get to see often enough. A cocktail party is a stylishly simple solution. And with this menu, which combines eggnog, Champagne, cocktails and delicious nibbles, the good cheer will commence with the first knock on the door.

Now, if you think planning food and drinks for 16 at this hectic time of year just sounds like more stress, think again. Every recipe here can be prepared ahead, and all are easy yet still elegant, like the Caviar Stars (purchased puff pastry, shaped into stars, baked and topped with sour cream and caviar). A savory cheesecake flavored with wild mushrooms and fresh crab makes a beautiful centerpiece, while homemade eggnog is a welcome indulgence.

So don't let another year slip by—this Christmas, raise a glass of Champagne and toast your friends.

CHICKEN, WILD RICE AND PECAN SALAD IN
ROMAINE SPEARS (IN GLASS COMPOTE);
SWEET AND SPICY OLIVES; AND CAVIAR STARS.

Sweet and Spicy Olives

START PREPARING THESE AT LEAST ONE DAY BEFORE
THE PARTY (AND UP TO TWO WEEKS AHEAD). THE
OLIVE OIL MARINADE MAKES A DELICIOUS DIP FOR
FRENCH BREAD; BREADSTICKS ADD CRUNCH.

makes about 3 cups

6 ounces imported black olives
   (such as Kalamata)
6 ounces imported green olives
   (such as Greek)
1½ cups olive oil
4 1 x 2-inch orange peel strips
4 1 x 2-inch lemon peel strips
1 tablespoon fennel seeds, lightly crushed in
   mortar with pestle
1 teaspoon dried crushed red pepper

Sliced French bread and breadsticks

Rinse olives; pat dry. Place 1 olive on work surface and crush with flat side of large knife until
skin begins to break. Repeat with remaining
olives. Place in medium bowl. Combine all
remaining ingredients except bread in heavy
small saucepan. Heat until oil bubbles around
the edge. Pour over olives. Let stand overnight,
stirring occasionally. *(Can be made 2 weeks
ahead. Cover and refrigerate. Bring olives to room
temperature before serving.)*

Drain oil from olives into small bowl. Place
olives in medium bowl. Serve olives, oil, bread
and breadsticks together.

Caviar Stars

THESE ELEGANT HORS D'OEUVRES (OPPOSITE) ARE
PERFECT FOR HOLIDAY ENTERTAINING. IF YOU HAVE
EXTRA TIME, PIPE THE SOUR CREAM DECORATIVELY
INTO THE CENTER OF THE PASTRIES USING A PASTRY
BAG FITTED WITH A MEDIUM STAR TIP.

makes 50

2 sheets frozen puff pastry (one 17.3-ounce
   package), thawed
2 eggs beaten with 2 teaspoons water
   (for glaze)

1⅓ cups chilled sour cream
2 2-ounce jars black or golden caviar
¼ cup chopped fresh chives or green onion tops

Preheat oven to 400°F. Roll out 1 puff pastry
sheet on lightly floured surface to 11-inch
square. Trim edges neatly, forming 10-inch
square. Cut dough into twenty-five 2-inch
squares. At each corner of 1 square, make
diagonal cut toward center (without cutting
through center). Fold every other point to center and press to seal. Repeat with remaining
squares. Repeat rolling and cutting with
remaining puff pastry sheet. Brush pastries
lightly with glaze; arrange on baking sheets.

Bake pastries until golden and puffed, about
12 minutes. Cool on sheets. *(Can be prepared
4 hours ahead. Let stand at room temperature.)*

Spoon sour cream into center of each pastry.
Place ¼ teaspoon caviar on top of each pastry
(reserve remaining caviar for another use).
Garnish with chives and serve.

Prosciutto-wrapped Asparagus

VARIATIONS OF THIS EASY APPETIZER HAVE BEEN
POPULAR ON THE CATERING CIRCUIT FOR YEARS.
ASPARAGUS ALWAYS MAKES ELEGANT FINGER FOOD,
AND THE PROSCIUTTO AND GARLICKY GOAT CHEESE
SPREAD ADD PLENTY OF FLAVOR. THIS CAN BE
SERVED WARM OR AT ROOM TEMPERATURE.

makes 32

2½ ounces soft fresh goat cheese
    (such as Montrachet)
1 garlic clove, minced
¼ teaspoon ground black pepper

32 asparagus spears, trimmed
16 paper-thin prosciutto slices

Mix goat cheese, garlic and pepper in small
bowl to blend. Set aside.

Cook asparagus in large pot of boiling salted
water until crisp-tender, about 5 minutes.
Transfer to bowl of ice water and cool. Drain
and pat dry. Arrange prosciutto slices on work
surface. Cut each in half crosswise. Spread
1 side of each prosciutto slice with cheese mixture. Place 1 asparagus spear at 1 short end of
each slice. Roll up tightly. Transfer to baking
sheet. *(Can be prepared 1 day ahead. Cover tightly
with plastic wrap and refrigerate.)*

Preheat oven to 400°F. Bake asparagus until
heated through, about 5 minutes. Transfer
asparagus to platter and serve.

Chicken, Wild Rice and Pecan Salad in Romaine Spears

PURCHASED ROASTED CHICKEN MAKES THIS
APPETIZER A SNAP TO PREPARE. GUESTS SCOOP THE
SALAD INTO LETTUCE LEAVES FOR EASY EATING.

16 servings

9 cups canned low-salt chicken broth
12 ounces wild rice

1 3½- to 4-pound roasted chicken, skinned,
    boned, meat cut into ⅓-inch pieces
1½ red bell peppers, chopped
3 bunches arugula, chopped
⅓ cup (generous) chopped green onions
4½ tablespoons soy sauce
4½ tablespoons rice vinegar
4½ tablespoons oriental sesame oil

3 cups pecans, toasted, chopped
5 heads romaine lettuce

Bring broth to boil in large saucepan. Add rice
and bring to boil. Reduce heat to low, cover and
cook just until tender, about 50 minutes. Drain.

Transfer rice to large bowl. Mix in chicken, bell
peppers, arugula and green onions. Whisk soy
sauce, vinegar and oil in small bowl. Pour over
salad and mix to coat. Season to taste with salt
and pepper. *(Can be prepared 4 hours ahead.
Cover and refrigerate.)*

Mix pecans into salad. Place salad in center of
platter. Reserve outer romaine leaves for
another use. Arrange inner leaves on platter
around salad and then serve.

Wild Mushroom and Crab Cheesecake

THIS ELEGANT APPETIZER CAN BE MADE ENTIRELY
THE DAY AHEAD AND REFRIGERATED.

16 servings

crust

1¾ cups fresh breadcrumbs from French bread
1 cup freshly grated Parmesan cheese
  (about 3 ounces)
6 tablespoons (¾ stick) butter, melted

filling

1 tablespoon olive oil
1 cup chopped onion
1 cup chopped red bell pepper
4 cups coarsely chopped assorted fresh wild
  mushrooms (such as crimini, oyster and
  stemmed shiitake)

3 8-ounce packages cream cheese,
  room temperature
1 4-ounce package cream cheese,
  room temperature
2 teaspoons salt
1 teaspoon ground black pepper
4 large eggs

½ cup whipping cream
10 ounces crabmeat (about 2 cups),
  drained well, picked over
1 cup (about 4 ounces) grated smoked
  Gouda cheese
½ cup chopped fresh parsley

1 French bread baguette, sliced, toasted

FOR CRUST: Preheat oven to 350°F. Mix all
ingredients in medium bowl until well blended.
Press mixture onto bottom (not sides) of 9-inch-
diameter springform pan with 2¾-inch-high
sides. Bake crust until golden brown, about
15 minutes. Cool crust while preparing filling.
Maintain oven temperature.

FOR FILLING: Heat 1 tablespoon oil in heavy
large skillet over medium-high heat. Add
chopped onion and bell pepper and sauté
2 minutes. Add mushrooms and sauté until
liquid evaporates and mushrooms begin to
brown, about 10 minutes. Cool.

Using electric mixer, beat cream cheese, salt
and pepper in large bowl until mixture is fluffy.
Beat in eggs 1 at a time, then whipping cream.
Mix in vegetable mixture, crabmeat, smoked
Gouda and chopped parsley.

Pour filling over crust. Place cheesecake on baking sheet. Bake until cake puffs and browns on
top but center moves slightly when pan is shaken,
about 1 hour 30 minutes. Transfer pan to rack
and cool. *(Cheesecake can be prepared 1 day ahead.
Cover with plastic and refrigerate.)*

Run small sharp knife around pan sides to loosen
cheesecake. Release pan sides. Transfer cheesecake to platter. Serve cold or at room temperature
with toasted baguette slices.

Cocktails, anyone?

THE BASIC BAR

Vodka
Gin
Bourbon
Scotch
Whiskey
Rum
Dry vermouth
Tequila
Bitters
Triple sec
An aperitif such as
    Lillet, Dubonnet
    or Campari
Red wine
White wine
Champagne

BASIC BAR TOOLS

Cocktail shaker
Cocktail strainer
Glassware: highballs, rocks,
    flutes, all purpose wine-
    glasses, Martini glasses and
    Margarita glasses
Ice bucket
Ice cracker
Cocktail napkins
Cocktail stirrers
Cutting board and small,
    sharp knife for fruit
Several dish towels
Tongs
Pitchers
Blender
Jiggers
Corkscrew
Bottle opener

BASIC CONDIMENTS

Cocktail olives
Cocktail onions
Lemon wedges and twists
Lime wedges
Orange wedges and twists
Prepared horseradish
Tabasco sauce
Worcestershire sauce
Kosher or sea salt
    (for Margaritas)
Celery seed and black pepper
    (for Bloody Marys)

BASIC MIXERS

Soda water
Tonic water
Mineral water
Cola
Diet cola
Ginger ale
Tomato juice
Orange juice
Rose's lime juice

Smoked Bluefish Dip

SMOKED WHITEFISH OR SMOKED TROUT WILL WORK
JUST AS WELL IN THIS RECIPE.

makes about 2 ¼ cups

- ½ cup sour cream
- ½ cup cream cheese (about 4 ounces), room temperature
- 2 tablespoons whipping cream
- 1½ tablespoons fresh lemon juice
- 3 garlic cloves, finely chopped
- 1 tablespoon chopped fresh dill
- ½ teaspoon Worcestershire sauce
- ½ teaspoon ground black pepper
- ½ teaspoon Old Bay seasoning
- 4 drops hot pepper sauce
- 1 pound smoked bluefish or smoked whitefish chubs,* skin and bones removed, flaked with fork
- 2 tablespoons chopped fresh chives
  Assorted crudités
  Toasted baguette slices

Beat first 10 ingredients in large bowl until well blended. Fold all but ¼ cup fish into dip. Transfer to serving bowl. Garnish dip with reserved ¼ cup fish and chives. *(Can be prepared 1 day ahead. Cover and refrigerate.)* Serve with crudités and baguette slices.

Available at specialty foods stores, some delicatessens and some supermarkets.

Holiday Eggnog

THE CLASSIC CHRISTMAS LIBATION (ABOVE), RICH
AND DELICIOUS. (BAKING ANGEL FOOD CAKES IS A
GREAT WAY TO USE THE LEFTOVER EGG WHITES.)

16 servings

- 6 cups whipping cream
- 6 cups half and half
- 24 large egg yolks
- 2 cups sugar
- 1 tablespoon ground nutmeg
- 1⅓ cups (about) bourbon
- ⅔ cup (about) dark rum

  Additional ground nutmeg

Bring cream and half and half to simmer in large deep pot. Whisk yolks and sugar in very large bowl. Gradually whisk in half of hot cream mixture. Return mixture to pot. Stir over medium-low heat until custard thickens and leaves path on back of spoon when finger is drawn across, about 5 minutes (do not boil). Strain into bowl. Stir in 1 tablespoon nutmeg. Cool slightly. Chill. *(Can be made 1 day ahead. Keep chilled.)* Mix in bourbon and rum to taste.

Divide eggnog among glasses or cups. Sprinkle with additional nutmeg.

Yuletide Dessert Party

MENU FOR TWELVE

CHAMPAGNE

CHOCOLATE-ORANGE
BÛCHE DE NOËL

RASPBERRY LINZER TART

CHRISTMAS TURTLES

GINGER AND SPICE
SHORTBREAD DIAMONDS

HOLIDAY FRUITCAKE

COFFEE

28

The days of December may be short, but their hours tend to be packed with pre-Christmas activity. There is shopping to do, gifts to wrap and school performances to attend. There are trees to trim, lights to string, wreaths to hang and snowmen to build. But at night, things slow down. The malls shut, the weary return home and everyone breathes a sigh. It's a perfect time for a gathering. And if you don't feel like hosting a sit-down dinner for twelve, a dessert party is a realistic alternative.

Preparations for this festive shindig can begin days, even a week beforehand. The centerpiece is a classic *bûche de noël,* the log-shaped cake that has graced Christmas spreads for generations. This version features an orange-cream filling and a rich chocolate ganache icing. Another favorite, fruitcake (here, filled with dates, pecans, walnuts and raisins), makes an appearance, along with a wonderful raspberry tart, shortbread, and some quickly made "turtle" candies. Offer Champagne to guests as they walk through the door, then coffee to go with their platefuls of treats. It's a Christmas respite of the sweetest kind.

HOLIDAY FRUITCAKE; CHRISTMAS TURTLES AND GINGER
AND SPICE SHORTBREAD DIAMONDS (ON TIERED PLATES);
AND CHOCOLATE-ORANGE BÛCHE DE NOËL.

Chocolate-Orange Bûche de Noël

THIS UPDATED VERSION OF THE CHRISTMAS CLASSIC (OPPOSITE) FEATURES ORANGE MOUSSE IN A FLOURLESS CHOCOLATE CAKE ROLL, CHOCOLATE ICING AND A DECADENT GARNISH OF TRUFFLES.

12 servings

cake

6 large eggs, separated
¼ teaspoon cream of tartar
12 tablespoons sugar

⅓ cup plus 1 tablespoon unsweetened cocoa powder, sifted

filling

2 tablespoons boiling water
1 teaspoon unflavored gelatin
1½ cups chilled whipping cream
¼ cup powdered sugar
1 teaspoon grated orange peel
½ teaspoon vanilla extract

ganache

½ cup whipping cream
6 ounces bittersweet (not unsweetened) or semisweet chocolate, chopped
2 tablespoons light corn syrup
1 tablespoon Grand Marnier or other orange liqueur

Powdered sugar
12 purchased chocolate truffles

FOR CAKE: Preheat oven to 350°F. Butter 15 x 10 x 1-inch jelly-roll pan. Line bottom with waxed paper, allowing 1-inch overhang on short sides. Butter paper. Lightly dust paper and pan with flour; tap out excess. Using electric mixer, beat egg whites in large bowl until foamy. Add cream of tartar and beat until soft peaks form. Gradually add 6 tablespoons sugar, beating until stiff peaks form. Set aside.

Beat egg yolks, ⅓ cup cocoa powder and remaining 6 tablespoons sugar in another large bowl until thick, about 2 minutes. Stir ¼ of whites into yolk mixture to lighten. Fold in remaining whites. Gently spread batter in prepared jelly-roll pan.

Bake until cake springs back when pressed in center, about 15 minutes. Transfer pan to rack. Cool completely. Sift remaining 1 tablespoon cocoa powder over cake. Line baking sheet with foil. Invert cake onto sheet. Peel off paper.

FOR FILLING: Place 2 tablespoons boiling water in small bowl. Sprinkle gelatin over. Let soften 10 minutes. Heat ¼ cup cream in small saucepan over medium-low heat just until warm. Add to gelatin mixture; stir until gelatin dissolves. Using electric mixer, beat remaining 1¼ cups chilled whipping cream, powdered sugar, orange peel and vanilla extract in large bowl until soft peaks form. Add gelatin mixture. Beat until stiff peaks form.

Spread filling over cake, leaving 1-inch border on sides. Using foil as aid and starting at 1 long side of cake, gently roll up cake, enclosing filling. Arrange roll, seam side down, on platter. Cover tightly and refrigerate until filling is set, at least 8 hours or overnight.

FOR GANACHE: Bring cream to simmer in heavy medium saucepan. Remove from heat. Add chocolate, corn syrup and liqueur. Stir until mixture is smooth. Let ganache stand until cool and thick.

Whisk ganache just until soft peaks form (do not overmix). Spread ganache over roll. Using tines of fork, draw lines through ganache to represent tree bark. (*Cake can be made 1 day ahead. Tent with foil and refrigerate.*)

Sift powdered sugar over roll. Surround with chocolate truffles and serve.

Raspberry Linzer Tart

IN THIS TAKE ON THE CLASSIC LINZERTORTE, AN
ALMOND-CINNAMON COOKIE CRUST IS THE
DELICIOUS BASE FOR LAYERS OF CHOCOLATE AND
RASPBERRIES. COOKIE-CRUST STARS TOP IT OFF.

12 servings

crust

⅔ cup (packed) golden brown sugar

½ cup (1 stick) unsalted butter,
room temperature

1 large egg

1½ cups all purpose flour

½ cup ground toasted blanched almonds
(about 2½ ounces)

¾ teaspoon ground cinnamon

½ teaspoon baking powder

½ teaspoon salt

filling

6 ounces semisweet chocolate chips
(about 1 cup)

1 ½-pint basket raspberries

½ cup seedless raspberry jam

Powdered sugar

1 cup chilled whipping cream

1 tablespoon sugar

FOR CRUST: Using electric mixer, beat sugar,
butter and egg in medium bowl until creamy.
Add flour, almonds, cinnamon, baking powder
and salt; beat just until well blended. Measure
¾ cup of dough; flatten into disk. Wrap in plastic; chill. Using floured fingertips, press
remaining dough over bottom and up sides of
9-inch-diameter tart pan with removable bottom. Pierce dough in several places with fork.
Chill at least 1 hour. *(Can be made ahead. Keep
chilled up to 1 day or freeze up to 1 week. If
frozen, let dough stand 1 hour at room temperature before continuing.)*

Preheat oven to 375°F. Bake crust until light
golden, piercing with toothpick if crust bubbles, about 15 minutes. Transfer to rack and
cool. Maintain oven temperature.

Roll out chilled dough disk on generously
floured surface to ⅛-inch thickness. Cut dough
into stars, using 2-inch and 3-inch star cookie
cutters. Transfer cookies to baking sheet. Bake
until cookies are light golden, about 6 minutes.
Transfer cookies to racks and cool. Maintain
oven temperature.

FOR FILLING: Melt chocolate chips in top of
double boiler set over simmering water, stirring
until smooth. Cool 5 minutes. Spread chocolate
over bottom of crust. Arrange berries over
chocolate, spacing evenly. Stir jam in heavy
small saucepan over low heat until melted and
smooth. Spoon jam over raspberries.

Bake tart until crust is golden brown, about
35 minutes (filling will still appear slightly liquid but will set up as tart cools). Transfer tart to
rack and cool. Arrange stars atop tart, overlapping points. *(Can be prepared 6 hours ahead.
Keep at room temperature.)* Dust with powdered
sugar. Beat whipping cream and sugar in large
bowl until stiff peaks form. Serve tart with
sweetened whipped cream.

Christmas Turtles

SURPRISINGLY SIMPLE TO MAKE, THESE CARAMEL, CHOCOLATE AND PECAN CANDIES (AT LEFT, WITH GINGER AND SPICE SHORTBREAD DIAMONDS, PAGE 34) ARE ALSO AN EXCELLENT PARTY FAVOR.

makes about 24

2 cups (about) pecan halves
1⅓ cups whipping cream
1 cup sugar
½ cup light corn syrup
⅓ cup milk
¼ cup (½ stick) butter
1 teaspoon vanilla extract

12 ounces bittersweet (not unsweetened) or semisweet chocolate, chopped

Butter 2 large nonstick cookie sheets. On prepared sheets, arrange pecan halves in clusters resembling turtles. Combine cream, sugar, corn syrup, milk and butter in heavy medium saucepan. Stir over low heat until sugar dissolves. Clip candy thermometer onto side of pan. Increase heat to high and boil without stirring until mixture turns golden, bubbles thickly and thermometer registers 234°F, swirling pan occasionally, about 15 minutes. Remove mixture from heat. Stir in vanilla. Immediately drop 1 tablespoon caramel mixture onto center of each pecan cluster. Cool slightly.

Stir chocolate in top of double boiler over simmering water until melted. Drizzle 1 tablespoon chocolate over each candy. Chill until chocolate sets, about 30 minutes. *(Can be prepared 1 week ahead. Cover and keep refrigerated.)*

Ginger and Spice Shortbread Diamonds

THE PROCESSOR-QUICK DOUGH FOR THESE COOKIES (BELOW) COMES TOGETHER IN MINUTES. SAVE THE LEFTOVER IRREGULAR PIECES TO ENJOY AS A SNACK.

makes about 21

10 tablespoons (1¼ sticks) chilled
   unsalted butter
½ cup powdered sugar
1¼ cups all purpose flour
5 teaspoons grated peeled fresh ginger
1 teaspoon vanilla extract
½ teaspoon ground cloves
½ teaspoon ground allspice
½ teaspoon ground nutmeg
¼ teaspoon salt

Additional powdered sugar (optional)

Preheat oven to 350°F. Line 8-inch square glass baking dish with foil. Blend butter and ½ cup powdered sugar in processor. Add flour, ginger, vanilla, cloves, allspice, nutmeg and salt and process until mixture forms moist clumps. Gather dough into ball. Transfer to prepared dish. Using waxed paper dipped into powdered sugar as aid, press out dough evenly in dish. Freeze 15 minutes. Using ruler as guide, cut dough into 6 equal strips. Turn dish 45° and cut again into 6 strips, creating diamond shapes. Pierce each diamond with fork.

Bake shortbread until golden brown and firm to touch, about 50 minutes. Immediately recut shortbread into diamonds. Cool completely in dish on rack. Sift powdered sugar over short-bread, if desired. *(Can be prepared 1 week ahead. Store in airtight container.)*

Holiday Fruitcake

FRUITCAKE NEVER TASTED SO GOOD. (THE RECIPE IS IDEAL FOR A PARTY LIKE THIS SINCE IT CAN BE MADE A COUPLE OF DAYS AHEAD.)

12 servings

3 cups all purpose flour
1 tablespoon baking powder
½ teaspoon salt
1⅔ cups chopped pitted dates
1 cup chopped pecans
1 cup chopped walnuts
½ cup raisins
½ cup golden raisins
2 cups sugar
1 cup (2 sticks) unsalted butter,
   room temperature
4 large eggs
2 teaspoons vanilla extract
¼ teaspoon lemon extract

Preheat oven to 325°F. Butter and then flour 10-inch-diameter angel food or tube pan. Combine first 3 ingredients in large bowl. Add dates, pecans, walnuts and all raisins and toss to coat. Using electric mixer, beat sugar and butter in another large bowl until light and fluffy.

Add eggs 1 at a time, beating well after each addition. Add both extracts. Fold in dry ingredients until just combined (batter will resemble cookie dough). Spoon batter into prepared pan. Smooth top. Bake until cake is golden and tester inserted near center comes out clean, about 1 hour 45 minutes. Cool cake in pan on rack 10 minutes. Using sharp knife, cut around edges of cake to loosen. Turn out cake onto rack; cool completely. *(Can be made 2 days ahead. Wrap tightly in plastic.)*

The scent of Christmas

A QUICK WHIFF of gingerbread, the simple smell of cedar and the tangy fragrance of oranges have the ability to evoke vivid memories of Christmases past. Filling the house with seasonal scents is a big part of conjuring up happy memories and creating new ones. However, pleasurable as they may be, most Christmas smells are assertive and can overpower the aromas of food. So place highly scented decorations like clove-studded pomanders away from the dining table.

FRAGRANT IDEAS

❋ Put a large pot of mulled cider on the stove to simmer about 30 minutes before guests are due to arrive so the smell of apples and spices will waft through the house.

❋ Place a basket of pomanders, bundles of cinnamon sticks and evergreen clippings by the front door and in the powder room.

❋ Time the last batch of spice cookies so that you take them from the oven just as guests arrive.

❋ Hang a fresh bay leaf wreath in the kitchen. The herb's clean, natural scent echoes those used in stuffing recipes and other seasonal dishes. It will cheer the cook, too.

❋ Wire stems of fresh greenery together (trimmings from the tree are fine) to make garlands. Drape the garlands over the tops of mirrors, over doorways and on the mantel, securing with small nails or push pins if necessary.

❋ Place pots of blooming narcissus near the front door, and give one to each guest on departure at the end of the evening.

❋ Light a fire in the fireplace; its woodsy scent will fill the room and create an aura of coziness.

❋ Light scented candles and place them in the powder room, near the front door and in other locations away from food. (Note: Always choose candles made with real oils and essences; their scent is more natural and will keep your home from smelling like a gift shop.)

Tree-Trimming Buffet

MENU FOR SIXTEEN

TORTILLA CHIPS WITH
SALSA AND GUACAMOLE

SPICY BEEF AND SAUSAGE
TACOS

CHICKEN AND CORN
ENCHILADAS

LAYERED RICE SALAD WITH
RED AND GREEN SALSAS

MEXICAN BEER AND SODAS

MOCHA MOUSSE TORTE

PUMPKIN SPICE COOKIES

MULLED CIDER WITH
WINTER SPICES

everyone loves to decorate the tree. It's the very symbol of Christmas, the icon of the season. Big or small, noble or Douglas fir, the tree *says* Christmas, and decorating it together with friends and family does, too. Creating a casual party around the activity is fun and makes excellent use of that rarest of Christmas commodities: time. The tree will look great, and you'll get to see favorite people.

This menu is an easy, Mexican-style buffet made up of foods everyone loves: chicken enchiladas (start with a purchased roast chicken to simplify things), beef and sausage tacos (don't forget all the tasty garnishes) and other south-of-the-border goodies. In keeping with that theme, you might line the outdoor entryway to your house with luminarias, the little lanterns made from sand, paper bags and candles. (Another strategic tip: String the lights on the tree in advance.) And when the last ornament has been hung in the perfect place, you can all gather near the tree for a slice of mocha cream torte, pumpkin cookies and hot spiced cider—admiring your handiwork with every bite.

SPICY BEEF AND SAUSAGE TACOS;
AND CHICKEN AND CORN ENCHILADAS.

Spicy Beef and Sausage Tacos

ALLOW GUESTS TO FILL THEIR OWN TACO SHELLS WITH THE SPICY FILLING AND ASSORTED TOPPINGS. IF YOU PREFER SOFT TACOS, USE WARM FLOUR TORTILLAS INSTEAD—OR OFFER BOTH VERSIONS. TO KEEP THINGS EASY, SERVE TORTILLA CHIPS WITH PURCHASED SALSA AND GUACAMOLE TO START.

makes 16

¼ cup olive oil
2 cups chopped red bell peppers
4 teaspoons minced garlic
1 pound ground beef
1 pound hot Italian sausages, casings removed
1 1¼-ounce package taco seasoning mix
½ cup chopped fresh cilantro
   Hot pepper sauce

16 purchased corn taco shells, warmed
   Grated cheddar cheese
   Chopped red onion
   Diced peeled avocado
   Chopped tomatoes
   Shredded lettuce
   Sour cream

Heat oil in heavy large skillet over medium-high heat. Add bell peppers and garlic and sauté 1 minute. Add beef and sausages; sauté until brown, breaking up pieces with back of spoon, about 5 minutes. Sprinkle seasoning mix over; sauté 3 minutes longer. Add cilantro. Season to taste with hot pepper sauce.

Transfer beef mixture to large bowl; place in center of platter. Surround with taco shells. Place cheese, onion, avocado, tomatoes, lettuce and sour cream in separate bowls and serve.

Chicken and Corn Enchiladas

FOR THIS EASY-TO-MAKE ENCHILADA FILLING, PURCHASE A WHOLE ROAST CHICKEN FROM THE SUPERMARKET AND SHRED OR CUT IT INTO PIECES (OPPOSITE, WITH THE LAYERED RICE SALAD WITH RED AND GREEN SALSAS, PAGE 40).

makes 16

3 cups shredded cooked chicken
1½ cups sliced red onions
1½ cups frozen corn kernels, thawed
¾ cup sour cream
½ cup chopped fresh cilantro
1 teaspoon ground cumin
2 cups grated hot pepper Monterey Jack cheese (about 8 ounces)
3 cups purchased thick and chunky mild salsa
3 cups red enchilada sauce

16 6-inch corn tortillas

Lightly oil 15 x 10 x 2-inch glass baking dish. Mix first 6 ingredients and 1 cup cheese in medium bowl. Season chicken filling to taste with salt and pepper. Mix salsa and enchilada sauce in large bowl.

Heat heavy medium skillet over high heat. Add 1 tortilla and cook until heated through, about 10 seconds per side. Brush tortilla with some of sauce mixture. Spoon ⅓ cup chicken filling into center of tortilla. Roll up. Place seam side down in prepared baking dish. Repeat with remaining tortillas, some sauce and remaining filling. *(Can be made 1 day ahead. Cover and chill enchiladas and remaining sauce separately.)*

Preheat oven to 350°F. Spoon remaining sauce over enchiladas. Sprinkle with remaining 1 cup cheese. Cover with foil. Bake until heated through, about 35 minutes (or up to 45 minutes for refrigerated enchiladas).

Layered Rice Salad with Red and Green Salsas

YOU'LL NEED A BIG GLASS BOWL OR A TRIFLE DISH TO SHOW OFF THIS BEAUTIFUL MAKE-AHEAD SALAD TO ITS BEST ADVANTAGE.

16 servings

rice

5½ cups water
1 tablespoon plus 1 teaspoon olive oil
1½ teaspoons salt
2 cups long-grain white rice

green salsa

9 tomatillos,* husked, coarsely chopped
1½ cups chopped green bell peppers
¾ cup chopped green onions
   (dark green parts only)
½ cup chopped fresh basil
2 tablespoons olive oil

beans

2 15-ounce cans black beans, drained, rinsed
2 teaspoons ground coriander
1 teaspoon onion salt

red salsa

1 cup purchased medium-hot red salsa
2 cups chopped red bell peppers
½ cup chopped red onion
⅓ cup chopped fresh parsley
1 tablespoon olive oil

1 cup sour cream
3 tablespoons thinly sliced fresh basil

FOR RICE: Combine 5½ cups water, oil and salt in large saucepan. Bring to boil. Add rice. Return to boil. Reduce heat to low. Cover saucepan and cook until liquid is absorbed and rice is tender, about 20 minutes. Fluff rice with fork. Transfer to baking sheet and cool completely. Season to taste with salt and pepper.

FOR GREEN SALSA: Combine all ingredients in large bowl. Toss to blend. Season to taste with salt and pepper.

FOR BEANS: Mix beans, coriander and onion salt in medium bowl.

FOR RED SALSA: Mix purchased salsa, bell peppers, onion, parsley and oil in another large bowl. Season to taste with salt and pepper.

Spoon 2 cups rice into 4-quart clear glass bowl. Spoon green salsa evenly over rice. Spoon another 2 cups rice evenly over salsa. Spread sour cream over rice. Spoon all but ¼ cup beans over sour cream. Spread remaining rice over beans. Spread red salsa over rice. Sprinkle remaining ¼ cup beans over salad. Cover and refrigerate at least 1 hour or up to 8 hours. Sprinkle with sliced basil.

A green tomato-like vegetable with a paper-thin husk. Available at Latin American markets and some supermarkets.

Mocha Mousse Torte

THIS IS THE CHOCOLATE LOVER'S DREAM DESSERT: RICH, CREAMY AND INTENSELY FLAVORED. MAKE IT TWO DAYS AHEAD AND YOU WON'T HAVE TO THINK ABOUT THE PARTY'S DESSERT AGAIN.

16 servings

crust

2½ cups ground chocolate wafer cookies
(from about 1⅓ 9-ounce packages)
1½ tablespoons instant coffee powder
6 tablespoons (¾ stick) unsalted butter, melted

fillings

12 ounces bittersweet (not unsweetened) or
semisweet chocolate, chopped
6 tablespoons (¾ stick) unsalted butter,
cut into pieces
6 teaspoons instant coffee powder

½ cup sugar
3 tablespoons water

5 large egg whites

2¾ cups chilled whipping cream
¼ cup powdered sugar
¼ teaspoon ground cinnamon

FOR CRUST: Preheat oven to 350°F. Blend ground cookies and coffee powder in processor. Set aside ¾ cup cookie crumb mixture. Add butter to remaining crumb mixture and process until crumbs are moist. Press mixture onto bottom and up sides of 9-inch-diameter springform pan with 2¾-inch-high sides. Bake crust until just firm to touch, about 10 minutes. Cool.

FOR FILLINGS: Stir chocolate, butter and 1 teaspoon coffee powder in heavy medium saucepan over medium-low heat until melted and smooth. Transfer to large bowl. Set chocolate mixture aside while preparing meringue.

Stir ½ cup sugar and 3 tablespoons water in small saucepan over low heat until sugar dissolves. Increase heat and boil syrup without stirring until candy thermometer registers 240°F, tilting pan slightly to submerge bulb, approximately 4 minutes.

Meanwhile, using electric mixer, beat whites in large bowl to soft peaks.

Gradually beat hot syrup into whites. Continue beating until medium-stiff peaks form, about 3 minutes. Fold ⅓ of meringue into lukewarm chocolate mixture to lighten. Fold in remaining meringue. Set chocolate meringue aside.

Combine ¼ cup cream and remaining 5 teaspoons coffee powder in large bowl; stir to dissolve. Add 2½ cups cream, powdered sugar and cinnamon and beat until firm peaks form. Fold 1½ cups coffee whipped cream into chocolate meringue, forming mocha mousse.

Spoon half of mocha mousse over bottom of crust. Sprinkle 3 tablespoons reserved crumb mixture over mousse. Spoon half of coffee whipped cream over crumbs. Sprinkle with 3 tablespoons crumbs. Repeat layering with remaining mocha mousse, half of crumbs, coffee whipped cream and remaining crumbs. Cover and refrigerate until set, about 4 hours. *(Can be made 2 days ahead; keep refrigerated.)* Run knife around pan sides to loosen torte. Remove pan sides from torte and serve.

Pumpkin Spice Cookies

THESE SIMPLE CAKE-LIKE COOKIES CAN BE PREPARED
A DAY AHEAD OF THE PARTY.

makes about 4 dozen

½ cup (1 stick) unsalted butter,
   room temperature
½ cup (packed) golden brown sugar
½ cup sugar
1 large egg
2 tablespoons pure maple syrup
1 cup canned pure pumpkin
1 teaspoon grated orange peel
1 teaspoon maple extract
1 teaspoon ground cinnamon
½ teaspoon ground allspice
2 cups all purpose flour
1 teaspoon baking soda
½ teaspoon salt
1 cup raisins

   Orange Glaze (see recipe at right)

Preheat oven to 350°F. Butter 2 heavy large
baking sheets. Beat first 5 ingredients in large
bowl until well blended. Add pumpkin, orange
peel, maple extract, cinnamon and allspice and
beat to blend. Mix flour, baking soda and salt in
small bowl. Add to pumpkin mixture and beat
just until combined. Mix in raisins.

Drop batter by rounded tablespoonfuls onto
prepared sheets. Bake cookies until edges are
golden brown and centers are firm to touch,
about 10 minutes. Transfer to racks; cool.

Drizzle glaze over cookies. Let stand until
glaze sets, about 30 minutes. *(Can be prepared
1 day ahead. Store between sheets of waxed paper
in airtight containers at room temperature.)*

Orange Glaze

THIS GLAZE WOULD ALSO BE TERRIFIC DRIZZLED
OVER SPICE CAKE OR ANGEL FOOD CAKE.

makes about ⅓ cup

1 cup powdered sugar
4 teaspoons orange juice
½ teaspoon orange peel
2 drops orange food coloring (optional)

Whisk all ingredients in bowl to blend.

Mulled Cider with Winter Spices

HERE'S A CLASSIC THAT'S GUARANTEED TO WARM UP
A CHILLY WINTER DAY. PASS THE BRANDY
SEPARATELY FOR THOSE WHO WANT IT. GARNISH
EACH DRINK WITH A CINNAMON STICK, IF DESIRED.

16 servings

18 cups apple cider
⅓ cup orange juice
   Peel (orange part only) from
   1 large orange, cut into strips
1 large bay leaf
1½ tablespoons (packed) brown sugar
3 cinnamon sticks
3 whole cloves
3 whole allspice
3 tablespoons fresh lemon juice
   Pinch of salt
2¼ cups applejack brandy (optional)

Mix first 10 ingredients in large saucepan.
Bring to boil. Reduce heat to medium-low and
simmer mixture 30 minutes to blend flavors.
Strain mulled cider into mugs. Serve cider,
passing applejack brandy separately, if desired.

Decorating the mantel

YOU MAY BE WILLING to let your guests trim the tree, but the mantel can be yours and yours alone, to decorate before the revelers arrive. And while the tree tends to be a product of your collection of ornaments (and wonderfully predictable in its sameness), the mantel can change its look, silver and gold one year, woodsy and rustic the next.

The mantel can be turned into a festive focal point with very little effort: All it takes are some clippings from the back yard, a few pieces of fresh produce, plus items you probably already have, such as candles, ornaments, photos, cards and maybe even a crèche.

HELPFUL HINTS

✲ To make the decorations last longer (up to two weeks), select the freshest greenery and fruits available.

✲ Use T-pins, a glue gun or florists' tape to hold everything—greenery, ornaments, cards etc.—in place so that nothing can fall into the fire.

✲ If using candles, replace them every few days or when they've burned down to within a few inches of the greenery.

INSTANT IDEAS

SOUTHERN HOSPITALITY: magnolia leaves, boxwood, fresh pineapples.

INTO THE WOODS: pinecones, cedar branches with berries, mistletoe.

ALL THAT GLITTERS: antique tree ornaments in silver bowls of varying sizes and heights with casually draped garlands of silver or gold beads over the entire mantel.

CALIFORNIA STYLE: mounds of fresh oranges and lemons on a bed of flat-leaf eucalyptus.

RED-AND-GREEN CLASSIC: red fruits (pomegranates, apples and red Bartlett pears) mounded on pine, spruce or cedar branches.

VICTORIANA: dried hydrangea and dried roses arranged casually along the length of the mantel, with tall silver candelabra and tall silver or glass candy dishes filled with old-fashioned hard candy.

GARDEN STYLE: terra-cotta pots of budding narcissus or amaryllis, and seasonal greens entwined around the pots.

Family Christmas Eve Dinner

MENU FOR SIX

LEMON-PARMESAN ARTICHOKE
BOTTOMS

CAESAR SALAD

BAKED PASTA WITH HAM,
TOMATOES AND CHEESE

CRUSTY ROSEMARY
BREADSTICKS

RED WINE FOR THE ADULTS;
MILK FOR THE KIDS

DOUBLE CHOCOLATE-MINT CHIP
ICE CREAM SUNDAES

In the eye of the Christmas hurri-
cane, even as Santa feeds Rudolph a
PowerBar and prepares to blast off for another of his around-the-world
endurance runs, why not do the unthinkable? Take a break. Resign yourself to the fact that if you haven't gotten to it by Christmas Eve, you may
not get to it (alternatively, send out your Christmas cards after the 25th),
and step out of the Christmas rush hour to enjoy a quiet night at home.

Give in to the urge to make something delicious (but easy!) for a
family dinner. This wonderful menu is as simple as a cheesy baked pasta
dish, Caesar salad and ice cream sundaes. If time allows, add on the
quick-cooking, do-ahead appetizer of artichoke bottoms topped with a
lemony pine nut-Parmesan mixture, and the rosemary-scented homemade breadsticks. The recipes serve six, doubling easily if your family is
bigger or includes visiting relatives, and all offer do-ahead tips. Set a nice
table or serve the meal on trays around the sparkling tree. Then go
ahead and let the kids open just one present.

BAKED PASTA WITH HAM, TOMATOES AND CHEESE; AND CRUSTY ROSEMARY BREADSTICKS.

Lemon-Parmesan Artichoke Bottoms

THIS EASY APPETIZER IS A NEW TAKE ON THE ARTICHOKE DIP THAT'S ALWAYS SO POPULAR. MAKE IT EARLY IN THE DAY, THEN SIMPLY BAKE FOR 20 MINUTES BEFORE SERVING.

makes 14 to 16

2 14-ounce cans artichoke bottoms, rinsed, drained, patted dry

1½ cups grated Parmesan cheese

½ cup mayonnaise

3 large garlic cloves, minced

2 teaspoons fresh lemon juice

1 teaspoon grated lemon peel

¼ cup pine nuts

Chopped fresh parsley (optional)

Lightly grease 8-inch square baking dish. Place artichoke bottoms, rounded sides down, in prepared dish. Combine Parmesan, mayonnaise, garlic, lemon juice and lemon peel in medium bowl; season to taste with salt and pepper. Mound mayonnaise mixture in artichokes. Sprinkle with pine nuts. *(Can be prepared 6 hours ahead. Cover and refrigerate.)*

Preheat oven to 375°F. Bake artichokes until heated through, about 20 minutes. Garnish with parsley, if desired, and serve.

Caesar Salad

HOMEMADE GARLICKY CROUTONS MAKE THIS SALAD CLASSIC EXTRA-DELICIOUS.

6 servings

croutons

4½ cups ¾-inch cubes sourdough bread with crust (about 4½ ounces)

1½ tablespoons olive oil

2 garlic cloves, minced

¾ teaspoon garlic salt

salad

2 small heads romaine lettuce, torn into bite-size pieces, chilled

4½ tablespoons olive oil

5 garlic cloves, chopped

4½ tablespoons fresh lemon juice

12 anchovy fillets, chopped

2¼ cups freshly grated Parmesan cheese
Freshly ground black pepper

FOR CROUTONS: Preheat oven to 325°F. Place bread in 15 x 10 x 2-inch baking dish. Sprinkle oil, minced garlic and garlic salt over; toss to coat well. Bake until bread just begins to dry, about 15 minutes. Cool croutons at least 15 minutes and up to 3 hours.

FOR SALAD: Place lettuce in large bowl. Whisk olive oil and garlic in small bowl to blend. Pour oil mixture over lettuce and toss to coat. Pour fresh lemon juice over lettuce and toss to coat. Add anchovies and toss. Add Parmesan cheese in 4 additions and toss to coat well after each addition. Season salad with salt and freshly ground pepper. Sprinkle croutons over salad and then serve.

Baked Pasta with Ham, Tomatoes and Cheese

EASIER THAN LASAGNA (MUCH) BUT EVERY BIT AS DELICIOUS, THIS BAKED PASTA DISH (BELOW) WILL LEAVE YOU PLENTY OF TIME TO WRAP EVERYTHING STILL UNDER THE BED COME CHRISTMAS EVE.

6 servings

12 ounces rigatoni

1½ cups diced ham (about 8 ounces)

4 large plum tomatoes, chopped

1 cup crumbled feta cheese (about 4 ounces)

1 cup (packed) grated mozzarella cheese (about 4 ounces)

1½ teaspoons dried thyme

1 cup whipping cream

Preheat oven to 375°F. Butter 13 x 9 x 2-inch glass baking dish. Cook pasta in large pot of boiling salted water until just tender but still firm to bite. Drain. Place in prepared baking dish. Mix in ham, tomatoes, feta cheese, mozzarella cheese and thyme. Pour cream over. Sprinkle pasta with salt and pepper and toss to blend. Cover dish with foil.

Bake pasta 15 minutes. Uncover and stir to coat pasta evenly with melted cheeses. Cover again. *(Can be prepared 2 hours ahead; chill.)* Bake until heated through, about 45 minutes longer.

Crusty Rosemary Breadsticks

THESE ITALIAN-STYLE BREADSTICKS (OPPOSITE) ARE A GREAT ADDITION TO YOUR CHRISTMAS EVE DINNER. (THE PURCHASED KIND WILL DO JUST FINE IF YOU'RE PRESSED FOR TIME.) USE A PLASTIC SPRAY BOTTLE FILLED WITH WATER TO MIST THE OVEN WHILE THE BREADSTICKS ARE BAKING: THE WATER HELPS TO MAKE THEM CRUSTY ON THE OUTSIDE AND SLIGHTLY SOFTER INSIDE.

makes 12

- 1¾ cups warm water (105°F to 115°F)
- 1 envelope dry yeast
  Pinch of sugar
- 1 tablespoon salt
- 1 tablespoon (generous) chopped fresh rosemary or 1 teaspoon dried
- 4 cups (or more) bread flour
- 2 tablespoons cold milk
- 2 tablespoons extra-virgin olive oil

  Cornmeal

- 12 fresh rosemary sprigs

- 1 egg, beaten to blend (glaze)
  Coarse salt (optional)

Place 1¾ cups warm water in large bowl of electric mixer fitted with dough hook. Add yeast and pinch of sugar; stir to blend. Let stand until foamy, about 10 minutes. Add 1 tablespoon salt and chopped rosemary; beat at medium speed until blended. Add 4 cups bread flour, 1 cup at a time, beating until well incorporated. Mix milk and olive oil in small bowl. With mixer running on low speed, gradually add milk mixture. Increase speed to medium; beat 6 minutes. Scrape dough from hook and sides of bowl (dough will be soft and sticky). Let dough rest 15 minutes.

Sprinkle 2 heavy large baking sheets generously with cornmeal. Turn out dough onto floured surface and knead until soft and slightly sticky, adding more flour if necessary. Divide dough into 12 equal pieces. Let dough rest 10 minutes.

Roll each dough piece between surface and palms of hands to 12-inch-long rope. Arrange 6 ropes on each baking sheet, spacing apart. Break small green clusters off rosemary sprigs. Insert stem end of rosemary clusters along top of breadsticks, spacing 2 inches apart. Using sprayer filled with cold water, lightly mist breadsticks. Let rise uncovered in warm draft-free area until puffy, about 30 minutes.

Position 1 rack in bottom third of oven and 1 rack in center and preheat to 450°F. Brush breadsticks lightly with egg glaze. Sprinkle very lightly with coarse salt, if desired. Place baking sheets on racks in oven and spray oven with water. Bake 15 minutes, spraying oven with water every 5 minutes. Continue baking without spraying until breadsticks are golden and sound hollow when tapped, about 15 minutes longer. Transfer breadsticks to racks; cool. *(Can be made ahead. Wrap tightly in foil and freeze up to 2 weeks. Thaw breadsticks. If desired, rewarm wrapped sticks in 350°F oven 15 minutes.)*

Seasonal centerpieces

WHETHER YOUR STYLE is country rustic or urban elegant, a festive centerpiece on the dining room table can make the house look a lot like Christmas and make holiday meals even more special. The term *centerpiece* is used loosely here; think beyond the typical arrangement of red and white flowers with a few greens. Your table decor could be a long row of pillar candles in saucers placed directly on the table, or small flower arrangements in silver mint-julep cups set at each guest's place.

HELPFUL HINTS

❧ Avoid highly scented flowers and greenery as they may overpower the aromas of the food.

❧ Centerpiece arrangements should be either below eye level or above it.

❧ For safety reasons, make sure candles are several inches higher than greenery, flowers or other elements of the table decor.

❧ Don't forget to protect your table with a cloth or plastic mat if you're creating your centerpiece right on the surface.

INSTANT IDEAS

❧ A display of fresh-cut greens and hardy fruits (apples, pears, pomegranates, oranges) will last up to two weeks. Spray greenery with water to keep it fresh, and replace it when it begins to wither.

❧ Try offbeat colors or jewel tones instead of red and green. A sapphire-colored vase filled with burgundy tulips, for example, can look very elegant and festive.

❧ Try a monochromatic look. Combine red fruits (pomegranates, apples, pears), red flowers (roses, tulips) and red tree ornaments for a striking display. An all-gold or all-green table arrangement would be equally appealing.

❧ Place small, fresh, whole fruit, such as kumquats, cranberries or clementines, in large, clear glass vases before adding your flowers of choice and then water.

❧ For an elegant party, fill an antique silver epergne with flowers (put them into florists' vials) and grapes, letting the grapes cascade over the sides of the epergne.

❧ For a country look, spread pine boughs and twigs on the table and casually arrange pinecones, nuts in the shell and pillar candles among the greenery.

Double Chocolate-Mint Chip Ice Cream Sundaes

PREPARED WITH PURCHASED ICE CREAM, THESE SUNDAES ARE A SNAP TO MAKE. IF THE KIDS DON'T WANT THE DRIED CHERRIES ON TOP, SPRINKLE THEIR SUNDAES WITH MARASCHINO CHERRIES OR CHOPPED PEPPERMINTS. NUTS WOULD MAKE A GOOD TOPPING TOO.

6 servings

2 ounces good-quality white chocolate (such as Lindt or Baker's), coarsely chopped

1½ cups dark chocolate ice cream, softened slightly

¾ cup water

1 cup unsweetened cocoa, sifted

6 tablespoons (¾ stick) unsalted butter, cut into pieces

¾ cup sugar

¼ cup (packed) golden brown sugar

3 tablespoons light corn syrup
   Pinch of salt

2 teaspoons vanilla extract

3 cups mint chip ice cream

⅓ cup dried tart cherries
   Fresh mint sprigs

Fold white chocolate chunks into dark chocolate ice cream in large bowl. Cover and freeze until firm, about 4 hours.

Bring ¾ cup water to boil in heavy medium saucepan. Whisk in cocoa. Add butter. Stir over low heat until mixture is smooth. Add both sugars, corn syrup and salt. Stir over low heat until sugars dissolve, about 5 minutes. Remove from heat. Stir in vanilla. (*Dark chocolate ice cream and sauce can be prepared 1 week ahead. Keep ice cream frozen. Cover sauce and refrigerate. Rewarm sauce over low heat.*)

Drizzle some warm chocolate sauce into bottom of 6 parfait glasses or wineglasses. Place 1 scoop mint chip ice cream in each glass. Spoon some chocolate sauce over ice cream. Spoon dark chocolate ice cream, then mint chip ice cream into glasses, spooning some sauce over each layer. Sprinkle dried cherries over. Garnish sundaes with fresh mint sprigs.

Elegant Christmas Eve Dinner

MENU FOR TWELVE

SPICED PECANS

PROSCIUTTO ROLLS WITH
ARUGULA AND FIGS

CHAMPAGNE

SWEET POTATO SOUP WITH LOBSTER
AND ORANGE CRÈME FRAÎCHE

CHARDONNAY

BEEF TENDERLOIN WITH ROASTED
SHALLOTS, BACON AND PORT

BUTTERED GREEN BEANS AND CARROTS

POTATO AND SHIITAKE
MUSHROOM GRATIN

BORDEAUX, MERLOT OR CABERNET SAUVIGNON

INDIVIDUAL FROZEN CAKE "PRESENTS"
WITH STRAWBERRY SAUCE

For some people, Christmas Eve is It. It's the night they've looked forward to all year, when the extended family gathers to open presents and indulge in the most spectacular, elegant and satisfying dinner possible. Christmas Day may be reserved for opening Santa's gifts (and putting them together); Christmas Eve, tradition holds, is the big event.

If your clan likes to pull out all the stops on the night before Christmas, consider this lovely menu, with its beef tenderloin center-piece. That striking roast is served with a sauce (components of which can be finished up ahead) of roasted shallots, bacon and Port. To go with it, there is a superb shiitake mushroom and potato gratin, along with green beans and carrots. The supper gets started with slender cylinders of prosciutto-wrapped dried figs (blue cheese and arugula complete the flavor mix), followed by a luxurious sweet potato soup with lobster. Dessert—individual frozen cake "presents," frosted in chocolate ganache—may turn out to be everyone's favorite gift of the evening.

SWEET POTATO SOUP WITH LOBSTER AND
ORANGE CRÈME FRAÎCHE.

Spiced Pecans

GREAT TO NIBBLE ON WITH CHAMPAGNE.

makes about 4 cups

¼ cup (½ stick) butter
½ cup (packed) golden brown sugar
¼ cup water
1 teaspoon salt
2 teaspoons Chinese five-spice powder
½ teaspoon ground cumin
½ teaspoon ground black pepper
4 cups pecan halves

Preheat oven to 350°F. Butter 2 large baking sheets. Melt ¼ cup butter in large skillet over medium heat. Add brown sugar, ¼ cup water, salt and spices; stir until sugar dissolves. Add nuts to sugar mixture and cook until syrup thickly coats nuts, stirring often, 5 minutes.

Transfer nuts to prepared sheets. Bake until golden, 10 minutes. Cool. *(Can be made 3 days ahead. Store airtight at room temperature.)*

Prosciutto Rolls with Arugula and Figs

THE TRICK HERE IS TO GET THIN PROSCIUTTO SLICES THAT AREN'T *TOO* THIN OR THEY WILL TEAR WHEN YOU SPREAD THE CHEESE MIXTURE ON THEM (BELOW). YOUR BEST BET IS A DELI THAT WILL SLICE THE PROSCIUTTO FOR YOU.

makes 24

¼ cup extra-virgin olive oil
2 tablespoons fresh lemon juice
4 teaspoons grated lemon peel
12 thin slices prosciutto (not paper-thin)
6 ounces Gorgonzola cheese, room temperature
6 ounces cream cheese, room temperature
16 dried black Mission figs, quartered
4 large bunches arugula, stems trimmed

Whisk oil, lemon juice and peel in medium bowl to blend. Lay prosciutto on work surface, spacing slices 2 inches apart. Mix cheeses in small bowl to blend. Spread cheese evenly over prosciutto. Arrange figs over cheese mixture, dividing and spacing evenly. Drizzle lemon mixture over. Sprinkle with pepper. Arrange 6 arugula leaves atop each prosciutto slice, alternating stems and tops and allowing tops to extend 1 inch over long sides of prosciutto.

Starting at 1 short end of each prosciutto slice, tightly roll up as for jelly roll. Cut rolls crosswise in half. Transfer rolls to platter. *(Can be made 2 hours ahead. Cover with damp paper towels, then plastic wrap; refrigerate.)*

Sweet Potato Soup with Lobster and Orange Crème Fraîche

THIS SOPHISTICATED FIRST-COURSE SOUP (RIGHT) CAN ALSO BE SERVED WITHOUT THE LOBSTER.

12 servings

1 cup whipping cream

½ cup sour cream

3 teaspoons minced peeled fresh ginger

1½ teaspoons grated orange peel

10 tablespoons (1¼ sticks) butter

3½ pounds red-skinned sweet potatoes (yams), peeled, cut into ½-inch pieces

1 tablespoon golden brown sugar

2 large leeks, chopped (white and pale green parts only)

1⅓ cups finely chopped celery

10 cups (or more) canned low-salt chicken broth

1⅓ cups orange juice

3 1-pound cooked lobster tails

2 tablespoons chopped fresh parsley

Mix cream, sour cream, 1½ teaspoons ginger and orange peel in medium bowl to blend. Let stand until thickened, about 3 hours. Cover crème fraîche and refrigerate.

Preheat oven to 400°F. Melt 4 tablespoons butter in large pot over medium heat. Remove from heat. Add sweet potatoes and sugar and toss to coat. Arrange sweet potatoes on 2 baking sheets. Roast until very tender and starting to brown, stirring occasionally, 30 minutes.

Melt 4 tablespoons butter in same pot over medium heat. Add leeks, celery and remaining

1½ teaspoons ginger and sauté until leeks begin to soften, about 5 minutes. Add roasted sweet potatoes and sauté 2 minutes. Add 10 cups broth and orange juice. Bring mixture to boil. Reduce heat and simmer until leeks and celery are very tender, about 20 minutes.

Working in batches, puree soup in processor. Return soup to pot. Thin with more broth, if desired. Season with salt and pepper. *(Crème fraîche and soup can be made 2 days ahead. Cover separately and refrigerate.)*

Remove lobster meat from shells. Slice into ⅓-inch-thick medallions. Melt remaining 2 tablespoons butter in heavy large skillet over medium heat. Add lobster medallions; sauté until heated through, about 1 minute.

Bring soup to simmer. Ladle into bowls. Spoon small dollops of crème fraîche atop soup. Draw skewer through crème fraîche to form design. Arrange lobster atop soup. Sprinkle with chopped parsley and serve immediately.

Beef Tenderloin with Roasted Shallots, Bacon and Port

HERE'S AN ELEGANT MAIN COURSE FOR CHRISTMAS EVE. COMPONENTS OF THE SAUCE CAN BE MADE AHEAD, AND THE BEEF COOKS IN UNDER AN HOUR.

12 servings

1½ pounds large shallots (about 24),
   halved lengthwise, peeled

  3 tablespoons olive oil

  6 cups canned beef broth
1½ cups tawny Port
  1 tablespoon tomato paste

  2 3- to 3¼-pound beef tenderloins (large ends),
   trimmed
  2 teaspoons dried thyme
  7 bacon slices, chopped

  6 tablespoons (¾ stick) butter,
   room temperature
1½ tablespoons all purpose flour

  1 large bunch watercress

Position rack in center of oven and preheat to 375°F. In 9-inch-diameter pie pan, toss shallots with oil to coat. Season with salt and pepper. Roast until shallots are deep brown and very tender, stirring occasionally, about 30 minutes.

Boil broth and Port in large saucepan until reduced to 3¾ cups, about 30 minutes. Whisk in tomato paste. *(Shallots and broth mixture can be made 3 days ahead. Cover separately; chill.)*

Pat beef dry; sprinkle with thyme, salt and pepper. In large roasting pan set over medium heat, sauté bacon until golden, about 4 minutes. Using slotted spoon, transfer bacon to paper

towels. Increase heat to medium-high. Add beef to pan; brown on all sides, about 7 minutes. Transfer pan to oven; roast beef until thermometer registers 125°F for medium-rare, 45 minutes. Transfer to platter. Tent with foil.

Spoon fat off top of pan drippings in roasting pan. Place roasting pan over high heat. Add broth mixture and bring to boil, scraping up any browned bits. Transfer to medium saucepan; bring to simmer. Mix 3 tablespoons butter and flour in small bowl to form smooth paste; whisk into broth mixture and simmer until sauce thickens, about 2 minutes. Whisk in 3 tablespoons butter. Stir in shallots and reserved bacon. Season sauce with salt and pepper.

Slice beef. Spoon some sauce over. Garnish with watercress. Pass remaining sauce.

Buttered Green Beans and Carrots

SIMPLE TO MAKE, AND VERY PRETTY ON THE PLATE.

12 servings

  2 pounds slender green beans, trimmed
  8 ounces carrots, peeled,
   cut into matchstick-size strips

  2 tablespoons (¼ stick) butter
  2 tablespoons olive oil

Cook beans in large pot of boiling salted water until crisp-tender, about 6 minutes. Using slotted spoon, transfer beans to bowl of ice water. Cook carrots in same boiling water until crisp-tender, about 1 minute. Transfer carrots to ice water with beans. Drain; pat dry. *(Can be made 1 day ahead. Wrap in paper towels; chill.)*

Melt butter with oil in large pot over medium-high heat. Add vegetables and toss until hot, about 2 minutes. Season with salt and pepper.

Potato and Shiitake Mushroom Gratin

POTATO GRATIN IS, OF COURSE, THE TRADITIONAL SIDE DISH WITH ROAST BEEF, AND THIS VERSION IS JUST RIGHT FOR A SPECIAL OCCASION LIKE CHRISTMAS EVE. PLACE A BAKING SHEET IN THE OVEN ON THE RACK BELOW THE GRATIN TO CATCH ANY LIQUIDS THAT MAY BUBBLE OVER.

12 servings

  6 tablespoons (¾ stick) butter
1½ pounds button mushrooms, coarsely chopped
1½ pounds fresh shiitake mushrooms, stemmed, caps coarsely chopped
  3 tablespoons minced garlic
  2 teaspoons dried thyme
  1 teaspoon dried rosemary leaves, finely crushed
  2 cups canned low-salt chicken broth

  3 pounds Yukon Gold or russet potatoes, peeled, cut into ⅛-inch-thick slices
  2 cups freshly grated Parmesan cheese (about 5½ ounces)
  2 cups half and half
  2 cups whipping cream
1¼ teaspoons salt
  1 teaspoon ground black pepper

Melt butter in large pot over high heat. Add all mushrooms and sauté until liquid evaporates, about 10 minutes. Add garlic, thyme and rosemary; sauté 1 minute. Add broth and simmer until liquid evaporates, stirring often, about 18 minutes. Season with salt and pepper. Cool.

Position 1 rack in middle of oven and another rack in bottom third of oven; preheat to 375°F. Butter 13 x 9 x 2-inch glass baking dish. Arrange ⅓ of potatoes in dish, overlapping slightly. Top with half of mushroom mixture. Sprinkle ⅓ of cheese over. Repeat layering with ⅓ of potatoes, remaining mushroom mixture and ⅓ of cheese. Arrange remaining potatoes atop cheese. Whisk half and half, cream, salt and pepper in large bowl to blend; pour over potatoes. Cover loosely with foil.

Place baking sheet on bottom rack in oven. Place baking dish on middle rack in oven and bake until potatoes are tender and liquid thickens, about 1 hour 15 minutes. Uncover. Using metal spatula, press on potatoes to submerge. *(Can be prepared 1 day ahead. Cool, cover and refrigerate. Bake covered at 375°F until heated through, about 40 minutes. Uncover before continuing.)* Sprinkle remaining cheese over potatoes; bake until cheese melts and gratin is golden at edges, about 15 minutes longer. Let stand 10 minutes before serving.

Individual Frozen Cake "Presents" with Strawberry Sauce

THESE INDIVIDUAL CAKES (AT RIGHT), WITH THEIR "RIBBONS" OF ICING, MAY BE THE BEST PRESENTS ANYONE RECEIVES. (AS AN ALTERNATIVE TO THE ICING HERE, USE PURCHASED, READY-MADE FONDANT FOR THE RIBBONS. IT'S AVAILABLE AT CAKE SUPPLY STORES.)

makes 18

cakes

2 cups all purpose flour
2 teaspoons baking powder
 Pinch of salt
1 cup milk
2 tablespoons (¼ stick) unsalted butter
4 large eggs, separated
2 cups sugar

fillings

3 cups whipping cream
1½ cups sugar
6 tablespoons fresh lemon juice
4½ tablespoons grated lemon peel

4½ cups purchased strawberry ice cream, softened slightly

ganache

2½ cups whipping cream
½ cup light corn syrup
2 pounds bittersweet (not unsweetened) or semisweet chocolate, chopped
¼ cup Cognac or brandy

ribbon icing

3½ cups powdered sugar
5 tablespoons water

 Strawberry Sauce (see recipe opposite)

FOR CAKES: Preheat oven to 350°F. Butter and flour two 8-inch square baking pans. Sift flour, baking powder and salt in medium bowl. Bring milk and butter to simmer in small saucepan over medium-high heat. Remove from heat; cover to keep hot. Beat yolks and 1 cup sugar in large bowl until pale, about 1 minute. Using clean dry beaters, beat egg whites in another large bowl until soft peaks form. Gradually add remaining 1 cup sugar, beating until stiff peaks form. Beat dry ingredients into yolks alternately with hot milk mixture, beginning and ending with dry ingredients. Fold in whites in 3 additions.

Divide batter between prepared pans. Bake cakes until tester comes out clean, about 30 minutes. Cool in pans 10 minutes. Turn out onto clean floured dish towels. Cool. Cut each cake horizontally into 3 equal layers.

FOR FILLINGS: Mix cream, sugar, lemon juice and lemon peel in medium bowl until sugar dissolves. Freeze lemon cream until slightly firm, about 2 hours.

Line 2 clean 8-inch square baking pans with plastic, overlapping sides. Place 1 cake layer in each prepared pan. Spread 2¼ cups strawberry ice cream over each. Top with second cake layer. Spread 2¼ cups lemon cream over each. Top with third cake layer, cut side down. Cover and freeze cakes overnight.

Turn 1 cake out onto baking sheet. Peel off plastic. Trim cake edges. Cut cake into nine 2½-inch squares; place squares in freezer. Repeat with remaining cake.

FOR GANACHE: Bring cream and corn syrup to simmer in large saucepan. Remove from heat. Add chopped chocolate; stir until melted. Stir in Cognac. Cool ganache until thickened slightly but still pourable.

Remove 3 cakes from freezer and place on wire rack set over baking sheet. Pour ⅓ cup ganache over top of 1 cake. Working quickly, spread ganache over sides of cake. Repeat with remaining 2 cakes. Return cakes to baking sheet in freezer. Glaze remaining cakes, 3 at a time. Freeze until glaze is firm, about 1 hour.

FOR RIBBON ICING: Whisk powdered sugar and 5 tablespoons water in medium bowl to blend. Transfer to pastry bag fitted with small plain tip. Remove 1 baking sheet from freezer. Pipe icing over top of each cake, forming bow. Return to freezer. Repeat with remaining cakes. Freeze until icing sets, 30 minutes. (Can be made 1 week ahead. Cover with plastic; keep frozen.)

Place 1 cake on each plate. Pour some of sauce around each. Serve, passing remaining sauce.

Strawberry Sauce

makes about 4 cups

2 16-ounce bags frozen sweetened strawberries, thawed
½ cup orange juice

Working in batches, puree strawberries and orange juice in blender until smooth. Transfer to pitcher. (Can be prepared 1 day ahead; chill.)

The art of cleanup

CHRISTMAS TREE NEEDLES, shattered ornaments, cookie crumbs and wrapping paper—there's a natural mess that comes with Christmas. Some messes, like candle wax on the tablecloth or red wine spills on the carpet, can't be avoided; others can. Stay ahead of the game with these tips.

HELPFUL HINTS

❆ As the holidays get under way, try to keep the kitchen organized from one week to the next. Take an extra ten minutes every day to put dishes and bakeware away.

❆ For large parties, consider having several big plastic tubs filled with hot, soapy water that can be used to hold dirty dishes for several hours.

❆ Designate a place for dirty glasses so they won't be knocked over. An easy solution: Place stemware horizontally in a large roasting pan lined with dish towels.

❆ When the table has been cleared after the first course, it's all right to quickly scrape the dishes and put them into the sink before serving the main course. However, do not wash them or put them in the dishwasher; the clank of dishes can make guests feel uncomfortable.

❆ After the main course, scrape the dishes and add them to the first-course dishes. At this point, if your dishwasher is a very quiet one, it can be loaded and started.

❆ If a guest offers to help clean up, unless it's a formal party, say yes.

❆ Once the last guest leaves, turn on the late evening news or put on some lively dance music to keep you energized as you begin cleaning up.

Christmas Breakfast

MENU FOR FOUR

ORANGE JUICE AND COFFEE

CREAMY SCRAMBLED EGGS
WITH HERBS

CINNAMON FRENCH TOAST

BACON

FRESH FRUIT SALAD

CANDY CANE WHITE
HOT CHOCOLATE

s exciting as it can be to have a house full of people providing a steady stream of sound and motion, Christmas morning, when there are only as many people around as there are beds in the house, can be a welcome break from all the activity. If you have kids, it will, of course, be hectic for the first couple of hours around sunrise; but once the gifts have been opened, everyone will remember their growling stomachs.

Celebrate the day and the time together with a menu of child-friendly breakfast foods that will also appeal to the grown-ups present. The dress code is strictly robes and slippers, and the dishes include cinnamon-scented French toast (which can chill overnight in its vanilla-flavored egg mixture), creamy scrambled eggs (these take less than five minutes to cook, so you might wait until everyone is at the table before you start) and a big bowl of seasonal fruits, cut into kid-size bites. And since it's Christmas, why not have dessert after breakfast—in this case hot chocolate made with white chocolate, topped with whipped cream and served with candy cane stirrers?

CREAMY SCRAMBLED EGGS WITH HERBS;
AND CINNAMON FRENCH TOAST.

Deck the halls

DECORATING FOR THE HOLIDAYS doesn't have to be time-consuming or costly. If you take advantage of what's available this time of year —evergreens, berries, pears and pomegranates, for example—decking the halls can be quick and easy. Take a pair of clippers to the back yard, pick up some produce from the market, add a few of your favorite ornaments and some ribbon, and your house is dressed for the season.

INSTANT IDEAS

❋ Fill an oversize bowl or basket with a single type of fruit. The visual impact of several dozen pomegranates or oranges is dramatic.

❋ Fill a large rustic basket with pinecones and place it near the fireplace.

❋ Fill a wood bowl or Shaker box with mixed nuts in the shell.

❋ Ivy makes a festive indoor plant, especially ivy topiaries. Add a big bow and let the ends trail down and wrap around the plant.

❋ Don't forget the chandelier if you have one; a few casually tied bows of beautiful ribbon can give it a Christmasy look. Bows on the backs of your dining chairs can also be fun.

❋ Place holiday cards on the mantel, interspersed with greenery (magnolia, boxwood, cedar or pine) or cover a bulletin board with fabric, crisscross with ribbons tacked into place, and slip cards into the corners.

❋ Put children's holiday drawings (of Santa, snowmen, etc.) into Plexiglas stand-up frames and place them around the house: on the mantel, the buffet table, the powder-room counter.

❋ Use greenery, ribbon and other decorative touches where you'd least expect them: in the closet, the laundry room, the pantry. The whole house will feel more festive for it.

Creamy Scrambled Eggs with Herbs

THESE QUICKLY COOKED EGGS GET THEIR FLAVOR FROM A MIX OF BASIL, PARSLEY AND OREGANO. BACON AND A BEAUTIFUL SALAD OF FRESH FRUIT WOULD ROUND OUT THE MENU.

4 servings

6 large eggs
4 ounces Neufchâtel cheese,* diced
¼ cup chopped green onions
¼ cup chopped fresh basil
2 tablespoons chopped fresh parsley
2 tablespoons milk
2 teaspoons chopped fresh oregano or
    ½ teaspoon dried
2 tablespoons (¼ stick) butter

Beat eggs in large bowl to blend. Beat in next 6 ingredients. Season with salt and pepper. Melt butter in heavy large skillet over medium-high heat. Add egg mixture and stir until eggs are scrambled, about 4 minutes. Serve immediately.

A light style of cream cheese available at most supermarkets across the country.

Cinnamon French Toast

MAKE THE CINNAMON-FLAVORED EGG MIXTURE THE
BREAD SOAKS IN DURING A CALM MOMENT ON
CHRISTMAS EVE, THEN REFRIGERATE OVERNIGHT.
YOU CAN DOUBLE THE RECIPE FOR TWO SLICES OF
FRENCH TOAST (OPPOSITE) PER PERSON.

4 servings

- 3 large eggs
- 6 tablespoons half and half
- 1 tablespoon sugar
- 3 teaspoons ground cinnamon
- ¼ teaspoon vanilla extract
- 4 ¾-inch-thick slices soft-crusted French bread
     or egg bread

- 2 tablespoons (¼ stick) butter
- ¼ cup powdered sugar
     Warm maple syrup (optional)

Beat eggs, half and half, sugar, 2 teaspoons cinnamon and vanilla extract in 13 x 9 x 2-inch
glass baking dish to blend. Add bread and turn
to coat. Cover and chill until bread absorbs egg
mixture, at least 30 minutes and up to 1 day.

Melt butter in heavy large skillet over medium
heat. Add bread and cook until golden and
cooked through, about 3 minutes per side.
Transfer to plates. Combine powdered sugar
with remaining 1 teaspoon cinnamon and sift
over toast. Serve with maple syrup, if desired.

Candy Cane White Hot Chocolate

A BREAKFAST "DESSERT" TO SIP WHILE THE REST OF
THE PRESENTS ARE BEING OPENED. INDULGE AND
TOP THE HOT CHOCOLATE (ABOVE) WITH WHIPPED
CREAM AND MORE CRUSHED PEPPERMINT CANDY.

4 servings

- 4 cups milk
- 3 ounces good-quality white chocolate (such as
     Lindt or Baker's), chopped
- ⅓ cup crushed red-and-white-striped
     candy canes or hard peppermint candies
     Pinch of salt
- ½ cup peppermint schnapps (optional)
     Whipped cream
     Additional crushed red-and-white-striped
     candy canes or hard peppermint candies

Bring milk to simmer in heavy medium
saucepan. Reduce heat to medium-low. Add
white chocolate, ⅓ cup candy and salt; whisk
until smooth. Add schnapps, if desired. Ladle
hot chocolate into mugs, dividing equally. Top
with whipped cream and additional candy.

New Year's Eve Dinner à Deux

MENU FOR TWO

OYSTERS ON THE HALF SHELL

CREAM OF ZUCCHINI AND
ANISE SOUP

PHYLLO-WRAPPED SALMON WITH
LEEKS AND RED BELL PEPPERS

PARSLIED RICE PILAF

SAUTÉED BABY VEGETABLES

CHAMPAGNE

MOLTEN CHOCOLATE CAKES

64

hatever the date attached to the
approaching year, there's something
about the final night of Earth's annual trip around the sun that puts
people in the mood for celebrating. The past can't touch us; the future
stretches hopeful and unblemished before us.

For some, the best way to mark the moment is by placing themselves in the center of the biggest crowd they can find, then rocking into
the wee hours of the night. But for others, celebration is something better
done on an intimate level, away from the throngs of partygoers. It is for
these quiet revelers that this very romantic, very elegant menu was
created: a Champagne dinner for two, beginning with oysters on the half
shell and ending with individual, soft-centered chocolate cakes topped
with espresso-flavored whipped cream. In between, there's a creamy
zucchini soup, phyllo-wrapped salmon fillets with bell peppers and leeks,
buttery rice pilaf and baby vegetables. Make the meal together, enjoy it
together, and save a little Champagne for the stroke of midnight, to toast
another year ahead—together.

PHYLLO-WRAPPED SALMON WITH LEEKS AND
RED BELL PEPPERS; AND PARSLIED RICE PILAF.

By candlelight

WHETHER YOU SET the table with thick pillar candles, slender tapers or classic votives, the soft glow of their light creates instant atmosphere.

HELPFUL HINTS

✻ For candles that burn more evenly and slowly, wrap them in a plastic bag or in foil and refrigerate for four to six hours before lighting.

✻ Store new and unused candles flat in a cool, dry place to keep them straight.

✻ Discard candles when they come within several inches of the decor around them.

VOTIVE CANDLES

✻ Instead of place cards, use acrylic paint to write guests' names on glass votive holders.

✻ Put votive candles in their glass holders in small terra-cotta pots that are one to two inches taller than the votive candle. The lit flame will cast an upward glow.

PILLAR CANDLES

✻ Place a homemade or purchased evergreen "wreath" around the base of a pillar candle.

✻ Place a pillar candle in a large, clear glass vase and fill the bottom with small silver and gold tree ornaments so they come halfway up the sides of the candle.

✻ Place pillars in medium-size terra-cotta pots so that the candles extend several inches above the tops of the pots and fill in the sides with fresh-cut cedar, spruce or boxwood.

CANDLESTICKS AND TAPERS

✻ Place candles in a candelabrum and weave lengths of fresh ivy in and out, letting some of the ivy cascade onto the dining table.

✻ Use floral adhesive to stick candles to the bottoms of tall, antique canning jars. Add three inches of cranberries or kumquats to the jars.

Cream of Zucchini and Anise Soup

FRESH OYSTERS WOULD BE A ROMANTIC START TO THIS SPECIAL MEAL. TO SHUCK THEM, GRASP ONE IN A KITCHEN TOWEL, HOLDING IT OVER A BOWL. INSERT AN OYSTER KNIFE BETWEEN THE SHELLS AT THE POINTED END AND TURN TO OPEN. USE THE KNIFE TO LOOSEN THE OYSTER FROM ITS SHELL. PLACE THE OYSTERS IN THEIR SHELLS ON A BED OF ROCK SALT OR ICE TO SERVE. (FOR MORE INFORMATION, SEE THE BOX ON PAGE 108.) THIS SOUP (OPPOSITE), WHICH MAKES AN EXCELLENT FOLLOW-UP TO THE OYSTERS, CAN ALSO BE SERVED CHILLED.

2 servings

- 1 tablespoon olive oil (preferably extra-virgin)
- 3 cups chopped zucchini (from about 3 medium zucchini)
- ½ large onion, chopped
- 1 cup water
- 2 garlic cloves, chopped
- 2 teaspoons fennel seeds
- 1 fresh thyme sprig
- 1 tablespoon crème fraîche or whipping cream
- 1 tablespoon Pernod or other anise-flavored liqueur

    Additional olive oil

Heat 1 tablespoon olive oil in medium saucepan over medium heat. Add chopped zucchini and chopped onion and sauté until onion is translucent, about 15 minutes. Add 1 cup water, chopped garlic, 2 teaspoons fennel seeds and thyme sprig. Stir in crème fraîche and Pernod. Simmer soup uncovered 20 minutes. Remove thyme sprig from soup.

Puree soup in processor until smooth. *(Can be prepared 1 day ahead. Cover and refrigerate.)* Return to saucepan and rewarm over medium heat. Season to taste with salt and pepper. Ladle soup into bowls. Drizzle with olive oil.

Phyllo-wrapped Salmon with Leeks and Red Bell Peppers

IN THIS ELEGANT MAIN COURSE (RIGHT), SALMON
FILLETS ARE TOPPED WITH SAUTÉED RED PEPPERS
AND LEEKS, THEN ROLLED UP IN PHYLLO PASTRY.
(YOU CAN MAKE THE PACKETS SEVERAL HOURS
AHEAD; BAKE THEM JUST BEFORE SERVING.)

2 servings

    4 tablespoons (½ stick) butter
1⅓ cups matchstick-size strips red bell peppers
    ⅔ cup matchstick-size strips leek (white and
       pale green parts only)
    3 tablespoons dry white wine
    ¼ teaspoon dried crushed red pepper
    3 tablespoons thinly sliced fresh basil
    ½ teaspoon (scant) salt

    4 sheets fresh phyllo pastry or frozen, thawed
    2 5-ounce (6 x 2 x 1-inch) skinless
       salmon fillets

Melt 1 tablespoon butter in heavy large skillet
over medium-high heat. Add bell peppers and
leek and sauté until leek is tender, about 6 minutes. Add wine and crushed red pepper to skillet. Simmer until liquid evaporates, about
3 minutes. Remove skillet from heat. Cool vegetable mixture. Stir in basil and salt.

Preheat oven to 400°F. Melt remaining 3 tablespoons butter in small saucepan. Place 1 pastry
sheet on work surface (keep remaining phyllo
sheets covered). Brush with some of melted
butter. Top with second pastry sheet; brush
with melted butter. Place 1 salmon fillet crosswise on pastry sheet, 5 inches in from 1 short
end. Top salmon fillet with half of vegetable

mixture. Fold 5-inch section of pastry over
salmon. Fold in sides. Roll up, forming rectan-
gular packet. Transfer to heavy small baking
sheet, vegetable side up. Brush packet all over
with melted butter. Repeat with remaining pastry sheets, melted butter, salmon fillets and vegetables. *(Can be prepared 6 hours ahead. Cover
with plastic wrap and refrigerate.)*

Bake salmon until pastry is pale golden and
salmon is cooked through, about 35 minutes.

Parslied Rice Pilaf

SAUTÉING THE RICE BEFORE BOILING IT ADDS
BUTTERY FLAVOR TO THIS SIDE DISH. YOU COULD
EXPERIMENT BY ADDING OTHER FRESH HERBS, OR
EVEN TOASTED NUTS. ROUND OUT THE MENU WITH
A COLORFUL MIX OF SAUTÉED BABY VEGETABLES.

2 servings

4 tablespoons (½ stick) butter,
cut into 4 pieces
½ teaspoon salt
1 cup long-grain white rice
2 cups water
Chopped fresh parsley

Melt 2 tablespoons butter in heavy medium
saucepan over medium-high heat. Mix in ½ teaspoon salt, then rice. Sauté until rice is golden,
about 8 minutes. Add 2 cups water. Boil until
water is absorbed, about 10 minutes. Mix in
remaining 2 tablespoons butter. Cover, reduce
heat to very low and cook until rice is tender,
stirring occasionally, about 10 minutes.
Transfer pilaf to bowl. Sprinkle with chopped
fresh parsley and serve.

Molten Chocolate Cakes

INDIVIDUAL WARM CHOCOLATE CAKES WITH SOFT
CENTERS, THESE WILL MAKE THE MEAL ONE TO
REMEMBER INTO THE NEXT YEAR.

2 servings

2½ ounces bittersweet (not unsweetened) or
semisweet chocolate, chopped
2 tablespoons (¼ stick) unsalted butter
½ tablespoon brandy

1 large egg
1 large egg yolk
2½ tablespoons sugar
½ teaspoon vanilla extract
¾ teaspoon instant espresso powder or
instant coffee powder
Pinch of salt
½ tablespoon all purpose flour

¼ cup chilled whipping cream

Generously butter two ¾-cup soufflé dishes or
custard cups. Arrange on baking sheet. Stir
chocolate and butter in heavy small saucepan
over low heat until smooth. Remove from heat;
stir in brandy. Cool 10 minutes, stirring often.

Using electric mixer, beat egg, yolk, 2 tablespoons sugar, vanilla, ½ teaspoon espresso powder and salt in medium bowl until very thick
ribbon falls when beaters are lifted, about
4 minutes. Sift flour over batter; fold in flour.
Fold in chocolate mixture. Divide batter
between dishes. *(Can be made 1 day ahead.
Cover loosely; refrigerate. Let stand at room
temperature 30 minutes before baking.)*

Preheat oven to 400°F. Bake cakes until tops
are puffed and dry and tester inserted into center comes out with moist batter still attached,
about 15 minutes. Cool cakes 5 minutes.

Beat cream, ½ tablespoon sugar and ¼ teaspoon
espresso powder in small bowl until firm peaks
form. Top cakes with whipped cream and serve.

New Year's Day Brunch

MENU FOR EIGHT

MIMOSAS

CORNMEAL BLINI WITH
SOUR CREAM AND CAVIAR

GOAT CHEESE, ARTICHOKE
AND HAM STRATA

SLICED ORANGES WITH
DRIED CRANBERRIES

CAPPUCCINO

CINNAMON-SUGAR BISCOTTI

DARK CHOCOLATE
HONEY-ALMOND FONDUE

70

Okay, you did it. You ushered in the New Year. You stayed up late, watched the ball drop, saw the calendar turn. Now it's the first morning of a new year, and you want to celebrate it with a meal that exemplifies your warmest wishes for yourself and your loved ones in the coming 12 months: simplicity, beauty and good company. This sophisticated brunch will fill that bill perfectly.

Get things off to a slow and rather late start with Mimosas, or any of your favorite brunch concoctions. To go with them, serve the little cornmeal pancakes known as blini, encouraging your guests to top them with sour cream, caviar and chives. The main course—a savory bread pudding-like strata of sourdough, smoked ham and three cheeses—can be made the day ahead, and baked while you're enjoying the blini. A festive salad of sliced oranges, dried cranberries and walnuts makes a good accompaniment. To top off this gem of a meal, there's a new take on fondue, this one made with chocolate and flavored with honey. Instead of bread, "dippers" include homemade biscotti and chunks of fruit. Add steaming cups of cappuccino for a gathering that has style and substance, and is a happy harbinger for the new year.

GOAT CHEESE, ARTICHOKE AND HAM STRATA; AND
SLICED ORANGES WITH DRIED CRANBERRIES.

The beverage bar

SINCE BRUNCH ESSENTIALLY combines two meals, you'll want to offer food and drink that appeal to guests who have just rolled out of bed as well as to early risers who have been up for several hours. A self-serve beverage bar takes the pressure off the host, eliminates the need for a bartender and encourages guests to mix and mingle.

THE BASICS

COFFEE: Have at least two thermoses of coffee (one for decaf, the other for regular) set out for guests to serve themselves.

TEA: Have a samovar or thermos of piping-hot water and a selection of teas (black, green, herbal) so guests can brew their own by the cup.

JUICES: Serve freshly squeezed orange juice in pitchers or carafes placed in a pretty bowl of ice. Tie a colorful napkin around the top of each pitcher to catch drips and spills.

WATER: Place large bottles of sparkling or still mineral water next to an ice bucket.

CHAMPAGNE: Have two bottles open and chilling in wine buckets; keep additional bottles in the refrigerator (it *is* New Year's, after all).

ADDITIONS TO THE BAR

MILK AND CREAM: in pitchers (keep more in the refrigerator and refill as needed).

SWEETENERS: sugar (cubes or granulated) and honey, for tea drinkers.

FRUIT: wedges of orange, lemon and lime.

LIQUEURS AND SYRUPS: brandy, coffee- and orange-flavored liqueurs, plus nonalcoholic syrups (available in specialty foods stores) for adding to sparkling water.

Cornmeal Blini with Sour Cream and Caviar

YOU COULD SET UP A "BLINI STATION" WITH A VOLUNTEER FLIPPING THE CORNMEAL PANCAKES, AND BOWLS OF SOUR CREAM, CHIVES AND CAVIAR FOR GUESTS TO TOP THEIR OWN.

makes about 30

½ cup whole milk
1 large egg yolk
½ cup yellow cornmeal
2 teaspoons all purpose flour
¼ teaspoon baking powder
⅛ teaspoon salt
3 tablespoons butter, melted

Sour cream
Minced chives
Caviar

Whisk milk and yolk in medium bowl to blend. Add cornmeal, flour, baking powder and salt and whisk to blend. Whisk in 1½ tablespoons melted butter. (*Batter can be prepared 1 hour ahead. Cover and refrigerate.*)

Preheat oven to 300°F. Heat heavy large skillet over medium heat. Brush skillet with some of remaining melted butter. Drop batter by generous teaspoonfuls into skillet, spreading slightly with back of spoon. Cook until bottoms of blini are brown, about 1 minute. Turn and cook until second sides are brown, about 1 minute. Transfer to baking sheet; keep warm in oven. Repeat, whisking batter to blend before cooking each batch and brushing skillet with butter as necessary. Transfer blini to platter. Top each with sour cream, chives and caviar.

Goat Cheese, Artichoke and Ham Strata

8 servings

2 cups whole milk
¼ cup olive oil
8 cups 1-inch cubes sourdough bread, crusts trimmed
1½ cups whipping cream
5 large eggs
1 tablespoon chopped garlic
1½ teaspoons salt
¾ teaspoon ground black pepper
½ teaspoon ground nutmeg
12 ounces soft fresh goat cheese, crumbled
2 tablespoons chopped fresh sage
1 tablespoon chopped fresh thyme
1½ teaspoons herbes de Provence

12 ounces smoked ham, chopped
3 6½-ounce jars marinated artichoke hearts, drained, halved lengthwise (about 2½ cups)
1 cup (packed) grated Fontina cheese
1½ cups (packed) grated Parmesan cheese

Preheat oven to 350°F. Butter 13 x 9 x 2-inch glass baking dish. Whisk milk and oil in large bowl. Stir in bread. Let stand until liquid is absorbed, about 10 minutes. Whisk cream and next 5 ingredients in another large bowl. Add goat cheese. Mix herbs in small bowl.

Place half of bread mixture in prepared dish. Top with half of ham, artichoke hearts, herbs and cheeses. Pour half of cream mixture over. Repeat layering with remaining bread, ham, artichoke hearts, herbs, cheeses and cream mixture. *(Can be made 1 day ahead. Cover; chill.)* Bake uncovered until firm in center and brown around edges, about 1 hour.

Sliced Oranges with Dried Cranberries

SPICED NUTS AND DRIED CRANBERRIES TOP CHILLED ORANGE SLICES FOR A CRUNCHY-SWEET-TANGY CONTRAST IN THIS COLORFUL DO-AHEAD SALAD.

8 servings

6 tablespoons honey
1½ tablespoons plus ¾ cup water
¾ teaspoon ground allspice
½ teaspoon salt
¼ teaspoon (generous) ground ginger
1 cup walnut halves and pieces
2 teaspoons sugar

¾ cup cranberry juice cocktail
½ cup dried cranberries

8 oranges, peel and white pith removed, sliced into ½-inch-thick rounds, chilled
Fresh mint sprigs (optional)

Preheat oven to 325°F. Line baking sheet with parchment paper. Mix honey, 1½ tablespoons water, allspice, salt and ginger in large bowl to blend. Add nuts; toss to coat well. Strain nuts, reserving liquid. Transfer nuts to baking sheet. Sprinkle nuts with sugar. Bake until golden brown, about 17 minutes. Cool completely.

Whisk ¾ cup water, cranberry juice and reserved liquid from nuts in medium saucepan to blend. Stir in dried cranberries. Bring to boil. Reduce heat to medium-low and simmer until cranberries soften and liquid is reduced to thin syrup, about 20 minutes. *(Can be made 3 days ahead. Store nuts airtight at room temperature. Cover and chill cranberry mixture.)*

Arrange orange slices on platter. Spoon cranberry mixture over. Sprinkle nuts over. Garnish with mint, if desired.

Cinnamon-Sugar Biscotti

THESE CRISP, TWICE-BAKED COOKIES (RIGHT) ARE
DELICIOUS DIPPED INTO THE CHOCOLATE FONDUE.

makes about 40

    2 cups all purpose flour
2½ teaspoons ground cinnamon
    1 teaspoon baking powder
 ¼ teaspoon salt
    1 cup plus 3 tablespoons sugar
    6 tablespoons (¾ stick) unsalted butter,
       room temperature
    2 large eggs
    1 large egg yolk
    1 teaspoon vanilla extract

Preheat oven to 325°F. Line 2 large baking
sheets with parchment paper. Mix flour, 1½ teaspoons cinnamon, baking powder and salt in
medium bowl to blend. Using electric mixer,
beat 1 cup sugar and butter in large bowl until
fluffy. Add 1 egg; beat well. Add egg yolk; beat
well. Mix in vanilla, then dry ingredients.

Transfer dough to work surface. Divide in half.
Shape each half into 9-inch-long, 1½-inch-wide
log. Transfer logs to prepared baking sheets.
Beat remaining egg in small bowl. Brush logs
with egg. Bake until golden and firm to touch
(dough will spread), about 50 minutes. Cool on
sheets. Maintain oven temperature.

Mix remaining 3 tablespoons sugar and 1 teaspoon cinnamon in small bowl to blend. Using
serrated knife, cut logs into ½-inch-wide diagonal slices. Place biscotti, cut side down, on
baking sheets. Sprinkle ¼ teaspoon cinnamon-
sugar mixture over each biscotti. Bake until
pale golden, about 20 minutes. Cool on racks.
*(Can be made 1 week ahead. Store in airtight con-
tainer at room temperature.)*

Dark Chocolate Honey-Almond Fondue

SILKY CHOCOLATE FONDUE (OPPOSITE) IS A GREAT
WAY TO FINISH OFF THIS BRUNCH. USE AN
ASSORTMENT OF FRUIT AS DIPPERS—OR EVEN THE
BISCOTTI (AT LEFT), IF YOU LIKE. TOBLERONE
CHOCOLATE WORKS WELL IN THE DISH, BECAUSE ITS
HONEY-NOUGAT BLEND ECHOES THE HONEY AND
ALMOND FLAVORS THAT ARE ALSO IN THE RECIPE.

8 servings

 ¾ cup whipping cream
    6 tablespoons honey
    4 3.52-ounce bars Toblerone bittersweet
       chocolate or 14 ounces semisweet
       chocolate, chopped
    2 tablespoons kirsch (clear cherry brandy)
 ½ teaspoon almond extract
       Assorted fresh fruits (such as whole
       strawberries, 1-inch-thick slices peeled
       banana, peeled pear wedges, sliced star fruit,
       grapes and orange segments)

Bring cream and honey to simmer in heavy
medium saucepan. Add chocolate; whisk until
melted. Remove from heat. Whisk in kirsch
and extract. Pour fondue into bowl; place on
platter. Surround with assorted fresh fruits.
Serve fondue with skewers.

New Year's Day Open House

MENU FOR THIRTY

PURCHASED PÂTÉ WITH CRACKERS

SMOKED SALMON WITH SOUR CREAM-CAPER SAUCE

HONEY-ROASTED HAM AND TURKEY WITH
DRIED CHERRY RELISH

SMOKED CHICKEN SALAD ON
CORN BREAD TRIANGLES

SNAPPY RED BELL PEPPER DIP WITH SHRIMP

MARINATED GREEN BEANS AND RED PEPPERS

BELGIAN ENDIVE WITH EGG SALAD

LAYERED POTATO, ONION AND
CELERY ROOT CASSEROLE

CHAMPAGNE, WINE AND ASSORTED BEERS

DESSERTS FROM THE BAKERY

New Year's Day is a great time to make a grand impression on a lot of good friends. They will be looking for a comfortable place to recover and refuel after the previous night's festivities, a place to greet and eat and, of course, watch a football game or two. This year, make your home the destination of choice for these comfort-seekers with this fun and informal meal for a crowd.

Designed to serve approximately 30 hungry guests, the menu doubles easily if you're planning to feed the neighborhood. It's easy in large part because it revolves around purchased honey-roasted turkeys and hams and bakery desserts. All of the appetizers and side dishes are quickly made by you (or you and your guests, if you decide to go the potluck route), among them sliced smoked salmon with a sour cream-caper sauce, a spicy red bell pepper dip for shrimp, and a wonderfully rich potato and celery root casserole. So plug in a couple of televisions, chill the beer and Champagne, assemble this terrific menu (look for the do-ahead tips to get a head start), and have a great time hosting what may well turn out to be the most memorable party of the season.

HONEY-ROASTED HAM AND TURKEY WITH
DRIED CHERRY RELISH; LAYERED POTATO, ONION
AND CELERY ROOT CASSEROLE; AND MARINATED
GREEN BEANS AND RED PEPPERS.

Smoked Salmon with Sour Cream-Caper Sauce

A SIMPLE BUT ELEGANT COLD DISH. THE SAUCE CAN BE MADE A DAY IN ADVANCE.

30 servings

    3 8-ounce containers sour cream
    1 cup chopped red onion
 1/3 cup drained capers
 1/4 cup chopped fresh Italian parsley
 1½ teaspoons ground black pepper

    3 pounds pre-sliced smoked salmon
    3 16-ounce loaves cocktail rye and/or
       pumpernickel bread
       Fresh Italian parsley sprigs

Mix sour cream, onion, capers, chopped parsley and pepper in large bowl. Season to taste with salt. *(Sauce can be made 1 day ahead. Cover with plastic wrap and refrigerate.)*

Place salmon on 2 platters, dividing equally. Arrange bread slices around salmon. Garnish with parsley and serve with sauce.

Honey-roasted Ham and Turkey with Dried Cherry Relish

THE MAIN COURSES, HAM AND TURKEY, ARE PURCHASED (AS ARE THE DESSERTS), MAKING A PARTY THIS SIZE DO-ABLE. THE HOMEMADE APPETIZERS AND SIDE DISHES, NOT TO MENTION THE DELICIOUS RELISH HERE (BELOW), GIVE THE OPEN HOUSE YOUR PERSONAL STAMP. THE COMPONENTS OF THIS RECIPE—HAM AND TURKEY, THE CHERRY RELISH (OPPOSITE, WITH LAYERED POTATO, ONION AND CELERY ROOT CASSEROLE, PAGE 82, AND MARINATED GREEN BEANS AND RED PEPPERS, PAGE 81) AND DINNER ROLLS—CAN BE COMBINED BY YOUR GUESTS TO MAKE LITTLE SANDWICHES.

30 servings

 3/4 cup crème de cassis (black currant-flavored
       liqueur) or cherry-flavored brandy
 3/4 cup water
 3/4 cup sugar
    3 cups dried tart cherries or dried Bing cherries
       or 1½ cups of each (about 15 ounces total)
 1¼ cups pecans, toasted, chopped (about
       4½ ounces)
    3 tablespoons grated orange peel

    1 6- to 8-pound spiral-cut honey-roasted ham
    1 12- to 14-pound honey-roasted turkey
       Small dinner rolls (optional)

Stir crème de cassis, 3/4 cup water and sugar in heavy large saucepan over medium heat until sugar dissolves. Bring to boil. Add dried cherries. Reduce heat; cover and simmer until cherries are plump, about 8 minutes. Mix in pecans and orange peel. Season relish lightly with salt. Transfer to bowl. Cool. *(Can be made 1 week ahead. Cover and refrigerate.)*

Place ham and turkey on platters. Place bowl with cherry relish alongside. Serve with dinner rolls to make sandwiches, if desired.

Smoked Chicken Salad on Corn Bread Triangles

IF YOU CANNOT FIND SMOKED CHICKEN, USE
SMOKED TURKEY INSTEAD.

makes about 60 appetizers

¾ cup mayonnaise

2 tablespoons fresh lime juice

4 teaspoons chopped canned chipotle chilies*

1 teaspoon ground cumin

3 cups finely chopped smoked chicken or
turkey (about 24 ounces)

1 cup finely chopped yellow bell pepper

1 cup finely chopped seeded tomato

1 cup finely chopped peeled jicama

½ cup finely chopped red onion

Green Chili Corn Bread (see recipe at right)

Fresh parsley leaves (optional)

Mix first 4 ingredients in large bowl to blend.
Mix in chicken, bell pepper, tomato, jicama and
onion. Season to taste with salt and pepper.
(Can be prepared 1 day ahead. Cover and chill.)

Preheat oven to 350°F. Cut corn bread into
⅓-inch-thick slices. Cut each slice diagonally in
half, forming 2 triangles. Working in batches,
place on 2 baking sheets. Bake until lightly
toasted, about 10 minutes. Cool.

Top each triangle with 1 tablespoon chicken
salad. Arrange on platter. Garnish each with
parsley leaf, if desired.

*Chipotle *chilies canned in a spicy tomato sauce,
often called* adobo, *are available at Latin
American markets and specialty foods stores.*

Green Chili Corn Bread

THE CORN BREAD IS GREAT ON ITS OWN, TOO.

makes 2 loaves

6 poblano chilies (about 14 ounces total)*

2 cups yellow cornmeal

2 cups all purpose flour

½ cup sugar

4 teaspoons baking powder

2 teaspoons baking soda

2 teaspoons salt

2 cups (packed) grated extra-sharp cheddar
cheese (about 8 ounces)

2 cups buttermilk

4 large eggs

½ cup (1 stick) unsalted butter, melted, cooled

Char chilies over gas flame or in broiler until
blackened on all sides. Enclose in paper bag; let
stand 10 minutes. Peel, seed and chop chilies.
*(Chilies can be prepared 2 days ahead. Cover with
plastic wrap and refrigerate.)*

Preheat oven to 400°F. Generously butter two
9 x 5 x 2¾-inch metal loaf pans. Whisk cornmeal and next 5 ingredients in large bowl to
blend. Stir in cheese. Whisk buttermilk, eggs
and butter in another large bowl to blend. Add
egg mixture to dry ingredients and stir just
until blended. Mix in chilies. Transfer batter to
prepared pans, dividing equally.

Bake breads until deep golden brown on top
and tester inserted into center comes out clean,
about 45 minutes. Cool in pans on rack 10 minutes. Turn breads out onto rack and cool completely. *(Can be prepared 2 weeks ahead. Wrap in
foil; freeze. Unwrap; thaw at room temperature.)*

Fresh green chilies, often called pasillas; *available at Latin American markets and also at some
supermarkets nationwide.*

Snappy Red Bell Pepper Dip with Shrimp

YOU CAN PREPARE THIS BRIGHTLY COLORED DIP UP TO TWO DAYS AHEAD OF TIME.

30 servings

    4 large garlic cloves, peeled
    6 7- to 7.25-ounce jars roasted red peppers,
      undrained
    2 8-ounce packages chilled cream cheese,
      cut into pieces
    3 teaspoons ground cumin
    1 cup chopped seeded tomato
    ½ cup chopped green onions
    3 tablespoons chopped seeded jalapeño chilies

    4 pounds cooked peeled deveined large shrimp

With machine running, drop 2 garlic cloves through feed tube of processor; chop finely. Add roasted peppers from 3 jars with their juices; puree until almost smooth. Add 8 ounces cream cheese and 1½ teaspoons cumin; blend until smooth. Transfer to large bowl. Repeat with remaining garlic, peppers, cream cheese and cumin. Mix in tomato, onions and jalapeños. Season with salt and pepper. Cover and refrigerate at least 4 hours and up to 2 days. Rewhisk dip before serving.

Place half of dip in bowl in center of platter. Surround with shrimp and serve. Replenish dip and shrimp as necessary.

Marinated Green Beans and Red Peppers

A CHRISTMASY SALAD (ABOVE) THAT CAN BE MADE THE MORNING OF THE PARTY.

30 servings

    6 large red bell peppers
    4 pounds slender green beans, trimmed

 1½ cups olive oil
    ⅔ cup red wine vinegar
    6 garlic cloves, minced
      Lettuce leaves (optional)

Char peppers over gas flame or in broiler until blackened on all sides. Enclose in paper bag; let stand 10 minutes. Peel and seed peppers. Cut into ½-inch-wide strips. Transfer to 2 large bowls. Cook beans in large pot of boiling salted water until crisp-tender, about 5 minutes. Drain. Transfer to bowl of ice water to cool. Drain thoroughly. Add green beans to bowls with peppers, dividing equally.

Whisk oil, vinegar and garlic in medium bowl to blend well. Pour over vegetables, dividing equally; toss. Season to taste with salt and pepper. Cover; chill up to 6 hours. Line 2 large bowls with lettuce. Fill with vegetables.

Belgian Endive with Egg Salad

WITH ENDIVE LEAVES ARRANGED IN CONCENTRIC CIRCLES ON THE PLATTER, THIS IS AN ESPECIALLY ATTRACTIVE ADDITION TO THE BUFFET TABLE.

30 servings

8 hard-boiled eggs, shelled, finely chopped
6 tablespoons mayonnaise
¼ cup Dijon mustard
1 teaspoon celery salt

12 heads Belgian endive
Paprika

Mix chopped eggs, mayonnaise, mustard and celery salt in medium bowl. *(Can be made 1 day ahead. Cover and refrigerate.)*

Cut off and discard root ends of endive. Separate leaves. Place 1 generous teaspoon egg salad mixture at wide end of each leaf. Sprinkle salad lightly with paprika.

On 2 large platters, arrange leaves in concentric circles resembling flowers. *(Can be made 4 hours ahead. Cover and refrigerate.)*

Layered Potato, Onion and Celery Root Casserole

RICH AND SATISFYING, THIS DISH (BELOW) IS SURE TO BE THE HIT OF THE PARTY.

30 servings

6 pounds celery roots (celeriac; about 8 medium), peeled, quartered, thinly sliced
6 pounds russet potatoes (about 8 large), peeled, thinly sliced
1 teaspoon ground nutmeg
2 large onions, thinly sliced
6 garlic cloves, minced
4 cups (packed) grated Gruyère cheese (about 1 pound)

4 cups canned low-salt chicken broth or canned vegetable broth
2 cups whipping cream

Preheat oven to 375°F. Generously butter two 13 x 9 x 2-inch glass baking dishes. Divide ⅓ of celery root slices between dishes. Top with ⅓ of potato slices, dividing equally. Sprinkle with salt and pepper, then ¼ teaspoon nutmeg over each. Top with half of onion slices, half of garlic, then half of cheese, dividing equally. Repeat layering 1 more time. Cover with remaining celery root, then potatoes.

Bring broth and cream to simmer in large saucepan. Pour over vegetables, dividing equally. Sprinkle generously with salt and pepper. Cover baking dishes with foil. Bake casseroles 1 hour. Remove foil. Bake until vegetables are very tender and liquid bubbles thickly and is slightly absorbed, about 55 minutes longer. Remove from oven. Let stand 15 to 20 minutes; serve. *(Can be made 2 hours ahead. Let stand at room temperature. Rewarm, covered with foil, in 350°F oven, about 25 minutes.)*

Planning a party

ALL PARTIES REQUIRE planning, but organization is even more important at holiday time when everyone is so busy. There are certain things to consider when planning any party, but large parties come with their own challenges. An open house is a good way to entertain a large number of friends, but to be a success it must have flow and flexibility, since some guests may arrive while others are getting ready to leave. A good rule is to keep the cocktail bar and the dessert table refreshed throughout and to either serve foods that can stand at room temperature for several hours or make plans to have hot foods continuously replenished. Here's a party countdown.

THREE WEEKS AHEAD

✻ Invite guests (by phone or written invitation).

✻ Book hired help (bartender, someone to answer the door and take coats, waitstaff to clear dishes and replenish platters).

✻ Order wine, liquor and specialty foods.

TWO WEEKS AHEAD

✻ Book cleaning service to clean house before and after the party.

✻ Have table linens cleaned and pressed.

✻ Order flowers.

ONE WEEK AHEAD

✻ Shop for nonperishables.

✻ Have wine and liquor delivered.

✻ Prepare anything that can be frozen.

✻ Confirm rentals and hired help.

TWO DAYS AHEAD

✻ Have house cleaned, silver polished, garden and yard tended.

✻ Set out platters, plates and glassware.

✻ Shop for perishable items.

✻ Prepare foods that can be refrigerated until the party.

✻ If you are not ordering ice, begin storing your own in plastic bags.

ONE DAY AHEAD

✻ Arrange flowers.

✻ Set the table.

✻ Place candles in the refrigerator so they'll burn longer.

✻ Select CDs for the party.

THE *Menu*

The big Christmas dinner is surely one of the most important meals of the year. You want everything to be perfect:

a sparkling table, a fabulous menu, and loved ones gathered together to enjoy it all. For many, the holidays are a time when tradition dictates everything— especially the menu. For others, it's an opportunity for culinary experimentation, revising old favorites or trying something completely new. In this section, you will find everything you need to meet any kind of menu demand.

Each chapter here is dedicated to a single course (starters, soups and salads, side dishes, breads and rolls, desserts, and the main course) and features a wide array of options. So whether your idea of the perfect centerpiece dish is goose, roast beef, turkey or a crown roast of pork, you'll find a recipe here (plus seven others, including a meatless lasagna). Begin with the entrée, then mix and match the rest of the menu from there, using our guide on page 86 or your own family favorites. And don't miss all of the advice scattered throughout this section, from tips on roasting (be it turkey, beef, ham or duck) to hints on shucking oysters. The big feast was never so easy.

Christmas Dinners

Everyone has a different idea of what, exactly, the perfect Christmas feast must include. While some insist on roast beef, others wouldn't consider anything other than turkey. Those options are included in this section, along with nine other main-course possibilities. Add to that more than 50 recipes for starters, soups and salads, side dishes, breads, and desserts and you have all the makings of a memorable meal. Mix and match dishes as you like, or use these menus as inspiration.

MENUS FOR SIX

Spiced Moroccan-Style Shrimp *(page 102)*

Creamy Leek Soup with Bacon and Shallots *(page 112)*

Herb-stuffed Leg of Lamb with Parsnips, Potatoes and Pumpkin *(page 94)*

Steamed Brussels Sprouts

Wild-Mushroom Bread Pudding *(page 123)*

Chocolate-Cranberry Poinsettia Cake *(page 140)*

✼

Winter Crudités with Walnut-Garlic Dip *(page 108)*

Hot Cucumber and Watercress Soup *(page 112)*

Red Snapper Roasted with Fennel and Breadcrumbs *(page 91)*

Rice Pilaf with Chestnuts *(page 119)*

Carrot Puree with Ginger and Orange *(page 124)*

Eggnog Custards *(page 136)*

✼

Baked Goat Cheese with Roasted Garlic and Caramelized Onion *(page 108)*

Wild Rice and Wild Mushroom Soup *(page 111)*

Garlic-studded Racks of Lamb *(page 93)*

Potato and Apple Galette with Sage *(page 125)*

Haricots Verts with Chopped Toasted Almonds

Sesame-Onion Crescent Rolls *(page 131)*

Poached Pears in Red Wine Sauce *(page 145)*

MENUS FOR EIGHT

Mushrooms Stuffed with Herbed Breadcrumbs *(page 107)*

Mixed Baby Greens with Balsamic Vinaigrette

Roasted Eggplant Lasagna with Broiled Tomato Sauce *(page 101)*

Peas with Caraway and Parmesan Butter *(page 118)*

Crusty Italian Bread

Chestnut Cheesecake *(page 144)*

✼

Cheddar Cheese Tartlets *(page 109)*

Curly Endive Salad with Radishes, Coriander and Bacon *(page 117)*

Roast Goose with Caramelized Apples *(page 99)*

Sautéed Swiss Chard

Carrot Puree with Ginger and Orange *(page 124)*

Sesame-Onion Crescent Rolls *(page 131)*

Honey-Pecan Pumpkin Pie *(page 138)*

✼

Steamed Artichokes with Butter and Lemon

Shrimp, Zucchini and Red Pepper Bisque *(page 110)*

Beef Wellington with Madeira Sauce *(page 96)*

Broccoli and Cauliflower with Chive Butter *(page 125)*

Red-skinned Potatoes with Rosemary

Christmas Pudding with Brandy Butter *(page 136)*

MENUS FOR TEN

Smoked Salmon and Goat Cheese
Crostini *(page 104)*

Herb-crusted Beef Tenderloin with
Bell Pepper Relish *(page 92)*

Baked Potatoes with Chives and Sour Cream

Corn and Winter Squash with Spinach *(page 119)*

Chocolate-Caramel Tart *(page 142)*

❊

Butternut Squash Soup with
Cider Cream *(page 114)*

Crown Roast of Pork with Apple Stuffing and
Cider Gravy *(page 90)*

Golden Mashed Potatoes with Parsnips and
Celery *(double recipe; page 124)*

Broccoli Florets with Toasted Pine Nuts

Mocha and Raspberry Trifle *(page 134)*

❊

Skewered Lamb with Almond-Mint
Pesto *(page 103)*

Orange- and Balsamic-glazed
Roast Duck *(page 100)*

Cranberry, Tangerine and
Blueberry Sauce *(page 100)*

Rice Pilaf with Chestnuts *(double recipe; page 119)*

Steamed Snow Peas

Warm Pear Shortcakes with Brandied
Cream *(page 146)*

MENUS FOR TWELVE

Crab Cakes with Chive and Caper
Sauce *(page 105)*

Spinach, Beet and Walnut Salad *(page 117)*

Marmalade-glazed Ham with
Pineapple Relish *(page 88)*

Brown Sugar-glazed Sweet Potatoes with
Marshmallows *(double recipe; page 123)*

Sautéed Collard Greens

Cheddar Cheese Biscuits with Dill
and Chives *(page 127)*

Gingerbread Cake with Maple Whipped
Cream *(page 139)*

❊

Smoked Salmon and Fennel Salad with
Horseradish Dressing *(double recipe; page 116)*

Honey-brined Turkey with
Cream Gravy *(page 98)*

Leek, Mushroom and Bacon Dressing *(page 120)*

Green Beans with Pearl Onions

Piquant Cranberry Sauce *(page 122)*

Mashed Potato Bread *(page 129)*

Chocolate-glazed Croquembouche *(page 147)*

Main Course

Whether the main course for your Christmas meal is a given or you are open to suggestions, this collection of entrées may well have just what you're looking for. If it has to be turkey, there's a wonderful one here; if it might be ham or duck or fish, you'll find versions of all three—plus seven other recipes, all festive and delicious.

Marmalade-glazed Ham with Pineapple Relish

FOR THIS RECIPE (OPPOSITE), USE A FULLY COOKED BONE-IN HAM THAT HAS THE NATURAL SHAPE OF THE LEG, AND HAS SOME FAT AND RIND STILL ATTACHED. DO NOT SUBSTITUTE A "RE-FORMED" OVAL CANNED HAM OR A DELI HAM.

12 servings

ham

  1 16- to 19-pound smoked fully cooked
    bone-in ham
36 (about) whole cloves

  1 cup orange marmalade
¼ cup Dijon mustard
  2 tablespoons plus 1½ cups water

sauce

2 cups water
4 orange-spice herb tea bags or black tea bags
2 cups canned low-salt chicken broth
1 cup orange juice
3 tablespoons orange marmalade
1 tablespoon Dijon mustard
1 tablespoon cornstarch dissolved in
  1 tablespoon water

Pineapple Relish (see recipe opposite)

FOR HAM: Position rack in center of oven and preheat to 325°F. Trim any rind and excess fat from upper side of ham, leaving ¼-inch-thick layer of fat. Using long sharp knife, score fat in 1-inch-wide diamond pattern. Insert 1 clove into center of each scored diamond. Place ham in heavy large roasting pan. Bake until thermometer inserted into center of ham registers 120°F, about 3 hours 45 minutes.

Melt 1 cup marmalade in heavy small saucepan over medium heat. Whisk in ¼ cup mustard and 2 tablespoons water. Boil until mixture thickens enough to coat spoon without dripping, about 6 minutes. Set mixture aside.

Transfer ham to cutting board. Increase oven temperature to 425°F. Place same roasting pan atop burner set on medium heat. Whisk remaining 1½ cups water into pan, scraping up browned bits from bottom. Transfer pan juices to 4-cup glass measuring cup. Freeze pan juices 15 minutes. Spoon fat off top of pan juices. Reserve pan juices in measuring cup.

Line same pan with foil. Return ham to pan. Generously spoon marmalade mixture over ham. Bake ham until glaze is set and begins to caramelize, about 20 minutes. Let ham stand 30 minutes at room temperature.

MEANWHILE, PREPARE SAUCE: Bring 2 cups water to boil in heavy medium saucepan. Add tea bags. Remove from heat; cover and let steep 10 minutes. Discard tea bags. Add chicken broth, orange juice and marmalade to tea. Boil mixture until reduced to 3 cups, about 12 minutes. Whisk in Dijon mustard and reserved pan juices. Return to boil. Whisk in cornstarch mixture. Boil until sauce thickens slightly, about 4 minutes. Season sauce to taste with pepper.

Carve ham; serve with sauce and relish.

Pineapple Relish

THIS REFRESHING CONDIMENT CAN BE MADE A DAY AHEAD OF TIME. IT'S GREAT WITH THE HAM, OR TRY IT WITH FISH OR CHICKEN.

makes 4 cups

½ large pineapple, peeled, cored, cut into
  ¼-inch pieces (about 3 cups)
½ cup finely chopped green bell pepper
½ cup finely chopped red onion
¼ cup chopped fresh mint
2 teaspoons grated lemon peel

Stir all ingredients in large bowl to blend. Season to taste with salt and pepper. (Can be made 1 day ahead. Cover; chill.)

Crown Roast of Pork with Apple Stuffing and Cider Gravy

A SIMPLY SPECTACULAR ENTRÉE (BELOW). ASK THE BUTCHER TO GRIND ANY PORK TRIMMINGS TO USE IN THE STUFFING. BEGIN PREPARING THE ROAST THE DAY BEFORE YOU PLAN TO SERVE IT.

10 servings

pork

1 8-pound crown roast of pork (12 ribs)
2 tablespoons vegetable oil
1 teaspoon salt
1 teaspoon sugar
1 teaspoon dried thyme
½ teaspoon crumbled dried sage
½ teaspoon ground black pepper

Apple Stuffing (see recipe opposite)

gravy

1½ cups canned beef broth
1 cup apple cider
4 teaspoons cornstarch
2 tablespoons applejack brandy or brandy

FOR PORK: Position pork atop 9- to 10-inch-diameter tart pan bottom. Transfer to large rimmed baking sheet. Brush pork with oil. Combine salt, sugar, thyme, sage and pepper in small bowl. Rub spice mixture over pork. Cover with plastic and refrigerate overnight.

Position rack in bottom third of oven and preheat to 450°F. Fill pork cavity with enough stuffing to mound in center. Cover tips of pork bones with foil. Roast pork 20 minutes. Reduce temperature to 325°F. Continue roasting until thermometer inserted into center of pork meat registers 150°F, about 1 hour 50 minutes. Remove foil from bones. Continue roasting until thermometer inserted into center of pork and stuffing registers 155°F, about 15 minutes longer. Carefully transfer roast atop tart pan bottom to serving platter.

FOR GRAVY: Add 1 cup broth to baking sheet and scrape up browned bits from bottom of baking sheet. Pour juices into 2-cup glass measuring cup; freeze 15 minutes. Spoon fat off top of pan juices. Transfer pan juices to medium saucepan. Add remaining ½ cup beef broth and apple cider. Bring to boil. Dissolve cornstarch into applejack in small bowl; whisk into broth mixture. Boil until gravy thickens slightly, about 3 minutes. Season with salt and pepper. Transfer gravy to sauceboat.

Carve roast between bones to separate chops. Serve with stuffing and gravy.

Apple Stuffing

PART OF THIS STUFFING IS USED TO FILL THE
CROWN ROAST OF PORK, AND THE REST IS BAKED
ALONGSIDE. IT SLICES FOR SERVING.

10 servings

    2 tablespoons vegetable oil
1¼ cups chopped celery
    ⅓ cup chopped shallots
    1 tablespoon minced garlic
    2 pounds ground pork
    1 cup plain dry breadcrumbs
    4 ounces dried apples, chopped
    ⅓ cup chopped fresh parsley
    2 teaspoons crumbled dried sage
    2 teaspoons salt
    ¾ teaspoon ground black pepper
    ¼ teaspoon ground allspice
    3 large eggs, beaten to blend
    1 cup (about) canned beef broth

Heat oil in heavy medium skillet over medium
heat. Add celery and sauté until tender, about
3 minutes. Add shallots and garlic; sauté until
shallots are tender, about 2 minutes. Transfer
mixture to large bowl. Mix in all remaining
ingredients except eggs and beef broth. *(Can be
prepared 1 day ahead. Cover and refrigerate.)* Add
eggs and enough broth to moisten stuffing.

Preheat oven to 375°F. Set aside enough stuffing to fill crown roast of pork cavity. Transfer
remaining stuffing to 8½ x 4½ x 2½-inch loaf
pan. Cover with foil. Bake stuffing in pan
alongside roast until thermometer inserted into
center registers 155°F, about 1 hour.

Invert stuffing in pan onto platter. Slice stuffing and serve with roast. *(Can be prepared
1 day ahead. Cover and refrigerate. Rewarm.)*

Red Snapper Roasted with Fennel and Breadcrumbs

IF ONE LARGE FISH IS DIFFICULT TO FIND, TWO
SMALLER ONES CAN BE SUBSTITUTED.

6 servings

    2 fresh fennel bulbs, trimmed, chopped
    6 large shallots or green onions, chopped
    ½ cup chopped fresh Italian parsley
    2 cups soft fresh breadcrumbs from
        French bread
    ¼ cup olive oil

    1 3½- to 4-pound headless red snapper
    ¼ cup dry white wine
        Olive oil

Combine first 3 ingredients in medium bowl.
Transfer 1 cup fennel mixture to large bowl.
Add breadcrumbs and ¼ cup oil to fennel mix-
ture in large bowl. Season with salt and pepper.
*(Can be made 1 day ahead. Cover fennel and
breadcrumb mixtures separately; chill.)*

Preheat oven to 450°F. Cut slashes 2 inches
apart almost to bone in both sides of fish.
Spread half of fennel mixture in bottom of
gratin dish or roasting pan. Sprinkle with wine.
Brush generous amount of oil over inside and
outside of fish. Season inside and out with salt
and pepper. Set fish atop fennel mixture in
gratin dish. Spread remaining fennel mixture
inside fish. Spread breadcrumb mixture over
top of fish, pressing to adhere.

Bake fish until just opaque in center, about
45 minutes. Serve with fennel mixture.

Herb-crusted Beef Tenderloin with Bell Pepper Relish

HERE'S A CENTERPIECE DISH (BELOW) THAT REALLY LIVES UP TO THE NAME. A PEPPER-AND-OLIVE RELISH ADDS BEAUTIFUL COLOR AND FLAVOR.

10 servings

    8 tablespoons olive oil
    2 2¼- to 2¾-pound pieces beef tenderloin
      (thick end), trimmed

    6 garlic cloves, minced
    2½ tablespoons minced fresh thyme
    2½ tablespoons minced fresh rosemary
    6 tablespoons Dijon mustard

    Bell Pepper Relish (see recipe at right)

Preheat oven to 375°F. Rub 1 tablespoon oil over each beef piece. Sprinkle with salt and pepper. Heat 2 large nonstick skillets over high heat. Add 1 beef piece to each; brown on all sides, about 5 minutes.

Place beef pieces in 1 large roasting pan. Mix 6 tablespoons oil, garlic, 2 tablespoons thyme and 2 tablespoons rosemary in small bowl. Coat top and sides of beef pieces with mustard, then with herb mixture. Roast until thermometer inserted into center of beef registers 125°F for medium-rare, about 45 minutes. Transfer to platter. Let stand 10 minutes.

Cut beef into ½-inch-thick slices. Sprinkle with remaining ½ tablespoon each of thyme and rosemary and serve with pepper relish.

Bell Pepper Relish

TRY THIS WITH ANY ROASTED MEAT OR AS A TOPPER FOR *CROSTINI*. BEGIN MAKING IT A DAY AHEAD.

makes about 2 cups

    2 tablespoons (¼ stick) butter
    2 tablespoons olive oil
    1 large onion, thinly sliced
    1 red bell pepper, coarsely chopped
    1 yellow bell pepper, coarsely chopped
    ⅓ cup coarsely chopped pitted Kalamata olives
    1 tablespoon Dijon mustard
    1 large garlic clove, chopped

Melt butter with oil in heavy large skillet over medium-high heat. Add onion; sauté until golden, about 5 minutes. Add peppers; sauté until just tender, about 3 minutes. Add olives, mustard and garlic. Stir 1 minute. Remove from heat. Season with salt and pepper. Transfer relish to bowl. Cool. Cover and refrigerate overnight. *(Can be made 2 days ahead. Keep refrigerated.)* Bring relish to room temperature before serving.

Garlic-studded Racks of Lamb

ASK YOUR BUTCHER TO REMOVE THE BACKBONES FROM THE RACKS AND TRIM TWO INCHES OF FAT STARTING FROM THE TIPS OF THE RIB BONES (THIS IS CALLED FRENCHING THE RACKS). SAVE THE BACKBONES TO MAKE THE STOCK FOR THE SAUCE.

6 servings

lamb

- ¾ cup olive oil
- ¼ cup red wine vinegar
- ¼ cup chopped fresh parsley
- 1 teaspoon Dijon mustard
- 1 teaspoon salt
- 1 teaspoon dried thyme
- 2 bay leaves, crumbled
- 3 racks of lamb with 6 ribs each, frenched, backbones reserved for Lamb Stock (see recipe at right)
- 4 garlic cloves, slivered

sauce

- ½ cup dry red wine
- ⅓ cup finely chopped shallots
- 1 cup Lamb Stock (see recipe at right)

  Cracked black pepper
- ⅓ cup olive oil
- 8 tablespoons (1 stick) chilled unsalted butter, cut into 8 pieces
- 2 tablespoons finely chopped fresh parsley

FOR LAMB: Mix oil, vinegar, parsley, mustard, salt, thyme and bay leaves in medium bowl. Cut small slits in lamb. Press garlic slivers into slits. Place lamb in large glass baking dish. Pour marinade over. Cover and refrigerate overnight, turning occasionally.

FOR SAUCE: Boil wine and shallots in heavy medium saucepan until liquid is reduced to 2 tablespoons. Add Lamb Stock and boil until liquid is reduced to ⅔ cup, about 5 minutes.

Preheat oven to 450°F. Remove lamb from marinade and pat dry. Rub with cracked pepper. Heat oil in heavy large roasting pan over medium heat. Add lamb and cook until brown, about 3 minutes per side. Transfer lamb in pan to oven and roast until meat thermometer inserted into center of meat registers 130°F for rare, about 25 minutes. Transfer racks to platter. Tent with foil to keep warm.

Pour off any fat from roasting pan. Place roasting pan over medium-high heat. Add reduced stock and bring to boil, scraping up any browned bits. Return mixture to same saucepan. Whisk in 2 pieces butter. Set pan over low heat and whisk in remaining butter 1 piece at a time, removing pan from heat briefly if drops of melted butter appear. (If sauce breaks down at any time, remove from heat and whisk in 2 tablespoons butter.) Season with salt and pepper. Mix in parsley.

Cut racks into individual chops. Place 3 on each plate. Spoon sauce over lamb chops.

Lamb Stock

makes 1 cup

- 2 tablespoons olive oil
  Backbones reserved from Garlic-studded Racks of Lamb (see recipe at left)
- 2 cups chicken stock or canned low-salt chicken broth
- 2 cups water

Heat oil in heavy large saucepan over medium-high heat. Add bones and brown well, stirring frequently, about 15 minutes. Pour off oil. Add stock and water to pan and bring to boil, scraping up any browned bits. Cook over medium-high heat until reduced to 1 cup. Strain into bowl. *(Can be made 3 days ahead; chill.)*

Herb-stuffed Leg of Lamb with Parsnips, Potatoes and Pumpkin

THIS BONELESS—ASK THE BUTCHER TO DO THAT
CHORE FOR YOU—ROAST (OPPOSITE) IS SPREAD
WITH A FRESH HERB BUTTER, THEN ROLLED, A STEP
THAT CAN BE DONE A DAY AHEAD. THE VEGETABLES,
A HEARTY MIX OF RED POTATOES, PARSNIPS AND
PUMPKIN OR BUTTERNUT SQUASH, COOK IN THE
DELICIOUS PAN JUICES WHILE THE ROAST LAMB RESTS.

6 servings

1 cup (packed) fresh parsley
⅓ cup (packed) fresh rosemary leaves
⅓ cup (packed) fresh oregano leaves
⅓ cup (packed) chopped fresh thyme
6 large garlic cloves
¼ cup (½ stick) butter, room temperature
1 5½-pound leg of lamb, boned

4 medium-size red-skinned potatoes, quartered
4 large parsnips, peeled, halved lengthwise,
   cut into 3-inch pieces
1 small pumpkin or medium butternut squash
   (about 1¾ pounds) peeled, seeded,
   cut into 2-inch pieces

Assorted fresh herbs

Combine first 6 ingredients in processor.
Process until herbs and garlic are finely
chopped. Open lamb and season with salt and
pepper. Reserve 2 tablespoons herb butter for
vegetables; spread remainder inside lamb. Roll
up lamb and tie with string at 3-inch intervals.

Bring large pot of water to boil. Add potatoes
and parsnips and boil 4 minutes. Add pumpkin
and continue to boil until vegetables are tender,
about 8 minutes. Drain. Refresh vegetables
under cold water; drain. *(Can be prepared 1 day
ahead. Cover lamb, vegetables and reserved herb
butter separately and refrigerate.)*

Preheat oven to 375°F. Season lamb with salt
and pepper. Set lamb in roasting pan. Roast
until thermometer inserted into thickest part
registers 130°F for rare, about 1 hour 10 minutes. Maintain oven temperature. Transfer
lamb to platter; tent with foil to keep warm.
Pour off fat from pan. Add vegetables to pan.
Season with salt and pepper. Add reserved
2 tablespoons herb butter and toss to coat. Bake
until vegetables begin to brown, about 25 minutes. Surround lamb with vegetables. Garnish
with assorted fresh herbs.

Roasting 101

As many cooks know, turning out a beautifully browned yet moist turkey or tender roast beef isn't as easy as following a chart with cooking times per pound. After all, roasting takes place in a dry oven at a relatively high temperature, making it easy to overcook. Follow these tips for perfect roasting every time.

HELPFUL HINTS

✻ Start with thawed meats that are close to room temperature; this keeps the outside from burning before the inside is done.

✻ Use a roasting rack underneath the meat or poultry so that it doesn't stick to the pan. If you don't have a rack, try roasting atop a bed of whole celery and peeled carrots.

✻ Don't rely on cooking times to determine when the meat is done. Instead, use the cooking time as a guideline, and begin testing for doneness as the end of that time approaches.

✻ If the meat or poultry is browning too quickly, cover it loosely with foil.

✻ When roasting whole poultry, check for doneness by piercing the bird's thigh. The juices should be clear, not pink. The USDA recommends an internal temperature of 180°F.

✻ To check doneness, insert an instant-read thermometer into the thickest part of the roast, making sure that it doesn't touch any bone. The USDA recommends the following temperatures: beef and lamb, 145°F; pork, 160°F.

✻ Remember that the meat or poultry's internal temperature will rise by 5 to 10 degrees after being removed from the oven.

Beef Wellington with Madeira Sauce

BEEF WELLINGTON, A CLASSIC SPECIAL-OCCASION ENTRÉE, CONSISTS OF BEEF TENDERLOIN THAT HAS BEEN SPREAD WITH LIVER PÂTÉ AND WRAPPED IN PASTRY. THIS VERSION IS ELEGANT, IMPRESSIVE AND ABSOLUTELY DELICIOUS—A PERFECT CENTERPIECE DISH FOR THE CHRISTMAS TABLE.

8 servings

chicken liver pâté

2 tablespoons (¼ stick) butter
1 pound chicken livers, trimmed
1 medium onion, chopped
1 tablespoon chopped fresh thyme
2 tablespoons brandy

beef

2 tablespoons vegetable oil
1 12- to 13-inch-long, 3- to 4-inch-diameter beef tenderloin (about 4 pounds), fat trimmed

1 17.3-ounce package frozen puff pastry (2 sheets), thawed
1 egg, beaten to blend (for glaze)

Madeira Sauce (see recipe opposite)

FOR CHICKEN LIVER PÂTÉ: Melt butter in heavy large skillet over high heat. Add chicken livers, onion and thyme and sauté until livers are cooked through and all liquid evaporates, scraping bottom of skillet often, about 8 minutes. Add brandy and simmer 1 minute, scraping up any browned bits from bottom of skillet. Puree mixture in food processor until smooth. Season with salt and pepper. Cool. *(Can be prepared 1 day ahead. Cover and refrigerate.)*

FOR BEEF: Heat oil in heavy very large skillet over high heat. Add beef to skillet and brown on all sides, about 8 minutes. Transfer beef to baking sheet and refrigerate until cool to touch, about 15 minutes.

Lightly flour another heavy large baking sheet. Roll out each pastry sheet on floured surface to 13-inch square. Overlap pastry sheets by ½ inch on prepared baking sheet, pressing overlapping edges to seal. Brush pastry with egg glaze. Spread half of liver pâté over bottom and sides of beef. Place beef, pâté side down, in center of pastry. Cover top and sides of beef with remaining pâté. Lift up long sides of pastry in center and overlap atop beef. Lightly brush edges with water and press together to seal. Press pastry against beef at short ends to cover completely and seal. Trim excess pastry from short ends. Crimp edges with fork to seal.

Gather scraps and reroll to 16-inch-long, 5-inch-wide rectangle (about ⅟₁₆ inch thick). Cut out three 16-inch-long, 1-inch-wide strips and one 2-inch-long, 1-inch-wide strip. Fold each 16-inch strip in half lengthwise, forming three 16-inch-long, ½-inch-wide strips. Press edges of each to seal.

Brush lengthwise and crosswise seams of beef Wellington lightly with water. Place 1 pastry strip lengthwise down center of beef Welling-ton, covering seam. Cut second pastry strip crosswise in half, forming two 8-inch strips. Place one 8-inch strip crosswise atop beef Wellington, covering center seam. Form ring with third 16-inch pastry strip and press ends together. Press to seal at center, creating 2 bow loops. Place bow loops atop center of beef.

Cut remaining 8-inch pastry strip crosswise in half. Attach both pieces at base of bow loops, forming ribbons. Fold 2-inch strip in half lengthwise. Press edges to seal. Cover center of bow loops and ribbons with strip, forming knot. Brush entire beef Wellington with egg glaze. *(Can be prepared 6 hours ahead. Cover with plastic wrap and refrigerate.)*

Position rack in center of oven and preheat to 450°F. Bake until pastry is golden and ther-mometer inserted into thickest part of meat registers 125°F for medium-rare, about 40 min-utes. Transfer baking sheet to rack. Using spat-ula, gently loosen bottom of beef Wellington from pan. Let stand in pan 10 minutes. Serve with Madeira Sauce.

Madeira Sauce

MADEIRA, LIKE PORT, IS A FORTIFIED WINE. ITS RICH AND COMPLEX FLAVOR ADDS DEPTH TO THIS SAUCE.

makes about 2 cups

  2 tablespoons (¼ stick) butter
  ½ cup chopped onion
  ¼ cup minced celery
  ¼ cup minced carrot
  2 tablespoons all purpose flour
  2 cups canned beef broth
  ½ cup chopped seeded tomatoes

  ½ cup Madeira
  ½ teaspoon chopped fresh thyme

Melt butter in heavy medium saucepan over medium heat. Add onion, celery and carrot; sauté until beginning to brown, about 25 min-utes. Add flour and stir until flour browns, about 8 minutes. Gradually whisk in broth. Bring to boil, whisking constantly. Reduce heat to low; add tomatoes and simmer until sauce begins to thicken, about 10 minutes. Remove from heat; cool slightly.

Puree sauce in blender in batches. Return to saucepan. Stir in Madeira and thyme. Bring to boil. Reduce heat; simmer until reduced to sauce consistency, whisking occasionally, about 5 minutes. *(Can be made 2 days ahead. Cover and chill. Reheat sauce before serving.)*

Honey-brined Turkey with Cream Gravy

HERE, THE TURKEY IS "BRINED" IN A MIX OF WATER, SALT, HONEY AND SEASONINGS. THE RESULTS (BELOW) ARE INCREDIBLY TENDER, BUT YOU DO NEED TO GET STARTED A DAY AHEAD.

14 to 16 servings

turkey

1 19- to 20-pound turkey, neck, heart and gizzard reserved for gravy

8 quarts water

2 cups coarse salt

1 cup honey

2 bunches fresh thyme

8 large garlic cloves, peeled

2 tablespoons coarsely cracked black pepper

2 lemons, halved

2 tablespoons olive oil

5 cups (about) canned low-salt chicken broth

gravy

Reserved turkey neck, heart and gizzard

6 cups water

3½ cups canned low-salt chicken broth

2 carrots, coarsely chopped

1 onion, halved

1 large celery stalk, chopped

1 small bay leaf

5 tablespoons butter

5 tablespoons all purpose flour

¼ cup whipping cream

FOR TURKEY: Line extra-large stockpot with heavy large plastic bag (about 30-gallon capacity). Rinse turkey; place in plastic bag. Stir 8 quarts water, 2 cups coarse salt and 1 cup honey in large pot until salt and honey dissolve. Add 1 bunch fresh thyme, peeled garlic cloves and black pepper. Pour brine over turkey. Gather plastic bag tightly around turkey so that bird is covered with brine; seal plastic bag. Refrigerate pot with turkey in brine at least 12 hours and up to 18 hours.

Position rack in bottom third of oven and preheat to 350°F. Drain turkey well; discard brine. Pat turkey dry inside and out. Squeeze juice from lemon halves into main cavity. Add lemon rinds and remaining 1 bunch fresh thyme to main cavity. Tuck wings under turkey; tie legs together loosely to hold shape. Place turkey on rack set in large roasting pan. Rub turkey all over with 2 tablespoons olive oil.

Roast turkey 1 hour. Baste turkey with 1 cup chicken broth. Continue to roast until turkey is deep brown and thermometer inserted into thickest part of thigh registers 180°F, basting with 1 cup chicken broth every 30 minutes and covering loosely with foil if turkey is browning too quickly, about 2½ hours longer. Transfer turkey to platter. Tent loosely with foil; let stand 30 minutes. Pour pan juices into glass measuring cup. Spoon off fat; reserve juices.

MEANWHILE, PREPARE GRAVY: Place reserved turkey neck, heart and gizzard into large saucepan. Add 6 cups water, 3½ cups chicken broth, carrots, onion, celery and bay leaf. Simmer over medium heat until turkey stock is reduced to 3 cups, about 2 hours. Strain turkey stock into bowl; reserve turkey neck and giblets. Pull meat off neck. Chop neck meat and giblets; set aside.

Melt 5 tablespoons butter in heavy large saucepan over medium heat. Add 5 tablespoons all purpose flour and whisk 2 minutes. Gradually whisk in turkey stock, cream and up to 1 cup reserved turkey pan juices (juices are salty, so add according to taste). Simmer gravy until thickened to desired consistency, whisking occasionally, about 5 minutes. Add chopped turkey neck meat and giblets; season to taste with pepper. Serve turkey with gravy.

Roast Goose with Caramelized Apples

A CHRISTMAS TRADITION IN MANY PLACES, ROAST GOOSE IS SURPRISINGLY EASY TO MAKE. HERE, BAKED APPLES MAKE A WONDERFUL SIDE DISH.

8 servings

1 13-pound goose, giblets and neck discarded
3 garlic cloves, thinly sliced

8 Gala or Golden Delicious apples, peeled, each cut into 6 wedges
¼ cup fresh lemon juice
6 tablespoons sugar
¼ cup apple juice
1½ teaspoons ground cinnamon

Position rack in bottom third of oven and preheat to 350°F. Rinse goose inside and out; pat dry with paper towels. Sprinkle goose inside and out with salt and pepper. Using knife, cut small slits all over goose, then place garlic slices into slits. Place goose on wire rack, breast side down, in large roasting pan.

Roast goose 2 hours 45 minutes, basting occasionally with drippings and removing excess fat; reserve 6 tablespoons fat. Turn goose over. Roast until brown and thermometer inserted into thickest part of thigh registers 175°F, basting occasionally, about 45 minutes longer.

Meanwhile, toss apple wedges and lemon juice in large bowl. Pour 6 tablespoons goose fat into 15 x 10 x 2-inch glass baking dish. Using slotted spoon, transfer apples to baking dish; toss apples in goose fat. Add sugar, apple juice and cinnamon to apples; toss. Bake apples alongside goose until very tender and golden, 1 hour.

Serve goose with caramelized apples.

Orange- and Balsamic-glazed Roast Duck

YOU WILL NEED TWO LARGE ROASTING PANS WITH RACKS FOR THIS RECIPE—AND AN OVEN BIG ENOUGH TO HOLD THEM. IF YOUR CHRISTMAS DINNER IS SMALLER, BUY JUST TWO DUCKS AND HALVE THE REMAINING INGREDIENTS TO SERVE SIX.

10 to 12 servings

4 5½-pound ducks, fresh or frozen, thawed (necks, hearts and gizzards discarded)
4 pink grapefruits, cut into large wedges
4 oranges, cut into large wedges

2 cups orange juice
1 cup balsamic vinegar
1 tablespoon chopped fresh rosemary

Cranberry, Tangerine and Blueberry Sauce (see recipe at right)

Position 1 rack in center and 1 rack on bottom shelf in oven and preheat to 400°F. Rinse ducks inside and out; pat dry with towels. Trim excess fat from cavities of ducks. Using fork, pierce duck skin in several places. Place 2 ducks, breast side up, on rack in each of 2 large roasting pans. Sprinkle salt and pepper over ducks and in cavities. Fill duck cavities with half of grapefruit wedges and half of orange wedges, dividing equally. Tie legs together with string to hold shape. Scatter remaining grapefruit and orange wedges around ducks in pans.

Roast ducks 50 minutes. Mix orange juice, vinegar and rosemary in bowl. Using baster, remove fat from pans. Turn ducks breast side down on racks. Pour orange juice mixture over ducks, dividing equally. Roast 25 minutes, basting occasionally with pan juices. Turn ducks breast side up. Roast until thermometer

inserted into inner thigh registers 180°F, basting occasionally, about 30 minutes longer.

Remove string from duck legs. Discard fruit from duck cavities. Transfer ducks to platter. Serve immediately with Cranberry, Tangerine and Blueberry Sauce.

Cranberry, Tangerine and Blueberry Sauce

makes about 3½ cups

6 large tangerines

1 cup (packed) golden brown sugar
1 tablespoon minced peeled fresh ginger
⅛ teaspoon ground cloves
Pinch of salt
1½ 12-ounce packages fresh cranberries (about 6 cups)
1½ cups frozen blueberries, thawed

Finely grate enough peel from tangerines to measure 2 tablespoons. Using small sharp knife, cut all peel and white pith from 1 tangerine. Cut between membranes to release segments. Set aside. Squeeze enough juice from remaining tangerines to measure 1½ cups.

Combine peel, juice, brown sugar, ginger, cloves and salt in heavy large saucepan. Bring to boil, stirring until sugar dissolves. Reduce heat and simmer 5 minutes. Add cranberries and cook until berries pop and juices thicken, stirring often, about 8 minutes. Add blueberries and tangerine segments. Stir until blueberries are heated through. Cool. Cover and refrigerate. *(Can be made 4 days ahead. Keep refrigerated.)* Serve cold or at room temperature.

Roasted Eggplant Lasagna with Broiled Tomato Sauce

THIS MEATLESS MAIN COURSE HAS WONDERFUL SMOKY FLAVORS AND JUST A TOUCH OF SWEETNESS.

8 servings

  2   1-pound eggplants, peeled, cut into
       1-inch pieces
  2   tablespoons olive oil

  2   pounds part-skim ricotta cheese
1¼   cups freshly grated Parmesan cheese
       (about 3 ounces)
  ½   cup chopped shallots
  1   tablespoon chopped fresh rosemary

       Broiled Tomato Sauce with Roasted Garlic
       (see recipe at right)
  9   no-boil or oven-ready lasagna noodles
  8   ounces smoked mozzarella cheese or smoked
       Gouda cheese, thinly sliced

Preheat oven to 375°F. Brush rimmed baking sheet with olive oil. Place eggplant pieces on paper towels. Sprinkle lightly with salt; let stand 20 minutes. Transfer eggplant to prepared sheet. Toss with 2 tablespoons olive oil. Roast eggplant until tender, stirring occasionally, about 30 minutes. Set eggplant aside. Maintain oven temperature.

Mix ricotta cheese, ½ cup Parmesan, shallots and chopped rosemary in large bowl. Season mixture with salt and pepper.

Oil 13 x 9 x 2-inch glass baking dish. Spread ½ cup tomato sauce in dish. Arrange 3 lasagna noodles crosswise in single layer in dish. Spread half of ricotta mixture over noodles. Arrange half of eggplant over. Sprinkle with salt and pepper. Spoon generous 1 cup sauce over. Arrange half of mozzarella over sauce. Repeat layering 1 more time. Top with 3 lasagna noodles. Spread remaining sauce over. Sprinkle with ¾ cup Parmesan. Cover with lightly oiled foil. *(Can be made 1 day ahead; chill.)*

Bake until noodles are tender and lasagna is heated through, about 45 minutes. Uncover; bake until cheese begins to brown and sauce is bubbling slightly at edges, about 15 minutes longer. Let stand 10 minutes before serving.

Broiled Tomato Sauce with Roasted Garlic

makes about 4 cups

  2   medium heads garlic, separated into cloves,
       unpeeled
  ¼   cup olive oil

  4   pounds plum tomatoes, halved lengthwise
  1   tablespoon red wine vinegar
  2   teaspoons honey

Preheat oven to 350°F. Combine garlic and oil in small glass baking dish. Cover with foil and bake until garlic is very tender, about 40 minutes. Using slotted spoon, transfer garlic to work surface; reserve oil. Peel garlic cloves.

Preheat broiler. Line 2 rimmed baking sheets with foil. Brush foil with some of reserved garlic oil. Arrange tomatoes, cut side down, on prepared sheets. Working in batches, broil tomatoes until skins are slightly charred, watching closely to avoid burning, about 10 minutes. Cool. Remove tomato skins and discard. Place tomatoes and any juices from baking sheets in processor. Add garlic, vinegar, honey and any remaining garlic oil. Puree sauce until smooth. Transfer to bowl. Season to taste with salt and pepper. *(Can be prepared 2 days ahead. Cover and refrigerate.)*

The Starters

For an occasion as special as Christmas, you might want to offer your guests something a little more special than chips and dip. That's where these ten recipes come in, ranging from smoked-salmon-topped *crostini* to a new take on stuffed mushrooms. And while these starters are elegant and tasty, they aren't complex, leaving you time to enjoy the pre-dinner festivities.

Spiced Moroccan-Style Shrimp

BEGIN PREPARING THIS A DAY AHEAD OF TIME.

makes 48

4 teaspoons ground coriander

1 tablespoon ground cumin

½ teaspoon turmeric

2 7.25-ounce jars roasted red peppers, well drained

⅓ cup chopped onion

5 teaspoons minced seeded serrano chilies

3 garlic cloves

¼ cup honey

¼ cup fresh lime juice

1 tablespoon grated lime peel

¼ cup plus 3 tablespoons olive oil

48 large uncooked shrimp (about 2 pounds), peeled, deveined

48 ¾-inch cubes peeled cored pineapple

48 6-inch bamboo skewers, soaked in water 30 minutes, drained

½ cup chopped green onions

3 tablespoons toasted sesame seeds

2 limes, cut into wedges

Stir coriander, cumin and turmeric in small skillet over medium heat until lightly toasted, about 3 minutes. Transfer to processor. Add red peppers, onion, chilies and garlic. Blend to form smooth paste. Mix in honey, juice and peel. With machine running, gradually blend in ¼ cup oil. Season with salt and pepper. Transfer to bowl. Cover; chill overnight.

Thread 1 shrimp and 1 pineapple cube on each skewer. Brush with 3 tablespoons oil. Sprinkle with salt and pepper. *(Can be made 8 hours ahead. Cover and refrigerate.)*

Preheat broiler. Arrange skewers in single layer on 3 baking sheets. Broil until shrimp are almost cooked through, about 2 minutes per side. Brush shrimp and pineapple with 1 cup dipping sauce. Broil 1 minute longer.

Arrange skewers on platter. Sprinkle with green onions and sesame seeds. Serve with lime wedges and remaining sauce.

Skewered Lamb with Almond-Mint Pesto

ALMONDS REPLACE THE MORE TRADITIONAL PINE NUTS, AND MINT ADDS EXTRA FLAVOR IN THIS NEW TAKE ON PESTO (BELOW). MAKE IT A DAY AHEAD.

makes about 26 skewers

¼ cup slivered almonds (about 1 ounce)
¼ cup freshly grated Parmesan cheese
1 large garlic clove
⅓ cup (or more) extra-virgin olive oil
1¼ cups chopped fresh mint leaves
¾ cup chopped fresh basil leaves

2 to 2½ pounds boneless leg of lamb, excess fat trimmed, meat cut into 4 x 1 x ¼-inch strips
26 (about) bamboo skewers, soaked in water 30 minutes, drained
Olive oil

Finely chop almonds, cheese and garlic in processor. Add ⅓ cup oil and process to form paste. Add mint leaves and basil leaves and process until well blended and smooth. Mix in more oil if necessary to loosen mixture. Season pesto with salt and pepper.

Thread 1 strip of lamb onto each skewer. Arrange in single layer on baking sheet. Lightly brush lamb with oil. Sprinkle with salt and pepper. *(Can be prepared 1 day ahead. Top pesto with ¼-inch-thick layer of olive oil. Cover pesto and lamb separately and refrigerate. Spoon off oil from top of pesto before serving.)*

Preheat broiler. Broil lamb just until cooked through, about 2 minutes per side. Transfer to platter. Serve with pesto.

Smoked fish primer

SMOKED SALMON AND smoked trout are excellent staples to have on hand throughout the holidays for impromptu hors d'oeuvres or to dress up simple salads, egg dishes and pastas.

Most smoked salmon is cold-smoked, which means it has been smoked at a temperature between 70° and 90°F. This process infuses the fish with flavor and preserves it. Smoked salmon is available in its fresh form in many specialty foods stores; both smoked salmon and smoked trout can be purchased in vacuum-sealed packages, which keep the fish fresh (unopened, and in the refrigerator) for several weeks (check the expiration date on the package). Once opened, the fish should be enjoyed within three days, which is also how long you can keep the fresh type. Save time by having the fishmonger slice the fresh smoked salmon for you. Smoked trout does not need to be sliced; it breaks into chevron-shaped pieces.

INSTANT SERVING IDEAS

❧ Smoked salmon on halved, boiled new potatoes, topped with a small dollop of sour cream and a sprinkling of minced fresh chives.

❧ Smoked salmon on thin-sliced pumpernickel bread that has been spread with sweet butter. Garnish with minced white onion and capers.

❧ Smoked salmon slices served alongside a mound of scrambled eggs for an indulgent breakfast. Sprinkle with capers.

❧ Smoked trout on thin-sliced rye bread that has been spread with sweet butter. Garnish with minced chives and grated lemon peel.

❧ Smoked trout on top of cucumber rounds, garnished with sour cream and fresh dill.

❧ Smoked trout on top of thick, waffle-cut potato chips topped with sour cream and caviar.

Smoked Salmon and Goat Cheese Crostini

A QUICK AND ELEGANT APPETIZER (BELOW).

10 servings

- 8 ounces soft fresh goat cheese
- 1½ tablespoons chopped fresh tarragon
- 1 tablespoon fennel seeds, finely crushed
- 2 teaspoons grated lemon peel
- ½ teaspoon coarsely ground black pepper

- 2½ tablespoons olive oil
- 30 slices French-bread baguette

- 12 ounces thinly sliced smoked salmon
   Lemon peel strips (for garnish)
   Tarragon sprigs (for garnish)

Preheat oven to 350°F. Mix first 5 ingredients in small bowl to blend. Set aside.

Brush oil over both sides of bread. Arrange bread in single layer on large baking sheet. Bake until bread is crisp, about 5 minutes per side. *(Can be made 2 days ahead. Cover cheese mixture and chill. Cool toasts; store airtight.)*

Spread cheese mixture over toasts. Top with salmon. Garnish with lemon and tarragon.

Crab Cakes with Chive and Caper Sauce

THERE ARE TWO DO-AHEAD STEPS HERE: YOU CAN MAKE THE CRAB CAKES (RIGHT) A DAY AHEAD, AND YOU CAN COOK THEM 30 MINUTES BEFORE SERVING.

makes about 40

½ cup minced green onions

½ cup finely chopped celery

¼ cup mayonnaise

¼ cup minced fresh basil

4 teaspoons fresh lemon juice

1 tablespoon Old Bay seasoning

2 teaspoons Dijon mustard

1 pound crabmeat, picked over

3 cups fresh breadcrumbs made from
    crustless French bread

2 large egg yolks, beaten to blend

¼ cup vegetable oil

    Chive and Caper Sauce (see recipe at right)
    Small basil sprigs

Mix first 7 ingredients in medium bowl. Add crabmeat; toss. Fold in 1 cup breadcrumbs. Season with pepper. Mix in yolks.

Place remaining 2 cups breadcrumbs on plate. Using 1 tablespoon crab mixture for each, form 1-inch-diameter patties. Coat each patty with breadcrumbs. Cover; chill at least 1 hour. *(Can be made 1 day ahead. Keep refrigerated.)*

Position rack 6 inches below broiler and preheat broiler. Brush 2 baking sheets with oil. Arrange crab cakes on sheets. Broil until golden brown and cooked through, about 3 minutes per side. *(Can be cooked 30 minutes before serving. Keep warm in 300°F oven.)*

Transfer cakes to platter. Top each with dollop of sauce and basil sprig.

Chive and Caper Sauce

makes about 1½ cups

1 cup mayonnaise

¼ cup chopped fresh parsley

¼ cup chopped fresh chives

2 tablespoons minced shallot

2 tablespoons fresh lemon juice

½ teaspoon hot pepper sauce

2 tablespoons drained capers

Mix first 6 ingredients in processor until pale green and well blended. Transfer to small bowl. Stir in capers. Season to taste with salt and pepper. Cover and chill. *(Can be made 1 day ahead.)*

Winter Crudités with Walnut-Garlic Dip

THE STAR OF THIS DISH IS *SKORDALIA*, A GARLICKY DIP THAT IS THE GREEK VERSION OF AIOLI.

makes about 3 cups

1 12-ounce russet potato, peeled, quartered

¾ cup walnuts, toasted
⅔ cup extra-virgin olive oil
⅓ cup fresh lemon juice
3 garlic cloves
1 tablespoon chopped fresh oregano
2 tablespoons cold water

⅓ cup finely chopped fresh parsley
  Assorted raw vegetables (such as carrots, radishes, and red and green bell peppers)

Cook potato in medium saucepan of boiling salted water until tender, about 15 minutes. Drain. Cool completely.

Combine walnuts, ⅓ cup oil, lemon juice, garlic and oregano in processor. Process until almost smooth. Add potato, remaining ⅓ cup oil and 2 tablespoons water. Using on/off turns, process just until potato is blended (do not over-process or mixture will become sticky).

Transfer mixture to medium bowl. Mix in parsley. Season with salt and pepper. *(Can be prepared 1 day ahead. Cover and refrigerate.)* Serve with vegetables.

Baked Goat Cheese with Roasted Garlic and Caramelized Onion

THIS SPREAD CAN BE MADE A DAY AHEAD AND BAKED JUST BEFORE SERVING.

6 servings

6 elephant garlic cloves or 12 large
  garlic cloves, peeled
1 tablespoon vegetable oil

2 tablespoons (¼ stick) butter
1 medium-size red onion, thinly sliced
1 tablespoon (packed) golden brown sugar
10 ounces soft fresh goat cheese (such as
  Montrachet), crumbled

1 tablespoon balsamic vinegar
¼ cup thinly sliced fresh basil
  Baguette slices

Preheat oven to 350°F. Arrange garlic cloves in glass baking dish. Drizzle with vegetable oil. Cover and bake until garlic is very tender, about 40 minutes for elephant garlic or 30 minutes for regular garlic. Transfer to rack; cool.

Melt butter in heavy large skillet over medium heat. Add onion and sauté until tender and beginning to brown, about 15 minutes. Add brown sugar; stir until melted. Remove from heat and cool. Arrange onion mixture on bottom of 8 x 8-inch glass baking dish. Sprinkle cheese over. Arrange roasted garlic atop cheese. *(Can be prepared 1 day ahead. Cover and chill.)*

Preheat oven to 350°F. Bake garlic mixture until cheese melts but mixture is not bubbling, about 25 minutes. Add balsamic vinegar; stir until well blended. Season to taste with salt and pepper. Transfer mixture to medium bowl. Sprinkle with basil. Serve warm or at room temperature with baguette slices.

Cheddar Cheese Tartlets

A RICH AND FLAVORFUL HORS D'OEUVRE (RIGHT, WITH MUSHROOMS STUFFED WITH HERBED BREAD-CRUMBS, PAGE 109) THAT CAN BE PREPARED ONE WEEK AHEAD AND THEN FROZEN.

makes 30

1 cup (packed) cottage cheese
 (about 8 ounces)
½ cup whipping cream
1¼ cups loosely packed grated sharp cheddar
 cheese (about 4 ounces)
2 large eggs
¾ teaspoon salt
¼ teaspoon cayenne pepper
⅓ cup finely chopped green onions

Cheddar Cheese Pastry (see recipe at right)

Blend cottage cheese and whipping cream in processor until smooth. Add 1 cup cheddar cheese, eggs, salt and cayenne and blend well. Transfer to medium bowl. Mix in green onions.

Preheat oven to 350°F. Butter 30 mini muffin cups. Roll out Cheddar Cheese Pastry on lightly floured surface to thickness of scant ⅛ inch. Cut out 2¾-inch rounds using cookie cutter. Gather scraps, reroll and cut out additional rounds, forming 30 total. Place 1 round in each muffin cup, pressing into cup. Spoon 1 heaping table-spoon filling into each pastry.

Bake tartlets until filling is almost set, about 30 minutes. Sprinkle remaining ¼ cup cheddar cheese over tartlets. Bake until cheese and crusts are golden and filling is set, about 10 minutes. Cool tartlets in pan on rack 10 minutes. Run small knife around tartlet sides. Using tip of knife, gently pry tartlets out of muffin cups. *(Can be prepared 1 week ahead. Place on baking sheet and cool, then cover and freeze. Rewarm uncovered in 350°F oven until heated through.)*

Cheddar Cheese Pastry

makes enough for 30 tartlets

1¼ cups all purpose flour
¼ teaspoon salt
¼ teaspoon cayenne pepper
1¼ cups loosely packed grated sharp cheddar
 cheese (about 4 ounces)
½ cup (1 stick) chilled unsalted butter, cut into
 ½-inch pieces
5 teaspoons (about) ice water

Blend flour, salt and cayenne in processor. Add cheese and butter and process using on/off turns until coarse crumbs form. Blend in enough water by teaspoonfuls to form small moist clumps. Gather dough into ball. Flatten into disk. Wrap in plastic and refrigerate 1 hour. *(Can be made 3 days ahead; keep chilled. Before rolling, soften slightly at room temperature.)*

All about oysters

ONE OF THE MOST luxurious of all culinary treats, raw oysters on the half shell are a special addition to a holiday party. They're at their peak of flavor in autumn and winter, so the timing is perfect. (Oysters spawn during the summer, making them less flavorful during the "non-R" months: May, June, July and August.) Always purchase fresh oysters from a reputable source, and keep them very cold.

BUYING: Make certain that every oyster is tightly closed. If any are partially open, tap them sharply with a knife. If they do not close up, do not buy them.

STORING: Place oysters in a jelly-roll pan or baking dish with the oyster's larger side facing down. Cover with a damp cloth and refrigerate up to three days.

PREPARING: Scrub the oysters well with a stiff brush, then rinse clean.

OPENING: Place a thick, folded towel in the palm of your hand and, working with one at a time, hold each oyster rounded side down. Use an oyster knife to pry into the oyster's hinge and pop off the top shell. Then use the knife to gently loosen the oyster from the bottom shell. (Alternatively, you can have the fishmonger shuck the oysters for you, but they should be served within a few hours of shucking.)

ARRANGING: Place the half shell with the loosened oyster in it on a bed of crushed ice or coarse sea salt, taking care that the ice or the salt does not get into the oysters.

SERVING: Purists enjoy freshly shucked oysters plain, but they can also be topped with a little bit of caviar, a squeeze of fresh lemon juice, a few drops of hot pepper sauce or a tangy mignonette sauce.

Broiled Oysters with Hazelnut Pesto

10 servings

1½ cups (packed) fresh basil leaves
 ¾ cup hazelnuts, toasted, husked
    (about 5 ounces)
 ¼ cup plain dry breadcrumbs
 ¼ cup freshly grated Parmesan cheese
 ¼ cup water
 1 tablespoon fresh lemon juice
 2 garlic cloves, peeled
 ½ cup (1 stick) butter, room temperature
 30 fresh oysters, shucked, shells reserved

Combine basil, hazelnuts, breadcrumbs, cheese, ¼ cup water, lemon juice and garlic in processor. Blend until mixture is finely chopped. Add butter and process until smooth paste forms. Season pesto to taste with salt and pepper. *(Can be made 2 days ahead. Cover and refrigerate. Bring to room temperature before continuing.)*

Preheat broiler. Arrange oysters in half shells on 2 large baking sheets. Top each oyster with 1½ teaspoons pesto. Working in batches, broil until pesto begins to brown, about 1½ minutes. Serve oysters immediately.

Shiitake Scrambled Eggs and Caviar on Toasts

AS SIMPLE AS SCRAMBLED EGGS AND TOAST, THESE ELEGANT APPETIZERS COMBINE THE TWO BREAKFAST FAVORITES IN A NEW WAY, ADDING WILD MUSHROOMS, SOUR CREAM AND CAVIAR FOR INTEREST.

14 servings

 6 tablespoons (¾ stick) butter
10 ounces shiitake mushrooms, stemmed, thinly sliced
 1 teaspoon grated lemon peel

10 large eggs
¼ cup minced fresh chives
½ teaspoon salt
½ teaspoon ground black pepper

28 ⅓-inch-thick diagonal slices baguette, toasted
   Sour cream
   Caviar

Melt 3 tablespoons butter in heavy large skillet over medium heat. Add mushrooms and sauté until tender and beginning to brown, about 6 minutes. Mix in lemon peel. *(Can be prepared 1 day ahead. Cover and refrigerate. Bring mushrooms to room temperature before continuing.)*

Whisk eggs, chives, salt and pepper in large bowl to blend. Melt 3 tablespoons butter in large nonstick skillet over medium heat. Add egg mixture and cook until eggs are softly set, stirring often, 2 minutes. Mix in mushrooms.

Spoon egg mixture onto toasts. Top with sour cream and caviar. Transfer to platter and serve.

Mushrooms Stuffed with Herbed Breadcrumbs

FRESH BREADCRUMBS MAKE ALL THE DIFFERENCE HERE. USE DAY-OLD FRENCH BREAD, CHOPPING PIECES IN THE PROCESSOR UNTIL CRUMBS FORM.

makes 24

24 1½-inch-diameter mushrooms
 2 tablespoons olive oil

 3 tablespoons butter
 1 medium onion, finely chopped
¾ teaspoon dried thyme
¾ cup dry Sherry
½ cup finely chopped fresh parsley
 2 teaspoons minced garlic
1¼ cups soft fresh breadcrumbs from French bread

   Additional finely chopped fresh parsley

Remove stems from mushrooms. Finely chop mushroom stems in processor. Transfer to medium bowl. Using melon baller, carefully scoop out center of each mushroom and discard. Place mushroom caps in large bowl. Drizzle with oil; toss to coat.

Melt butter in heavy large skillet over medium heat. Add chopped mushroom stems, onion and thyme. Sauté until tender and brown, about 7 minutes. Remove skillet from heat; add Sherry. Boil until liquid evaporates, about 5 minutes. Mix in ½ cup parsley and garlic. Mix in breadcrumbs. Season to taste with salt and pepper. Spoon scant tablespoon stuffing into each mushroom cap. Place mushroom caps on rimmed baking sheet. *(Can be prepared up to 6 hours ahead. Cover mushrooms and refrigerate.)*

Preheat oven to 350°F. Bake mushrooms until tender and stuffing browns, about 25 minutes. Transfer mushrooms to platter. Sprinkle with additional chopped parsley and serve.

The Soups & Salads

Think of these soups and salads as fill-in fare, rounding out a menu where it needs it most. Any of them would make a fine sit-down start to the Christmas meal; many of the salads would be a lovely addition to the main course, a touch of green and crunch in the mix. All of them contain do-ahead advice, making these recipes as easy as they are versatile.

Shrimp, Zucchini and Red Pepper Bisque

HERE IS A LIGHT AND ESPECIALLY FESTIVE WAY TO INTRODUCE A SIT-DOWN HOLIDAY MEAL.

8 servings

1 pound uncooked large shrimp

7 tablespoons butter
¾ cup chopped onion
¾ cup chopped celery
3 cups cold water
2 cups bottled clam juice
1 cup dry white wine
2 fresh parsley sprigs
¼ teaspoon dried thyme
¼ teaspoon whole black peppercorns

¼ cup all purpose flour
¼ cup Madeira
3 tablespoons tomato paste
¾ cup half and half

1 medium zucchini, cut into ¼-inch cubes
1 medium-size red bell pepper, cut into ¼-inch cubes

Peel and devein shrimp; reserve shells. Coarsely chop shrimp. Place shrimp in small bowl; cover with plastic and refrigerate.

Melt 1 tablespoon butter in heavy medium saucepan over medium heat. Add onion and celery. Cover and cook until tender, stirring occasionally, about 5 minutes. Add reserved shrimp shells, 3 cups cold water and next 5 ingredients. Bring to boil. Reduce heat to low and simmer until reduced to 5 cups, about 30 minutes. Strain shrimp stock; discard solids.

Melt 4 tablespoons butter in heavy large pot over medium heat. Add flour and whisk until mixture bubbles but does not brown, about 3 minutes. Whisk in Madeira and tomato paste, then shrimp stock. Simmer until mixture thickens slightly, about 8 minutes. *(Can be prepared 1 day ahead. Cool slightly. Cover and refrigerate. Bring to simmer before continuing.)* Mix in half and half. Cook until soup is heated through (do not boil). Season with salt and pepper.

Meanwhile, melt remaining 2 tablespoons butter in heavy large skillet over medium-high heat. Add zucchini and red bell pepper. Sauté until vegetables are crisp-tender, about 3 minutes. Add reserved shrimp. Sauté just until shrimp are cooked through and vegetables are tender, about 3 minutes longer. Season shrimp mixture with salt and pepper.

Spoon ⅓ cup shrimp mixture into center of each bowl. Ladle soup around shrimp mixture and serve immediately.

Wild Rice and Wild Mushroom Soup

DRIED AND FRESH WILD MUSHROOMS, GARLIC AND CHIVES FLAVOR THIS LOVELY LOW-FAT SOUP.

6 servings

 1 ounce dried porcini mushrooms*
 1 tablespoon butter
 ½ cup finely chopped onion
 ⅓ cup wild rice
6⅓ cups canned chicken broth
 4 large garlic cloves, thinly sliced
 6 ounces fresh shiitake mushrooms, stems removed, caps sliced

 1 carrot, cut into matchstick-size strips
 1 3.5-ounce package enoki mushrooms
 ½ bunch fresh chives, cut into 1-inch lengths

Place dried porcini in strainer; shake strainer from side to side, allowing grit to fall through. Melt butter in heavy large saucepan over medium heat. Add onion and rice and sauté 2 minutes. Stir broth and porcini into onion and rice. Cover and simmer 25 minutes, stirring occasionally. Add garlic, cover and simmer until rice is almost tender, about 15 minutes. Add shiitake mushrooms. Cover and simmer until rice is very tender, about 10 minutes longer. *(Can be prepared 2 days ahead. Cover and chill. Bring to simmer before continuing.)*

Stir carrot into soup. Cover and simmer until carrot is crisp-tender, about 2 minutes. Season to taste with salt and pepper. Remove stems from enoki mushrooms and reserve for another use. Ladle soup into bowls. Sprinkle with enoki caps and chives and serve.

*Dried porcini are available at Italian markets and specialty foods stores.

Creamy Leek Soup with Bacon and Shallots

THIS SPECTACULAR SOUP IS THICKENED WITH
PUREED POTATO INSTEAD OF CREAM.

8 servings

7 large leeks (about 4¾ pounds)
¼ cup (½ stick) butter
1 large onion, chopped
2 tablespoons sugar
2 teaspoons dried thyme
3 14½-ounce cans (or more) vegetable broth
1 12-ounce russet potato, peeled, quartered
1½ cups sliced green onions (about 1 bunch)

6 slices hickory-smoked bacon, cut into
    1-inch pieces
4 large shallots, cut into ¼-inch-thick slices
Pinch of sugar

Cut dark green tops from leeks. Thinly slice 2 leeks. Set aside to use later as garnish. Coarsely chop remaining 5 leeks. Melt butter in heavy large pot over medium heat. Add coarsely chopped leeks, onion, 2 tablespoons sugar and thyme and sauté until leeks begin to soften, about 8 minutes. Stir in broth and potato. Cover and simmer until potato is tender, about 25 minutes. Add green onions and simmer 3 minutes. Using slotted spoon, transfer half of vegetables to processor and puree until smooth. Gradually add half of cooking liquid to puree in processor and blend well. Transfer puree to large saucepan. Repeat with remaining vegetables and cooking liquid. Season soup to taste with salt and pepper. *(Can be prepared 1 day ahead. Cover and refrigerate sliced leeks for garnish and soup separately.)*

Preheat oven to 350°F. Sauté bacon in heavy large skillet over medium heat until crisp, about 4 minutes. Using slotted spoon, transfer bacon to paper towels and drain. Reserve bacon drippings. Arrange shallots on half of large baking sheet and sliced leeks on remaining half. Drizzle with bacon drippings. Sprinkle with pinch of sugar. Season to taste with salt and pepper. Bake until vegetables are light golden, stirring occasionally, about 20 minutes. Cool on baking sheet. *(Can be made 4 hours ahead. Let stand at room temperature.)*

Bring soup to simmer. Thin with more broth, if desired. Ladle soup into bowls. Garnish with bacon and roasted shallots and leeks.

Hot Cucumber and Watercress Soup

MAKE THIS REFRESHING SOUP (OPPOSITE) TWO
DAYS AHEAD AND REWARM IT JUST BEFORE SERVING.

6 servings

3 tablespoons butter
3 large leeks (white and pale green parts only),
    chopped (about 4 cups)
3 cucumbers (about 2 pounds total), peeled,
    seeded, diced
1 large russet potato (about 12 ounces),
    peeled, diced
1 large bunch watercress, trimmed, chopped
    (about 2½ cups)
5 cups canned low-salt chicken broth

Whipping cream
Chopped fresh chives

Melt butter in heavy large pot over medium heat. Add leeks and sauté until almost tender, about 7 minutes. Add cucumbers and sauté 3 minutes. Add potato and watercress and sauté

until hot, about 3 minutes. Add broth and bring to boil. Reduce heat and simmer until vegetables are tender, about 30 minutes.

Working in batches, puree soup in blender. Return soup to same pot. Season to taste with salt and pepper. *(Can be prepared 2 days ahead. Cover and refrigerate.)*

Bring soup to simmer. Ladle soup into bowls. Drizzle with cream. Sprinkle with chives.

Soup on the menu

SOUP IS A WELCOME thing this time of year, not only because it's hot and comforting but also because many soups can be prepared in advance and frozen, making party day easier on the cook. The foundation of a good soup is stock, the clear, savory essence made by simmering meats and/or vegetables and herbs with water. Homemade stock can be prepared several weeks ahead and frozen, but if time is short, take advantage of the many excellent canned broths available at supermarkets.

HELPFUL HINTS

✳ The flavor of the stock (chicken, beef, fish, etc.) will flavor the soup, so don't use fish stock for chicken soup—or vice-versa—unless that is the effect you want.

✳ Soups reduce in volume as they simmer, and the flavors become concentrated. This is why you always want to salt sparingly at first.

✳ Ground black pepper loses its clean, spicy perfume as it cooks, so add it just before serving.

QUICK GARNISHES

Soups can easily be embellished for added flavor and texture, but remember that a garnish should always complement the flavors in the soup or echo one or more of the recipe's ingredients.

CROUTONS: The homemade kind always taste best.

MINCED FRESH HERBS: Use an herb that enhances flavors in the soup (for example, minced fresh chives sprinkled on a soup that has onions in it).

DICED, COOKED VEGETABLES: These work best when the vegetable on top is also in the soup (for example, sweet potatoes on a sweet potato bisque; corn kernels atop corn chowder).

SOUR CREAM, CRÈME FRAÎCHE OR LIGHTLY WHIPPED UNSWEETENED CREAM: Swirl any of these additions into the soup just before serving.

CRUMBLED, COOKED BACON, DICED COUNTRY HAM OR SLIVERED PROSCIUTTO: These smoky garnishes are especially good on pea, lentil, winter squash or sweet potato soups.

Butternut Squash Soup with Cider Cream

APPLES AND APPLE CIDER LEND A PLEASANT SWEET-
NESS TO THIS BEAUTIFUL SOUP (OPPOSITE).

10 servings

5 tablespoons butter
2½ pounds butternut squash, peeled, seeded,
cut into ½-inch pieces (about 6 cups)
2 cups chopped leeks (white and pale green
parts only)
½ cup chopped peeled carrot
½ cup chopped celery
2 small Granny Smith apples, peeled,
cored, chopped
1½ teaspoons dried thyme
½ teaspoon crumbled dried sage leaves
5 cups chicken stock or canned
low-salt chicken broth
1½ cups apple cider

⅔ cup sour cream

½ cup whipping cream
Chopped fresh chives

Melt butter in heavy large saucepan over
medium-high heat. Add squash, leeks, carrot
and celery; sauté until slightly softened, about
15 minutes. Mix in apples, thyme and sage.
Add stock and 1 cup cider and bring to boil.
Reduce heat to medium-low. Cover and simmer until apples are tender, stirring occasionally, about 30 minutes. Cool slightly.

Working in batches, puree soup in blender.
Return soup to pan.

Boil remaining ½ cup cider in heavy small
saucepan until reduced to ¼ cup, about 5 minutes. Cool. Place sour cream in small bowl.

Whisk in reduced cider. *(Soup and cider cream
can be prepared up to 2 days ahead. Cover separately and then refrigerate.)*

Bring soup to simmer. Mix in whipping cream.
Ladle soup into bowls. Drizzle with cider
cream. Top with chives.

Mixed Green Salad with Oranges, Dried Cranberries and Pecans

FRESH FLAVORS STAR IN THIS SALAD (OPPOSITE).

6 servings

1 cup plus 3 tablespoons orange juice
6 tablespoons dried cranberries

3½ tablespoons olive oil
2 tablespoons white wine vinegar
1 tablespoon grated orange peel

6 cups mixed baby greens
3 oranges, peel and white pith removed,
segmented
¾ cup pecans, toasted

Bring 1 cup orange juice to simmer in heavy
small saucepan. Remove from heat. Mix in
dried cranberries. Let stand until softened,
30 minutes. Drain well; discard soaking juice.

Whisk oil, vinegar, orange peel and remaining
3 tablespoons orange juice in small bowl to
blend. Mix in cranberries. Season dressing to
taste with salt and pepper. *(Can be prepared
1 day ahead. Cover and refrigerate. Bring to room
temperature before using.)*

Place greens in large bowl. Toss with ⅔ of
dressing. Divide greens among 6 plates. Add
orange segments to bowl; toss with remaining
dressing. Top salads with orange segments and
pecans and serve.

A salad's place

SERVED AS A FIRST COURSE, a side dish or before dessert, salads are a welcome addition to the holiday menu. They're refreshing and healthful and add color to the buffet table, and everyone (except the most finicky eater) likes them. Now that pre-washed lettuces are readily available in bags, salads are easier and more convenient than ever.

A salad served as a first course or side dish can be as simple as a bowl of lettuce with a home-made dressing or as flavorful as a mix of various vegetables, fruits, nuts and cheeses.

If, however, you are planning to serve a salad between the main course and dessert, keep the recipe simple: This salad is meant as a transi-tion, taking the diner gently and deliciously from main course to dessert. For this palate-refreshing salad, choose Boston, Bibb or green leaf lettuce simply dressed with a light vinai-grette. And unless your goal is a strong, Mediterranean flavor, hold the garlic.

INSTANT IDEAS

❧ Toss red leaf or oakleaf lettuce with a vinai-grette, then top with sliced fresh mushrooms and homemade croutons.

❧ Cut canned, drained beets into half-inch pieces and drizzle with balsamic vinaigrette. Top with crumbled goat cheese and toasted walnuts and serve on a bed of red leaf lettuce.

❧ Dress arugula with a lemon vinaigrette and top with sliced pears and crumbled blue cheese.

❧ Toss baby spinach leaves with a basic vinai-grette. Top with cooked, crumbled bacon and hard-boiled-egg slices.

❧ Mix watercress and chopped fresh fennel with a basic vinaigrette and top with orange slices and pomegranate seeds.

Smoked Salmon and Fennel Salad with Horseradish Dressing

TYPICAL HOLIDAY INGREDIENTS COME TOGETHER IN AN ATTRACTIVE DO-AHEAD SALAD.

6 servings

½ cup olive oil
3 tablespoons fresh lemon juice
2½ tablespoons prepared extra-hot white horseradish
2 tablespoons whole grain mustard
6 slices smoked salmon (about 6 ounces)

6 ounces haricots verts or green beans
2 large heads Belgian endive, thinly sliced
1 large bunch watercress, tough stems removed
1 medium fennel bulb, trimmed, thinly sliced

1 bunch chives, cut into 1-inch lengths

Whisk olive oil, lemon juice, horseradish and mustard in medium bowl to blend. Season dressing to taste with salt and pepper. Trim each salmon slice to 1 x 4-inch rectangle. Coarsely chop trimmings. Set aside. Tightly roll salmon rectangles into cigar shapes. Cut each roll in half diagonally. *(Dressing, salmon trim-mings and rolls can be prepared up to 2 days ahead. Cover separately and refrigerate.)*

Cook haricots verts in pot of boiling salted water until just crisp-tender, about 2 minutes. Drain. Rinse under cold water; drain well. Combine haricots verts, endive, watercress and fennel in large bowl. *(Can be prepared 4 hours ahead. Cover and refrigerate.)*

Toss salad with enough dressing to coat. Divide among 6 plates. Sprinkle with chopped salmon trimmings. Garnish with salmon rolls and chives. Drizzle with remaining dressing.

Curly Endive Salad with Radishes, Coriander and Bacon

TOASTED CORIANDER SEEDS AND RADISHES GIVE THIS SALAD—A TWIST ON THE CLASSIC *FRISÉE AUX LARDONS*—AN APPEALING SPICINESS. ACCOMPANY IT WITH *FOUGASSE*, A LARGE PROVENÇAL FLATBREAD, OR OTHER FRENCH BREAD.

8 servings

    1 tablespoon whole coriander seeds
    1 large shallot, chopped
    6 tablespoons red wine vinegar
   10 tablespoons olive oil

    3 bacon slices

   16 cups bite-size pieces curly endive
      (from 1 large head)
    1 bunch radishes, trimmed, thinly sliced

Place coriander seeds in heavy small skillet. Heat over medium-high heat until fragrant and dark in color, about 4 minutes. Remove from heat and cool. Place in blender. Add shallot and vinegar. Blend until coriander seeds are chopped, about 1 minute. Add oil and blend well. *(Can be prepared 1 day ahead. Cover with plastic wrap and refrigerate. Bring mixture to room temperature before using.)*

Cook bacon in large nonstick skillet over medium heat until crisp. Transfer bacon to paper towels; reserve bacon drippings. Whisk bacon drippings into dressing. Season dressing with salt and pepper. Crumble bacon.

Combine curly endive, radishes and bacon in large bowl. Add enough dressing to coat salad; toss to blend. Serve immediately.

Spinach, Beet and Walnut Salad

THIS CONTEMPORARY SALAD (ABOVE) TAKES ITS INSPIRATION FROM THE FAMILIAR WALDORF SALAD.

12 servings

  1½ pounds medium beets, trimmed
   ½ cup walnut oil or olive oil
   ¼ cup Sherry wine vinegar
    2 large shallots, minced

    2 6-ounce packages baby spinach
    4 heads Belgian endive, thinly sliced crosswise
    1 cup walnuts, toasted, coarsely chopped
    6 ounces soft fresh goat cheese, crumbled

Preheat oven to 400°F. Wrap beets in foil and bake until tender when pierced with knife, about 1 hour 30 minutes. Cool slightly, then peel. Cut each beet into 8 wedges. Place in medium bowl; cover.

Whisk oil and vinegar in small bowl. Mix in shallots. Pour 3 tablespoons dressing over warm beets; toss. Cool. *(Can be made 1 day ahead; chill beets and remaining dressing separately.)*

Combine spinach, endive and ¾ cup nuts in large bowl. Pour remaining dressing over; toss. Season with salt and pepper. Divide among 12 plates. Sprinkle goat cheese over. Top with beets and remaining ¼ cup nuts.

The Side Dishes

In the rush to get the big feast on the table, it's often the side dishes that get over-looked. And while steamed carrots or broccoli are fine, you may want to take things a step further on Christmas Day. These recipes do just that, without adding lots of extra time or energy to the preparations. Do-ahead hints add to their usefulness, too.

Peas with Caraway and Parmesan Butter

8 to 10 servings

7 tablespoons freshly grated Parmesan cheese
6 tablespoons (¾ stick) butter, room temperature
1 teaspoon caraway seeds
¾ teaspoon grated lemon peel
½ teaspoon freshly cracked black pepper

¾ cup chopped shallots
3 10-ounce packages frozen petite peas, unthawed
⅓ cup canned beef broth or water
⅓ cup chopped fresh Italian parsley

Mix Parmesan, 4 tablespoons butter, caraway seeds, lemon peel and pepper in small bowl. *(Can be made 3 days ahead. Cover; chill.)*

Melt remaining 2 tablespoons butter in heavy large skillet over medium-high heat. Add shallots; sauté until tender, about 3 minutes. Add peas, broth and parsley and stir until peas are heated through, 8 minutes. Add Parmesan butter; stir until melted. Season with salt.

Rice Pilaf with Chestnuts

6 servings

6 cups water

1 teaspoon salt

½ cup wild rice (about 3 ounces)

2 tablespoons (¼ stick) butter

⅔ cup minced celery

⅔ cup minced onion

⅔ cup coarsely chopped vacuum-packed
   chestnuts (about 5 ounces)

½ cup white basmati rice or
   long-grain white rice

1 bay leaf

1 cup canned low-salt chicken broth

1 tablespoon chopped fresh thyme

2 tablespoons chopped fresh parsley

Combine 6 cups water and 1 teaspoon salt in
heavy medium saucepan over high heat. Bring
to boil. Stir in wild rice. Reduce heat to low
and simmer until rice is tender, stirring occasionally to keep rice from sticking to bottom of
pan, about 1 hour. Drain well.

Meanwhile, melt butter in heavy large skillet
over medium-low heat. Add celery and onion.
Cover skillet and cook until vegetables are tender, stirring occasionally, about 15 minutes.
Add chestnuts, basmati rice and bay leaf and
sauté 1 minute. Bring broth to boil in heavy
small saucepan. Stir hot broth and thyme into
basmati rice mixture. Reduce heat to low.
Cover skillet and cook until rice is tender,
about 18 minutes. Remove from heat. Let stand
5 minutes. Discard bay leaf.

Stir wild rice and parsley into basmati rice mixture. Season to taste with salt and pepper and
serve. *(Can be prepared 8 hours ahead. Cover and
chill. Rewarm in microwave oven.)*

Corn and Winter Squash
with Spinach

A LOVELY DISH (ABOVE) THAT'S A SNAP TO PREPARE.

10 to 12 servings

9 bacon slices, chopped

2 cups chopped onions

2½ pounds butternut squash, peeled, seeded,
   cut into ⅓-inch pieces

1½ 6-ounce packages baby spinach leaves

1 16-ounce package frozen corn kernels,
   thawed

6 tablespoons chopped fresh basil

Sauté bacon in large pot over medium heat
until crisp, about 10 minutes. Add onions and
squash. Sauté until squash is almost tender,
about 12 minutes. *(Can be prepared 1 day ahead.
Cover and refrigerate. Stir over medium heat until
squash is just heated through, about 6 minutes,
before continuing.)* Add spinach and corn. Toss
until spinach wilts and corn is heated through,
about 5 minutes. Stir in basil. Season with salt
and pepper. Transfer to bowl and serve.

Wild Rice Dressing with Pearl Onions, Dried Cherries and Apricots

SWEET AND SAVORY FLAVORS COME TOGETHER IN THIS MIXED-RICE DRESSING (OPPOSITE).

8 to 10 servings

    6 tablespoons (¾ stick) butter
   18 ounces pearl onions, blanched in boiling
        water 1 minute, peeled

 4½ cups canned low-salt chicken broth
    3 tablespoons chopped fresh thyme
 1¼ cups wild rice (about 6½ ounces)
 1¼ cups long-grain white rice

    1 6-ounce package dried apricots,
        coarsely chopped
    1 cup dried tart cherries
    1 cup raisins
    1 cup pecans, toasted, chopped

Melt 2 tablespoons butter in large skillet over medium heat. Add onions and sauté until brown, about 15 minutes. Set aside.

Bring broth and 1 tablespoon thyme to boil in large saucepan. Add wild rice; bring to boil. Reduce heat; cover and simmer 30 minutes. Add white rice; cover and simmer until liquid is almost absorbed, about 15 minutes longer.

Stir apricots, cherries, raisins and 2 tablespoons thyme into rice; cover and simmer 3 minutes. Stir in onions and 4 tablespoons butter. Mix in pecans. Season with salt and pepper.

Butter 13 x 9 x 2-inch glass baking dish. Transfer dressing to prepared dish. *(Can be made 1 day ahead; chill.)* Preheat oven to 350°F. Cover dish with buttered foil, buttered side down. Bake until heated through, 30 minutes.

Leek, Mushroom and Bacon Dressing

LOTS OF MUSHROOMS AND BACON FLAVOR THIS TRADITIONAL BREAD DRESSING.

12 to 14 servings

    1 24-ounce loaf sliced buttermilk bread, crust
        trimmed, bread cut into ½-inch cubes
        (about 11 cups)

    1 pound bacon slices, cut into ½-inch pieces

    7 cups chopped leeks (white and pale green
        parts only)
 1½ pounds button mushrooms, coarsely chopped
   12 ounces shiitake mushrooms, stemmed,
        caps coarsely chopped
    4 cups coarsely chopped celery
    3 tablespoons chopped fresh tarragon or
        1½ tablespoons dried
    2 large eggs, beaten to blend

        Canned low-salt chicken broth

Preheat oven to 350°F. Spread bread cubes on 2 rimmed baking sheets. Bake until bread is almost dry, 15 minutes. Cool. Transfer to bowl.

Sauté bacon in large pot over medium-high heat until crisp, about 12 minutes. Drain bacon on paper towels. Reserve 6 tablespoons drippings in pot; discard remaining drippings.

Add leeks and button mushrooms to same pot. Sauté over medium-high heat until beginning to soften, about 5 minutes. Add shiitake mushrooms and sauté 4 minutes. Add celery and sauté until leeks and mushrooms are tender but celery is still slightly crisp, about 6 minutes longer. *(Bread, bacon and sautéed vegetables can be prepared 1 day ahead. Cover separately. Store bread at room temperature; refrigerate bacon and vegetables.)* Mix bacon, sautéed vegetables and tarragon into bread. Season generously with salt and pepper. Mix eggs into dressing.

Stuffing versus dressing

WHETHER IT'S COOKED inside the bird or in a baking dish, the seasoned, bread-based or rice-based side dish known both as stuffing and as dressing is a frequent addition to the Christmas menu. The two are, in fact, the same; it's how they are cooked that distinguishes one from the other. Stuffing is literally stuffed inside the bird's cavity and removed before serving. Dressing, on the other hand, is baked in an ovenproof dish at the same time as the turkey.

Both stuffing and dressing are served hot as a side dish. They are usually made with corn bread or cubes of white or whole wheat bread. The bread cubes can be fresh or dry; fresh cubes yield a softer mixture than dry cubes, which result in a dish with coarser texture. Whether you opt for dressing or stuffing, additions such as sautéed onions, cooked chopped giblets, beaten eggs, butter, stock, herbs, mushrooms, sausage and oysters add flavor, texture and your own personal touch to the meal.

HELPFUL HINTS

※ Figure on about half a cup of stuffing for each pound of turkey.

※ Do not mix wet and dry stuffing ingredients until you are ready to stuff the bird. It should be trussed and roasted immediately after stuffing.

※ Stuffed birds take 20 to 30 minutes longer to cook than unstuffed ones.

※ For food safety, use an instant-read thermometer to make sure the stuffing inside the turkey reaches 165°F.

※ When the bird is done, use a long-handled spoon to remove the stuffing to a serving dish; keep warm while you carve the turkey.

※ Leftover stuffing or dressing can be chilled and reheated in a 350°F oven until hot in the center and golden brown on top, 20 to 30 minutes.

※ To save time, chop stuffing ingredients (onions, celery, etc.) a day in advance, chilling them in separate resealable bags.

※ Cook bacon or sausage (if desired) a day in advance, and refrigerate the cooked bacon or sausage separately from the drippings.

※ Nuts can be toasted, skinned and chopped, then frozen up to two weeks ahead of time.

※ Bread cubes can be toasted a day in advance. Store in plastic bags at room temperature.

Preheat oven to 350°F. Generously butter 15 x 10 x 2-inch glass baking dish. Add enough broth to dressing to moisten (about ¾ to 1 cup). Transfer dressing to prepared dish. Cover with buttered foil, buttered side down. Bake until heated through, 30 to 35 minutes. Uncover and bake until top is slightly crisp, 20 minutes.

The cranberry course

Whether it's served uncooked, jellied, or in a spoonable, sauce-like form, the tart-sweet taste and cool temperature of cranberry relish make it a delicious counterpoint to the mild flavor of roast poultry. This American native berry also adds bright jewel-like color to a Christmas menu.

Fresh cranberries are available from October through December. They keep in the refrigerator for up to a month and freeze well, so stock up on them if you're an enthusiast. Buy firm berries; remove any leaves or twigs and rinse well before using them. Fresh cranberries are too hard and tart to eat in their raw, whole form, but they can be added to stuffings, muffins, relishes and chutneys. Cranberry sauce is made by simmering fresh cranberries in a water-sugar mixture until the skins burst. Their natural pectin gives the sauce a jelly-like consistency.

INSTANT IDEAS

Mix any of the following ingredients into a basic cranberry sauce or canned whole-berry cranberries to add spiciness, texture or heat.

FRESH OR DRIED FRUIT: chopped fresh apples or pears, or dried apricots or cherries.

CITRUS PEEL: lemon, orange or tangerine (colored part of the peel only).

SPICES: ground cinnamon, cloves, cardamom, allspice or nutmeg, to taste.

NUTS: coarsely chopped toasted hazelnuts, walnuts or pecans.

HERBS: fresh thyme, parsley or rosemary.

FLAVORINGS: grated fresh ginger, prepared horseradish or minced fresh or canned chilies.

SPIRITS: Grand Marnier, Madeira, Marsala, sweet Sherry or Port.

Piquant Cranberry Sauce

THE PIQUANCY HERE (BELOW) COMES FROM FRESH THYME AND JUST A BIT OF DIJON MUSTARD.

makes 2 1/2 cups

1 cup water
1 cup (packed) dark brown sugar
1 12-ounce package cranberries
1 tablespoon chopped fresh thyme
1 teaspoon Dijon mustard
Pinch of salt

Combine 1 cup water and brown sugar in heavy medium saucepan. Bring to boil, stirring until sugar dissolves. Add cranberries. Simmer until berries burst, stirring occasionally, about 8 minutes. Remove from heat. Stir in thyme, mustard and salt. Cool completely. *(Can be made 3 days ahead. Cover and refrigerate.)*

Brown Sugar-glazed Sweet Potatoes with Marshmallows

THIS TRADITIONAL SIDE DISH HAS MARSHMALLOWS AND BROWN SUGAR TO KEEP THE YOUNGSTERS HAPPY, AND "BIG KIDS" WILL LIKE THE ADDITION OF ALMONDS AND SPICES.

8 servings

4 pounds red-skinned sweet potatoes (yams), peeled, cut into 1-inch pieces
⅔ cup (packed) golden brown sugar
5 tablespoons butter
1 teaspoon ground cinnamon
½ teaspoon salt
¼ teaspoon ground nutmeg
    Pinch of ground ginger

2 cups miniature marshmallows
½ cup sliced almonds

Preheat oven to 375°F. Arrange potatoes in 13 x 9 x 2-inch glass baking dish. Combine sugar, butter, cinnamon, salt, nutmeg and ginger in heavy small saucepan over medium heat. Bring to boil, stirring until sugar dissolves. Pour over potatoes; toss to coat. Cover tightly with aluminum foil.

Bake potatoes 50 minutes. Uncover; bake until potatoes are tender and syrup thickens slightly, basting occasionally, about 20 minutes. *(Can be prepared 1 day ahead. Cool; cover and refrigerate. Rewarm potatoes in 350°F oven until heated through, about 20 minutes, before continuing.)* Increase oven temperature to 500°F. Top potatoes with marshmallows and nuts. Return to oven; bake until marshmallows begin to melt and nuts begin to brown, about 3 minutes.

Wild-Mushroom Bread Pudding

BREAD PUDDING GOES SAVORY IN THIS RICH AND SATISFYING SIDE DISH.

6 servings

3 tablespoons olive oil
6 ounces shiitake mushrooms, stemmed, caps thickly sliced
6 ounces oyster mushrooms, thickly sliced
6 ounces crimini mushrooms, thickly sliced
2 portobello mushrooms, stems and gills removed, caps thickly sliced
4 teaspoons chopped garlic
1 tablespoon chopped fresh basil
1 tablespoon chopped fresh parsley
1 teaspoon dried rubbed sage
1 teaspoon dried thyme

5 large eggs
2 cups whipping cream
1 cup whole milk
¼ cup plus 2 tablespoons freshly grated Parmesan cheese
¾ teaspoon salt
½ teaspoon ground black pepper
6 cups 1-inch cubes crustless day-old French bread (about 6 ounces)

Preheat oven to 350°F. Butter 8 x 8 x 2-inch glass baking dish. Heat oil in heavy large pot over medium-high heat. Add all mushrooms, garlic, basil, parsley, sage and thyme and sauté until mushrooms are tender and brown, about 15 minutes. Remove from heat. Season with salt and pepper. *(Can be made 1 day ahead. Cover and refrigerate.)*

Whisk eggs, cream, milk, ¼ cup Parmesan, salt and pepper in large bowl to blend. Add bread cubes; toss to coat. Let stand 15 minutes. Stir in mushroom mixture. Transfer to prepared dish. Sprinkle 2 tablespoons cheese over. Bake until set in center, about 1 hour. Serve warm.

Carrot Puree with Ginger and Orange

WITH ITS BRIGHT ORANGE COLOR, THIS DO-AHEAD PUREE MAKES A LOVELY ADDITION TO THE MEAL.

8 servings

3 pounds carrots, peeled, cut into ½-inch rounds
4 tablespoons sugar

⅓ cup fresh orange juice
½ cup (1 stick) butter, cut into pieces, room temperature
1½ tablespoons minced peeled fresh ginger
1 tablespoon grated orange peel
1 tablespoon fresh lemon juice

Cook carrots and 3 tablespoons sugar in large pot of boiling salted water until carrots are very tender, about 25 minutes. Drain well. Return carrots to same pot; stir over medium heat until any excess moisture evaporates.

Meanwhile, bring orange juice to simmer in heavy small saucepan over medium heat. Add butter, minced ginger and orange peel; whisk until butter melts. Whisk in lemon juice and remaining 1 tablespoon sugar.

Puree half of carrots and half of juice mixture in processor until smooth. Transfer to large bowl. Repeat with remaining carrots and juice mixture. Season to taste with salt and pepper. *(Can be prepared 1 day ahead. Cover and refrigerate. Rewarm puree in microwave oven on high about 4 minutes or rewarm in saucepan over medium-low heat, stirring.)*

Golden Mashed Potatoes with Parsnips and Parsley

IF YOU USE THE PARSLEY ROOT, MINCE THE TOPS AND ADD THEM TO THE DISH WHEN THE INSTRUCTIONS CALL FOR MINCED FRESH PARSLEY.

6 servings

1½ pounds Yukon Gold potatoes, peeled, cut into 2-inch pieces
1 pound parsnips, peeled, cut into 1½-inch pieces
3 ounces trimmed parsley root (about 3 medium), peeled, cut into 1-inch pieces (optional)
1 large garlic clove, halved
3 cups (or more) water
1 14½-ounce can low-salt chicken broth

¼ cup whipping cream
2 tablespoons (¼ stick) butter
2 tablespoons minced fresh parsley or parsley root tops
Additional minced fresh parsley

Combine potatoes, parsnips, parsley root (if desired) and garlic in heavy large saucepan. Add 3 cups water and broth; if necessary, add additional water to cover by 1 inch. Boil uncovered until vegetables are tender, about 25 minutes. Drain vegetables, reserving liquid.

Return vegetables to pot. Add cream and butter. Set over low heat; mash until mixture is smooth and fluffy, adding enough reserved cooking liquid to thin to desired consistency. Mix in 2 tablespoons parsley. *(Can be made ahead. Cover; let stand at room temperature up to 2 hours or refrigerate overnight. Rewarm over low heat, stirring, or in microwave.)* Transfer to bowl. Top with additional parsley.

Potato and Apple Galette with Sage

A SOPHISTICATED DISH (BELOW) THAT IS IDEAL FOR MOST ANY HOLIDAY FEAST.

6 servings

5 tablespoons warm melted butter
1 6- to 7-ounce Golden Delicious apple, peeled, halved, cored, cut into ⅛-inch-thick slices
3 teaspoons minced fresh sage
3 6- to 7-ounce russet potatoes, peeled, cut into ⅛-inch-thick rounds

Position rack in bottom third of oven and preheat to 450°F. Brush 9-inch-diameter cake pan with 1½-inch-high sides with ½ tablespoon butter. Line bottom of pan with parchment; brush parchment with ½ tablespoon butter. Place apple slices, 1 tablespoon butter and 1 teaspoon minced sage in small bowl. Sprinkle with salt and pepper; toss to coat. Place potatoes, remaining 3 tablespoons butter and 2 teaspoons minced sage in medium bowl. Sprinkle with salt and pepper; toss to coat.

Arrange 1 layer of neatest potato slices in concentric circles in prepared pan, overlapping potatoes in outermost circle (this will become top of galette). Top with second layer of potatoes. Top with apple slices. Cover with remaining potatoes. Pour over any butter from bowls used to toss potatoes and apple.

Bake galette until potatoes are tender when tested with tip of sharp knife and top is beginning to brown, about 1 hour. Remove galette from oven. Turn out onto 9- or 10-inch tart pan bottom; peel off parchment. *(Can be made 2 hours ahead. Let stand at room temperature.)*

Preheat broiler. Broil until top is golden, about 2 minutes. Transfer to platter. Cut into wedges.

Broccoli and Cauliflower with Chive Butter

8 servings

½ cup (1 stick) butter, room temperature
2 tablespoons Dijon mustard
1 tablespoon grated lemon peel
⅓ cup plus 1 tablespoon chopped fresh chives

1 1½-pound whole cauliflower, trimmed, cut into florets
2½ pounds broccoli, stems trimmed, cut into florets

Using fork, blend butter, mustard and lemon peel in small bowl. Mix in ⅓ cup chives. Season with salt and pepper.

Cook cauliflower in large pot of boiling salted water 2 minutes. Add broccoli and cook until vegetables are crisp-tender, about 3 minutes. Drain. Transfer to bowl of ice water. Drain.

Combine butter mixture and vegetables in large pot. Toss gently over medium heat until vegetables are heated through and coated with butter mixture, about 5 minutes. Transfer to bowl. Sprinkle with remaining chives.

The Breads & Rolls

The Christmas season brings out the baker in all of us, an urge that encompasses everything from cookies and cakes to breads and rolls. And for many, the perfect holiday feast includes a golden loaf straight from the oven. These simple recipes will make that ideal possible, especially when you note how many of them include shortcuts and do-ahead steps.

Poppy Seed Dinner Rolls

THESE ALL-AMERICAN ROLLS ARE SO FLAKY AND BUTTERY THAT EVERYONE WILL WANT SECONDS. BE SURE TO BEGIN PREPARING THE DOUGH A DAY BEFORE BAKING BECAUSE IT NEEDS TO BE REFRIGERATED OVERNIGHT.

makes 24

1 cup warm water (105°F to 115°F)
2 envelopes dry yeast
¼ teaspoon plus ⅓ cup sugar

⅔ cup whole milk, room temperature
1 large egg
2½ teaspoons salt
¼ cup (½ stick) unsalted butter, melted, cooled
5 cups (or more) all purpose flour
1 cup (2 sticks) chilled unsalted butter, cut into thin slices

1 egg beaten with 1 tablespoon cold water (for glaze)
Poppy seeds

Place warm water in large bowl. Sprinkle yeast and ¼ teaspoon sugar over and stir to blend. Let stand until yeast dissolves and mixture is slightly foamy, about 8 minutes.

Whisk milk, 1 egg, salt and remaining ⅓ cup sugar into yeast mixture. Add melted butter and whisk until smooth. Add 1 cup flour and mix until smooth. Combine 4 cups flour and 1 cup chilled butter in processor. Using on/off turns, process until mixture resembles coarse meal. Add to yeast mixture and stir until dry ingredients are moistened. Knead in bowl until smooth dough forms, adding more flour if dough is sticky, about 5 minutes.

Cover bowl with plastic. Chill dough overnight. *(Can be made 2 days ahead; keep chilled.)*

Butter twenty-four ⅓-cup nonstick muffin cups. Turn dough out onto floured surface; knead briefly until smooth and elastic, about 3 minutes. Divide dough into 4 equal portions. Place 1 dough portion on work surface; cover and chill remaining dough. Roll out 1 dough portion on floured surface to 13 x 11-inch rectangle (about ⅛ inch thick). Cut rectangle lengthwise into 6 strips, each a scant 2 inches wide. Stack strips atop one another, forming 6 layers and pressing slightly to adhere. Cut strips crosswise into 6 equal stacks, each about 2 inches long. Place 1 dough stack, 1 cut side down, into each muffin cup (dough will fan out slightly and fill muffin cups as dough rises). Repeat with remaining chilled dough pieces.

Cover rolls with kitchen towel. Let rise in warm draft-free area until rolls are puffed and doubled in volume, about 1 hour 15 minutes.

Position 1 rack in center and 1 rack in top third of oven; preheat to 350°F. Brush rolls gently with egg glaze. Sprinkle with poppy seeds. Bake until rolls are golden brown, switching top and bottom muffin pans halfway through baking, about 25 minutes total. Transfer pans to rack and cool rolls 5 minutes. Remove rolls from pans and cool on racks. Serve warm or at room temperature. *(Can be made 1 week ahead. Wrap in foil; freeze. Rewarm thawed wrapped rolls in 350°F oven about 10 minutes.)*

Cheddar Cheese Biscuits with Dill and Chives

makes about 18

  3 cups all purpose flour
4½ teaspoons baking powder
  1 tablespoon sugar
1½ teaspoons dry mustard
  1 teaspoon salt
  ¼ cup (½ stick) chilled unsalted butter, cut into pieces
  ¼ cup chilled vegetable shortening, cut into pieces
  1 cup plus 2 tablespoons milk
  ¼ cup chopped fresh chives or green onions
  3 tablespoons (packed) chopped fresh dill or 1 tablespoon dried dillweed
2½ cups lightly packed grated extra-sharp cheddar cheese (about 8 ounces)

Position rack in center of oven and preheat to 450°F. Mix flour, baking powder, sugar, mustard and salt in large bowl to blend. Add butter and shortening; rub in with fingertips until mixture resembles coarse meal. Whisk milk, chives and dill in medium bowl. Pour into dry ingredients; stir until moist dough forms. Mix in 2 cups grated cheese.

Turn dough out onto floured surface; knead lightly to distribute cheese evenly. Roll out dough to generous ½-inch thickness. Using floured 2½-inch cookie cutter, cut out biscuits. Gather scraps; roll out to generous ½-inch thickness and cut out additional biscuits.

Transfer biscuits to heavy large ungreased baking sheet. Top with ½ cup cheese. Bake until biscuits are golden, about 15 minutes. Transfer to platter. Serve warm or at room temperature. *(Can be made 6 hours ahead. Let stand at room temperature. If desired, wrap biscuits in foil and rewarm in 350°F oven 5 minutes.)*

Bread, ahead

HAVING FRESH, HOMEMADE bread with the big Christmas meal sounds all the more possible when you consider the many ways in which it can be made ahead.

HELPFUL HINTS

❄ Dry ingredients can be pre-measured, mixed, then stored in a resealable plastic bag at room temperature for several weeks.

❄ Since the refrigerator is not cold enough to kill yeast (the chill just retards it), most yeast doughs can be mixed, kneaded, risen once and punched down, then refrigerated for one day. Oil the bowl well and keep the dough covered with oiled plastic wrap.

❄ When ready to bake refrigerated dough, if it hasn't risen at all in the refrigerator, let it stand at room temperature until doubled in volume, two to three hours. Punch the dough down, shape, then proceed as for unrefrigerated dough. If the dough has risen once in the refrigerator, punch it down, knead it and then shape it. Let it rise for about two hours, then bake.

❄ Biscuits can be rolled, shaped and cut, then placed on a baking sheet and put in the freezer. When frozen, place the dough cutouts in resealable plastic bags and keep frozen.

REHEATING NOTES

Breads, muffins and rolls can be baked, cooled, wrapped and frozen until ready to serve. Thaw and follow these reheating instructions.

ROLLS: Place on a baking sheet and rewarm for about 10 minutes at 350°F.

MUFFINS: Place on a baking sheet, then rewarm for about 8 minutes at 350°F.

QUICK BREADS OR YEAST BREADS: Wrap in foil and rewarm for about 15 minutes at 350°F.

THE MENU

Chili Cornmeal Muffins

CORN AND CHILI POWDER LEND A SOUTHWESTERN ACCENT TO THESE MUFFINS (OPPOSITE). IF YOU HAVE ANY LEFTOVERS AFTER THE HOLIDAY MEAL, THEY WOULD ALSO BE NICE WITH CHILI.

makes 12

½ cup (1 stick) unsalted butter
1 cup frozen corn kernels, thawed
4 teaspoons chili powder
1 cup buttermilk
2 large eggs

1 cup yellow cornmeal
1 cup all purpose flour
3 tablespoons sugar
2 teaspoons baking powder
1 teaspoon salt
½ teaspoon baking soda

Preheat oven to 400°F. Butter twelve ⅓-cup metal muffin cups. Melt butter in heavy medium skillet over medium heat. Add corn and chili powder. Sauté 3 minutes. Transfer to medium bowl. Mix in buttermilk, then eggs. Cool completely.

Whisk cornmeal, flour, sugar, baking powder, salt and baking soda in large bowl to blend. Add buttermilk mixture; stir just until blended.

Divide batter among prepared muffin cups. Bake until tester inserted into center of muffins comes out clean, about 20 minutes. Transfer muffins to rack. Cool slightly. *(Can be made 2 weeks ahead. Cool completely. Wrap in foil, seal in plastic bag and freeze. Rewarm thawed muffins wrapped in foil in 350°F oven until heated through, about 8 minutes.)*

Mashed Potato Bread

MAKE THE POTATO SOURDOUGH STARTER FOR THIS
TENDER, CRUSTY BREAD (BELOW) ONE DAY AHEAD.

makes 2 loaves

1 9- to 11-ounce russet potato, peeled, cut into
   1-inch pieces
2 cups (or more) water
2 teaspoons dry yeast

¼ cup warm water (105°F to 115°F)

2 tablespoons (¼ stick) unsalted butter, melted
1 tablespoon honey
1 teaspoon salt
½ cup whole wheat flour
3¾ cups (about) unbleached
   all purpose flour

1 large egg white, beaten to blend

Boil potato in 2 cups water in medium saucepan until very tender, about 15 minutes. Strain 1½ cups cooking liquid into large bowl (add more water if needed to measure 1½ cups). Cool liquid to 105°F to 115°F. Mash potato in small bowl until smooth. Add mashed potato and 1 teaspoon yeast to cooking liquid. Cover bowl with plastic and let starter stand at room temperature overnight.

Pour ¼ cup warm water into small bowl. Sprinkle remaining 1 teaspoon yeast over; stir to blend. Let mixture stand until yeast dissolves, about 10 minutes.

Stir yeast mixture into starter. Stir in melted butter, honey and salt. Mix in whole wheat flour. Mix in enough all purpose flour, ½ cup at a time, to form soft dough. Turn dough out onto floured work surface. Knead until smooth and elastic, about 4 minutes. Form into ball.

Butter large bowl. Place dough in bowl; turn to coat. Cover with plastic. Let dough rise in warm draft-free area until doubled, 1 hour.

Lightly flour 2 large baking sheets. Punch down dough. Turn dough out onto floured work surface and knead until smooth, about 3 minutes. Divide dough in half. Roll each half between palms and work surface into 14-inch-long loaf. Transfer to prepared baking sheets. Cover with dry towel. Let rise in warm draft-free area until almost doubled, 30 minutes.

Position 1 rack in center and 1 rack in top third of oven and preheat to 500°F. Using sharp knife, cut 5 diagonal slashes in surface of each loaf. Brush loaves with egg white. Bake loaves 10 minutes. Reduce oven temperature to 400°F. Bake until loaves are brown and sound hollow when tapped on bottom, switching and rotating baking sheets halfway through baking, about 15 minutes longer. Cool on racks. *(Can be prepared 2 weeks ahead. Cool completely. Wrap loaves separately in foil, seal in plastic bag and freeze. Thaw loaves, then rewarm, wrapped in foil, in 350°F oven 15 minutes.)*

Steamed Pumpkin Bread with Walnuts and Dates

NOTE THAT THIS BREAD (OPPOSITE) NEEDS TO COOK IN AN EMPTY 28-OUNCE FOOD CAN.

makes 1 loaf

½ cup all purpose flour
½ cup whole wheat flour
½ cup yellow cornmeal
1 teaspoon baking soda
½ teaspoon salt
¼ cup chopped dates
¼ cup chopped walnuts
⅔ cup buttermilk
½ cup canned pure pumpkin
½ cup honey
1 large egg yolk

Generously butter 1 empty 28-ounce can. Place rack on bottom of large pot. Pour water into pot to depth of 3 inches. Bring to boil.

Mix first 5 ingredients in large bowl. Stir in dates and walnuts. Whisk buttermilk, pumpkin, honey and yolk in medium bowl. Add to dry ingredients. Stir just until blended. Transfer to can. Cover can with buttered foil, buttered side down. Secure foil tightly by tying kitchen string around can just below top rim.

Place can on rack in pot; pour enough additional hot water into pot so that water level is ⅔ up sides of can. Bring water to boil. Cover pot; reduce heat to medium-low and simmer until wooden skewer inserted into center comes out clean, occasionally adding more hot water to pot to maintain water level, about 1½ hours.

Using tongs, transfer can to another rack. Cool 10 minutes. Remove foil. Run knife around sides of bread. Gently shake can to remove bread. Cut into slices. Serve warm.

Buttermilk Corn Bread with Bacon

START PREPARING THIS (OPPOSITE) ONE DAY AHEAD.

12 to 16 servings

2 cups buttermilk
1¼ cups polenta (coarse cornmeal)*
8 ounces bacon (about 10 slices),
   cut into ½-inch pieces

1¾ cups all purpose flour
1½ tablespoons baking powder
1 teaspoon salt
¼ teaspoon baking soda
½ cup (packed) golden brown sugar
3 large eggs
2 tablespoons honey
2 tablespoons (¼ stick) butter, melted
2½ cups frozen corn kernels, thawed

Stir buttermilk and polenta in medium bowl. Cover; let stand at room temperature overnight.

Preheat oven to 350°F. Cook bacon in heavy large skillet until crisp. Using slotted spoon, transfer bacon to paper towels to drain. Spoon 2 tablespoons drippings into 13 x 9 x 2-inch metal baking pan. Tilt pan to coat bottom and sides of pan with bacon drippings. Place pan in oven until drippings are hot, 6 minutes.

Meanwhile, sift flour, baking powder, salt and baking soda into large bowl. Stir in brown sugar. Whisk eggs, honey and butter in another large bowl to blend. Stir in polenta mixture. Add to dry ingredients. Stir just until blended. Stir in corn. Transfer batter to prepared pan. Sprinkle bacon over; press gently to submerge.

Bake until tester inserted into center comes out clean and top is golden, about 45 minutes. Transfer to rack. Cool 15 minutes. Cut into squares; serve warm or at room temperature.

Available at Italian markets, natural foods stores and some supermarkets.

Sesame-Onion Crescent Rolls

SAUTÉED ONIONS FILL THESE ROLLS (RIGHT), WHILE
SESAME SEEDS MAKE FOR A CRUNCHY EXTERIOR.

makes 16

1 cup warm water (105°F to 115°F)

1 envelope dry yeast

1 cup lukewarm milk

1 large egg

1 tablespoon sugar

5 cups (about) unbleached all purpose flour

2 tablespoons olive oil

2½ teaspoons salt

3 tablespoons unsalted butter

3 cups finely chopped onions

1 large egg beaten with 1 tablespoon
   whole milk (for glaze)

2 tablespoons sesame seeds

Pour ¼ cup warm water into small bowl.
Sprinkle yeast over; stir to blend. Let stand
until yeast dissolves, about 10 minutes. Whisk
remaining ¾ cup warm water, lukewarm milk,
1 egg and sugar in large bowl to blend. Stir in
yeast mixture. Add 3 cups flour and stir vigorously with wooden spoon until smooth thick
batter forms, about 2 minutes. Cover bowl with
kitchen towel; let rest 15 minutes.

Stir 2 tablespoons oil and salt into batter. Using
wooden spoon, mix in enough flour, ½ cup at a
time, to form firm and nearly smooth dough.
Turn dough out onto floured work surface.
Knead until dough is smooth and elastic,
adding more flour if dough is too sticky, about
10 minutes. Form dough into ball.

Oil large bowl. Place dough in bowl; turn to
coat with oil. Cover bowl with plastic wrap,
then towel. Let dough rise in warm draft-free
area until doubled, about 1 hour 15 minutes.

Meanwhile, melt butter in heavy large skillet
over medium heat. Add onions and sauté until
tender and golden, about 15 minutes. Set aside.

Punch down dough. Turn dough out onto
floured work surface. Divide dough in half.
Knead each half into ball. Cover loosely with
plastic; let rest on floured surface 10 minutes.

Using rolling pin, roll 1 dough ball to 14-inch
round. Spread half of onions over, leaving
1-inch border. Cut dough round into 8 wedges.
Starting at wide end of each wedge, roll up
toward point. Place rolls on ungreased heavy
large baking sheet, shaping into crescents and
spacing evenly. Loosely cover rolls with plastic
wrap. Repeat with remaining dough ball and
onions. Let rolls rise in warm draft-free area
until almost doubled, about 30 minutes.

Position 1 rack in center and 1 rack in top third
of oven; preheat to 375°F. Brush rolls with egg
glaze. Sprinkle with sesame seeds. Bake until
rolls are golden and sound hollow when tapped
on bottom, switching top and bottom baking
sheets halfway through baking, about 25 minutes total. Transfer rolls to racks and cool. *(Can
be made 2 weeks ahead. Cool completely. Wrap in
aluminum foil and freeze.)*

Cranberry-Walnut Braid

THIS IS THE PERFECT HOLIDAY BREAD (OPPOSITE) FOR THOSE WHO LOVE THE CRANBERRY RELISH AS MUCH AS THE TURKEY. IT HAS ALL THE RIGHT FLAVORS—CRANBERRIES, WALNUTS AND ORANGE— AND IT LOOKS BEAUTIFUL.

makes 1 loaf

3 cups (or more) bread flour

¼ cup sugar

2 envelopes quick-rising dry yeast

1½ teaspoons salt

½ cup buttermilk

2 large eggs

2 tablespoons (¼ stick) unsalted butter, melted, hot

1½ tablespoons orange extract

⅓ cup (about) hot water (120°F to 130°F)

1 cup dried cranberries

½ cup coarsely chopped walnuts

1 large egg, beaten to blend (for glaze)

Stir 3 cups flour, sugar, yeast and salt in large bowl to blend. Add buttermilk, 2 eggs, melted butter and orange extract and stir vigorously until well blended. Gradually stir in enough hot water to form soft, slightly sticky dough. Transfer dough to floured work surface. Knead dough until smooth and slightly tacky but not sticky, adding more flour if necessary, about 7 minutes. Knead in dried cranberries ⅓ cup at a time; then knead in walnuts. Form dough into ball.

Oil large bowl. Add dough to bowl, turning to coat with oil. Cover bowl with plastic wrap, then towel. Let dough rise in warm draft-free area until doubled in volume, about 1½ hours.

Lightly oil heavy large baking sheet. Punch down dough. Turn dough out onto floured surface. Divide dough into 4 equal pieces; then divide 1 dough piece into 3 equal pieces and reserve. Using palms of hands, roll out each of remaining 3 large pieces on work surface to 13-inch-long ropes. Braid ropes together. Tuck ends under and pinch together. Transfer braid to prepared baking sheet. Roll out each of reserved 3 small dough pieces to 10-inch-long ropes. Braid ropes together. Tuck ends under and pinch together. Brush large braid with some of egg glaze. Place small braid atop center of large braid. Brush small braid with some of egg glaze. Let loaf rise on baking sheet uncovered in warm area until almost doubled in volume, about 1 hour 15 minutes.

Preheat oven to 325°F. Brush loaf again with egg glaze. Bake until loaf is deep golden brown and sounds hollow when tapped on bottom, about 45 minutes. Transfer loaf to rack and cool at least 45 minutes before slicing. *(Can be prepared ahead. Cool completely. Wrap tightly in foil and freeze up to 2 weeks. Uncover and thaw at room temperature.)*

Desserts

For some, dessert is the best part of the day. The presents are touching, the mood is uplifting, and the meal is great, but it's dessert that's the capper. That's likely because a Christmas dessert is special by definition, a pull-out-all-the-stops confection of favorite flavors—chocolate, eggnog, gingerbread, caramel, and the like. Here are ten-plus recipes for the dessert of all desserts.

Mocha and Raspberry Trifle

DEFINITELY NOT YE OLDE ENGLISH CLASSIC, BUT VERY DELICIOUS AND VERY CONTEMPORARY NONETHELESS (OPPOSITE). USING STORE-BOUGHT SPONGE CAKE (FROM YOUR SUPERMARKET BAKERY) OR PURCHASED POUND CAKES SIMPLIFIES ASSEMBLY.

12 servings

syrup

    3 tablespoons water
    2 tablespoons sugar
    3 tablespoons Cognac or other brandy

mocha pastry cream

    2 cups whole milk
    1 tablespoon instant espresso powder
    1 vanilla bean, split lengthwise

    6 large egg yolks
    ¾ cup sugar
    ¼ cup cornstarch
    3 ounces bittersweet (not unsweetened) or
      semisweet chocolate, chopped

1¾ cups chilled whipping cream

assembly

2 purchased 8-inch-diameter, 1- to 1¼-inch-
thick round sponge cakes, each cut
horizontally in half

¾ cup raspberry preserves (about 10 ounces)

2 cups fresh or frozen raspberries (unthawed)

2 cups fresh raspberries

2 tablespoons red currant jelly, melted with
1 tablespoon water

1½ teaspoons sugar
Red currant bunches or red grape clusters
(optional)

FOR SYRUP: Combine 3 tablespoons water and
sugar in small saucepan. Bring to boil over
medium-high heat, stirring until sugar dissolves. Remove from heat. Mix in Cognac.
Cool syrup completely.

FOR MOCHA PASTRY CREAM: Combine milk
and espresso powder in heavy medium
saucepan. Scrape in seeds from vanilla bean;
add bean. Bring to simmer. Remove from heat.
Discard vanilla bean.

Using electric mixer, beat yolks and sugar in
large bowl until very thick, about 3 minutes.
Sift in cornstarch; beat to blend well. Gradually
beat hot milk mixture into egg mixture. Return
mixture to saucepan. Whisk over medium heat
until mixture comes to boil, about 3 minutes.
Remove from heat. Add chocolate. Whisk until
chocolate melts and mixture is smooth. Transfer to medium bowl. Place plastic wrap directly
onto surface of pastry cream. Refrigerate until
cold, about 3 hours. *(Can be made 2 days ahead.
Cover syrup and store at room temperature. Keep
pastry cream refrigerated.)*

Whisk cold pastry cream until smooth. Using
electric mixer, beat whipping cream in large
bowl until medium-stiff peaks form. Transfer

1½ cups whipped cream to another medium
bowl; set aside to use as topping. Stir ⅓ of
remaining whipped cream from large bowl into
pastry cream to lighten. Fold remaining
whipped cream from large bowl into pastry
cream in 2 more additions.

FOR ASSEMBLY: Place 1 cake layer in bottom
of 8-inch-diameter, 3-quart trifle bowl. Brush
¼ of syrup over cake. Spread 3 tablespoons
raspberry preserves over cake. Spread 1 cup
pastry cream over. Arrange ½ cup fresh or
frozen raspberries atop pastry cream. Repeat
layering 3 more times with remaining cake layers, syrup, preserves, pastry cream and 1½ cups
fresh or frozen raspberries.

Spread reserved 1½ cups whipped cream over
trifle. Top whipped cream with 2 cups fresh
raspberries. Lightly brush red currant jelly
mixture over raspberries. Sprinkle with 1½ teaspoons sugar. Garnish with red currant bunches or grape clusters, if desired. Cover and
refrigerate at least 3 hours. *(Can be prepared
8 hours ahead. Keep refrigerated.)*

Eggnog Custards

A FAVORITE CHRISTMAS DRINK IS TRANSFORMED INTO THESE LOVELY CUSTARDS (WHICH, CONVENIENTLY, CAN BE PREPARED THREE DAYS AHEAD).

6 servings

2½ cups half and half
3 tablespoons bourbon
1 vanilla bean, split lengthwise

8 large egg yolks
⅓ cup sugar
⅛ teaspoon ground nutmeg
   Pinch of salt

   Additional ground nutmeg
6 whole strawberries

Preheat oven to 325°F. Place half and half and bourbon in heavy medium saucepan. Scrape in seeds from vanilla bean; add bean. Bring to simmer. Remove from heat. Cover; steep 15 minutes. Discard vanilla bean.

Whisk yolks, sugar, ⅛ teaspoon nutmeg and salt in large bowl to blend. Gradually whisk in hot half and half mixture. Strain custard into 4-cup glass measuring cup.

Place six ¾-cup custard cups or soufflé dishes in roasting pan. Divide custard equally among cups. Cover each cup with foil. Pour enough hot water into pan to come halfway up sides of custard cups. Bake until custard is just set around edges but still soft in center, about 45 minutes. Remove cups from water. Remove foil and cool. Cover custards and refrigerate until cold, at least 2 hours. *(Can be prepared 3 days ahead. Keep refrigerated.)*

Sprinkle additional nutmeg over custards. Garnish with strawberries.

Christmas Pudding with Brandy Butter

THIS VERSION OF THE HOLIDAY FAVORITE INCLUDES DRIED CURRANTS, CANDIED CHERRIES, PRUNES AND ALMONDS. A SWEET AND POTENT BRANDY BUTTER IS DELICIOUS WITH THE WARM PUDDING.

10 servings

brandy butter

¾ cup (1½ sticks) unsalted butter, room temperature
1 cup powdered sugar
5 tablespoons brandy

pudding

1⅔ cups dried currants (about 8 ounces)
¾ cup candied cherries or other chopped dried fruit such as apricots or figs (about 4 ounces)
¾ cup pitted prunes, chopped (about 4 ounces)
¼ cup chopped candied orange peel
1½ teaspoons ground cinnamon
¾ teaspoon ground ginger
½ teaspoon ground nutmeg
½ teaspoon salt
½ cup dark rum

3 cups fresh white breadcrumbs
½ cup (packed) golden brown sugar
6 tablespoons all purpose flour

¼ cup finely chopped almonds
½ teaspoon baking powder
½ cup (1 stick) unsalted butter, melted, cooled slightly
3 large eggs
¼ cup milk
2 teaspoons vanilla extract
½ teaspoon almond extract

FOR BRANDY BUTTER: Using electric mixer, beat butter until smooth. Beat in powdered sugar. Gradually beat in brandy. *(Can be prepared 1 week ahead. Cover and refrigerate. Bring to room temperature before serving.)*

FOR PUDDING: Mix currants, candied cherries, prunes, orange peel, cinnamon, ginger, nutmeg and salt in large bowl. Pour rum over and stir to blend. Let stand 30 minutes.

Mix breadcrumbs, brown sugar and flour in medium bowl. Add to dried fruit mixture and stir to blend. Cover dried fruit mixture and let stand at room temperature overnight.

Generously butter 2-quart pudding mold with lid. Mix almonds and baking powder in medium bowl. Whisk melted butter, eggs, milk, vanilla extract and almond extract in large bowl. Stir in almond mixture. Stir butter mixture into dried fruit mixture. Spoon batter into prepared pudding mold. Smooth top. Cover pudding mold with lid.

Place pudding mold on rack in large pot. Add enough boiling water to pot to come halfway up sides of mold. Cover pot and steam pudding over medium-low heat until tester inserted into center comes out clean, adding more boiling water to pot if necessary, about 2 hours. Transfer mold to rack and cool 5 minutes. Turn out pudding. *(Can be made 1 week ahead. Cool. Wrap tightly in plastic and refrigerate. To reheat pudding, unwrap and return to buttered mold; cover mold. Place mold on rack in large pot. Add enough hot water to pot to come halfway up sides of mold. Cover pot and steam pudding over medium-low heat until heated through, about 45 minutes. Transfer mold to rack. Let stand 5 minutes. Turn out pudding.)*

Transfer pudding to platter. Serve pudding warm with brandy butter.

A sweet tradition

CHOCK-FULL OF NUTS, spices and glacéed or dried fruits, and redolent of brandy or other spirits, fruitcake and plum pudding (which doesn't contain plums but does feature prunes—dried plums) are traditional sweets that seem out of place any other time of year. The two desserts have much in common: They contain similar ingredients, can be prepared well in advance, and make excellent gifts. While some find it easier to purchase these holiday favorites, others make them year after year.

PLUM PUDDING TIPS

❧ To reheat plum pudding, return it to the mold and steam until heated through.

❧ Present plum pudding on a footed cake stand. Pour warm brandy over it and ignite.

❧ Serve with hard sauce (powdered sugar, butter and spirits or vanilla extract), custard sauce or unsweetened whipped cream.

❧ To give as a gift, wrap the pudding—mold and all—in clear cellophane tied with a bow. Include a recipe card with instructions on how to reheat and serve.

FRUITCAKE TIPS

❧ Try using dried fruits (pears, peaches, apricots) instead of red and green glacéed cherries for a more contemporary—and less cloyingly sweet—fruitcake.

❧ For "white fruitcake," a southern specialty, use dried pineapple, coconut and blanched almonds. White fruitcake is more delicately spiced than traditional fruitcakes.

❧ To infuse a fruitcake with a spirit, wrap it in cheesecloth that has been soaked in brandy, rum or bourbon, then in foil and keep in a cool place for two to three weeks.

Honey-Pecan Pumpkin Pie

AN EXTRA BATCH OF THE HONEYED PECANS WOULD
BE A GREAT SNACK OR HOLIDAY HOSTESS GIFT.

8 servings

pecans

6 tablespoons sugar

3 tablespoons honey

3 tablespoons unsalted butter
Pinch of salt

1 cup pecan halves (about 4 ounces)

pie

1 Easy Pastry Dough disk (see recipe at right)

½ cup sugar

1 tablespoon cornstarch

1½ teaspoons ground cinnamon

¾ teaspoon ground allspice

¼ teaspoon salt

⅛ teaspoon ground ginger

1 15-ounce can pure pumpkin

⅓ cup honey

1 cup whipping cream

4 large eggs

topping

1 cup chilled whipping cream

2 tablespoons honey

FOR PECANS: Place large piece of foil on work surface. Stir sugar, honey, butter and salt in heavy medium skillet over medium-low heat until sugar dissolves, butter melts and syrup comes to simmer. Add pecans. Cook until syrup turns deep caramel color and bubbles thickly, stirring occasionally, about 9 minutes. Scrape onto foil. Working quickly, separate nuts with spoon. Cool completely. Place in airtight container. *(Can be made 3 days ahead.)*

FOR PIE: Position rack in bottom third of oven and preheat to 350°F. Roll out dough disk on floured surface to 12- to 13-inch round. Transfer to 9-inch-diameter glass pie dish. Fold overhang under; crimp edge, forming high-standing rim.

Stir sugar and next 5 ingredients in large bowl. Whisk in pumpkin and honey, then cream and 3 eggs. Beat 1 egg in small bowl to blend. Brush inside of crust with some of beaten egg. Pour pumpkin filling into crust.

Bake pie until filling is slightly puffed and begins to crack at edges, covering crust with foil if browning too quickly, about 1 hour. Cool on rack. *(Can be prepared up to 8 hours ahead. Store pie at room temperature.)*

FOR TOPPING: Using electric mixer, beat cream and honey in medium bowl until stiff peaks form. Spoon into pastry bag fitted with star tip. Pipe rosettes of cream atop pie. Garnish with candied nuts. Serve, passing extra nuts.

Easy Pastry Dough

makes enough for 2 crusts

2½ cups all purpose flour

¾ cup (1½ sticks) chilled unsalted butter,
cut into 1-inch pieces

2 tablespoons sugar

¾ teaspoon salt

¼ cup frozen vegetable shortening,
cut into large pieces

1 large egg

3 tablespoons (about) ice water

Blend first 4 ingredients in processor 10 seconds. Add shortening; process just until very coarse meal forms. Beat egg with 2 tablespoons water; add to processor. Blend until large moist clumps form, adding more water if dry. Gather dough into ball; divide in half. Flatten each piece into disk. Wrap in plastic; chill at least 1 hour. *(Can be made 2 days ahead.)*

Gingerbread Cake with Maple Whipped Cream

THERE'S AN EXTRA HIT OF FLAVOR FROM CRYSTAL-
LIZED GINGER IN THIS LAYER CAKE (RIGHT).

14 to 16 servings

cake

Nonstick vegetable oil spray
3 cups all purpose flour
2 tablespoons ground ginger
2 teaspoons baking soda
1¼ teaspoons ground cinnamon
¾ teaspoon ground cloves
½ teaspoon ground nutmeg
¼ teaspoon salt
⅓ cup minced crystallized ginger

10 tablespoons (1¼ sticks) unsalted butter,
room temperature
1 cup (packed) golden brown sugar
3 large eggs
1 cup mild-flavored (light) molasses
1 cup boiling water
2½ teaspoons grated orange peel

filling and frosting

3 cups chilled whipping cream
½ cup pure maple syrup

1 tablespoon finely chopped crystallized ginger
Orange peel strips

FOR CAKE: Position rack in center of oven and
preheat to 350°F. Spray 10-inch-diameter cake
pan with 2-inch-high sides with nonstick spray.
Line bottom of pan with parchment paper;
spray paper. Sift flour and next 6 ingredients
into medium bowl. Mix in crystallized ginger.

Using electric mixer, beat butter in large bowl
until fluffy. Beat in brown sugar. Beat in eggs

1 at a time. Gradually beat in molasses, then
1 cup boiling water. Mix in grated orange peel.
Gradually mix in dry ingredients.

Transfer batter to prepared pan. Bake until
tester inserted into center of cake comes out
clean, about 1 hour. Transfer pan to rack and
cool 15 minutes. Run knife around pan sides.
Turn cake out onto rack; peel off paper. Cool.
(Cake can be prepared 1 day ahead. Wrap in plastic and store at room temperature.)

FOR FILLING AND FROSTING: Beat cream
and syrup in large bowl to stiff peaks.

Cut cake horizontally into 3 equal layers.
Transfer 1 cake layer, cut side up, to platter.
Spread 1½ cups whipped cream mixture over.
Repeat layering with 1 cake layer and 1½ cups
whipped cream mixture. Top with remaining
cake layer, cut side down. Spread remaining
whipped cream over top and sides of cake.
Sprinkle ginger atop cake around edge.
Garnish with peel. Cover with cake dome;
refrigerate at least 1 hour and up to 6 hours.

Chocolate-Cranberry Poinsettia Cake

HERE'S A GRAND FINALE TO A GRAND CHRISTMAS SUPPER. IF YOU ARE SHORT ON TIME, PLAIN WHITE CHOCOLATE LEAVES ARE ALSO NICE ON THIS CAKE (BELOW), IN PLACE OF THE MARBLEIZED ONES.

8 servings

cake

    1 cup cake flour
    ½ teaspoon baking powder
    ½ teaspoon baking soda
    ⅛ teaspoon salt
    ½ cup orange juice
    3 ounces semisweet chocolate, chopped

    1 cup sugar
    ¼ cup (½ stick) unsalted butter, room temperature
    1½ teaspoons grated orange peel
    2 large eggs
    ½ cup sour cream
    ½ teaspoon vanilla extract

cranberries and syrup

    ⅔ cup sugar
    ⅓ cup water
    2 cups fresh or frozen cranberries

frosting

    1½ cups whipping cream
    12 ounces semisweet chocolate, chopped

    Marbleized White Chocolate Leaves (see recipe opposite)
    Fresh mint leaves

FOR CAKE: Position rack in center of oven; preheat to 350°F. Butter two 9-inch-diameter cake pans with 1½-inch-high sides. Line bottoms of pans with parchment or waxed paper. Dust pans with flour; tap out excess. Stir flour, baking powder, baking soda and salt in medium bowl to blend. Bring orange juice to boil in heavy small saucepan. Remove from heat. Add chocolate; whisk until melted and smooth. Cool to barely lukewarm.

Using electric mixer, beat sugar, butter and orange peel in large bowl until blended. Add eggs 1 at a time, beating well after each addition. Add sour cream, vanilla and melted chocolate mixture and beat until well blended. Add dry ingredients; beat just until blended.

Divide batter equally between prepared pans; smooth tops. Bake cakes until tester inserted into center comes out clean, about 25 minutes. Cool cakes in pans on rack.

FOR CRANBERRIES AND SYRUP: Combine sugar and water in heavy medium saucepan. Stir over medium heat until sugar dissolves. Add cranberries; bring to boil. Using slotted

spoon, immediately transfer about 20 glazed cranberries to plate. Reserve for garnish; chill. Continue to boil remaining cranberries until berries pop, about 5 minutes. Using slotted spoon, transfer poached berries to small bowl. Pour cranberry syrup in pan into another bowl and reserve for Marbleized White Chocolate Leaves (see recipe at right). *(Can be prepared 1 day ahead. Wrap cakes and cover glazed cranberries, poached cranberries and syrup separately; store at cool room temperature.)*

FOR FROSTING: Bring cream to boil in heavy medium saucepan. Remove from heat. Add chocolate and stir until melted and smooth. Chill frosting until just thick enough to spread but still glossy, about 1 hour 20 minutes.

Invert 1 cake layer onto platter. Peel off parchment. Spread ½ cup chilled chocolate frosting over cake. Spoon poached cranberries in bowl evenly over frosting. Invert second cake layer onto work surface. Peel off parchment; place cake atop cranberries. Spread remaining chocolate frosting over top and sides of cake. Refrigerate until cake is well chilled, about 2 hours. *(Can be made 1 day ahead. Cover with cake dome and chill.)*

Working quickly, arrange Marbleized White Chocolate Leaves in center of cake, forming poinsettia flower. Place 3 glazed cranberries in center of flower. Arrange fresh mint leaves and remaining glazed cranberries around cake. Refrigerate cake until ready to serve.

Marbleized White Chocolate Leaves

THESE LEAVES ARE VERY FRAGILE, SO THE RECIPE YIELDS A FEW EXTRA TO ALLOW FOR BREAKAGE.

makes 20

8 ounces good-quality white chocolate (such as Lindt or Baker's), finely chopped

20 camellia or lemon leaves, wiped clean
Wooden skewers
Cranberry syrup reserved from Chocolate-Cranberry Poinsettia Cake (see recipe opposite)

Line large baking sheet with waxed paper. Stir white chocolate in top of double boiler set over hot water until melted and smooth. Remove from over water. Cool to barely lukewarm.

Using small metal spatula or spoon, spread chocolate between $^1/_{16}$ and $^1/_8$ inch thick on veined underside of 1 leaf, being careful not to drip over edges. Using flat end of wooden skewer, dab 4 tiny dots of cranberry syrup randomly on leaf. Using pointed end of same skewer, gently draw syrup into chocolate to marbleize. Place leaf on prepared baking sheet. Repeat with remaining leaves. Freeze until chocolate is completely set, about 30 minutes. Starting at stem end, gently peel chocolate off 1 leaf. Place on foil-lined sheet; freeze. Repeat with remaining leaves, freezing each after peeling to keep leaves from softening. *(Can be prepared up to 3 days ahead. Keep frozen.)*

Chocolate-Caramel Tart

12 servings

crust

- 1 cup all purpose flour
- 3 tablespoons sugar
- 1 teaspoon grated lemon peel
- 1/8 teaspoon salt
- 1/2 cup (1 stick) chilled unsalted butter,
  cut into 1/2-inch pieces
- 1 large egg yolk
- 1/2 teaspoon vanilla extract

chocolate filling

- 3/4 cup whipping cream
- 6 ounces bittersweet (not unsweetened) or
  semisweet chocolate, finely chopped

caramel filling

- 3/4 cup sugar
- 1/3 cup water
- 1/3 cup whipping cream
- 5 tablespoons unsalted butter
- 1/2 teaspoon vanilla extract
- Pinch of salt

FOR CRUST: Blend flour, sugar, lemon peel
and salt in processor 5 seconds. Add butter,
yolk and vanilla and process until large moist
clumps form. Gather dough into ball; knead
briefly to combine well. Flatten into disk. Wrap
in plastic; refrigerate dough until firm enough
to roll, about 30 minutes.

Roll out dough between sheets of plastic wrap
to 11- to 12-inch round. Peel off top sheet of
plastic. Turn dough over; press into 9-inch-
diameter tart pan with removable bottom. Peel
off plastic. Fold in any excess dough, forming
double-thick sides. Pierce crust all over with
fork. Freeze 15 minutes. *(Can be prepared
1 week ahead; keep frozen.)*

Preheat oven to 400°F. Bake crust 10 minutes.
Using back side of fork, press crust flat if bottom bubbles. Continue to bake until crust is
golden, about 10 minutes (crust sides may
shrink slightly). Transfer to rack and cool.

FOR CHOCOLATE FILLING: Bring cream to
boil in heavy small saucepan. Remove pan from
heat. Add chocolate and whisk until smooth.
Spread 1 cup chocolate filling in prepared crust.
Refrigerate until firm, about 45 minutes.
Reserve remaining filling in saucepan.

FOR CARAMEL FILLING: Stir sugar and 1/3 cup
water in heavy medium saucepan over low heat
until sugar dissolves. Increase heat and boil
until syrup is amber color, brushing down sides
with wet pastry brush and swirling pan occasionally, about 8 minutes. Remove from heat.
Add cream, butter, vanilla and salt (mixture
will bubble up). Return pan to very low heat;
stir until caramel is smooth and color deepens,
about 5 minutes. Refrigerate uncovered until
cold but not firm, about 20 minutes.

Spoon caramel filling over chocolate filling.
Pipe or drizzle reserved chocolate filling decoratively over caramel (if chocolate is too firm to
pour, warm slightly over low heat). Refrigerate
tart until caramel is firm, at least 1 hour. *(Can
be made 2 days ahead. Cover; keep chilled.)*

The Christmas nut

AT HOLIDAY TIME, edible chestnuts are available in the shell; at other times of year they are sold dried (reconstitute in water), or canned or in jars in sugar syrup or water. Rich in flavor and rather starchy in texture, chestnuts appear in both sweet and savory dishes. They can also—as the famous Christmas carol attests—be roasted on an open fire. (An ordinary oven will do if an open fire is not an option.)

The earthy flavor of chestnuts marries well with brussels sprouts, winter squash, sweet potatoes and leafy winter greens like kale. Chestnuts are also a delicious complement to game. And for dessert, they can be glacéed, dipped in chocolate or stewed in wine. But chestnuts are, perhaps, most famous for their role in Mont Blanc, a recipe in which they are pureed and piled high in a mountain shape, then topped with whipped cream.

HELPFUL HINTS

WHEN SHOPPING FOR CHESTNUTS: Look for glossy smooth shells and nuts that feel heavy in relation to their size.

TO ROAST AND SHELL CHESTNUTS: Preheat oven to 400°F. Make an X cut into the shell on the flat side of each nut. Place nuts in a shallow roasting pan and sprinkle with water. Roast 30 minutes. Wrap nuts in kitchen towel and squeeze to crush shells. Keep the nuts wrapped for five minutes before removing the outer shell and the brown skin inside. Sprinkle the chestnuts with coarse salt and serve with mulled wine, spiced cider or glögg.

Chestnut Cheesecake

EVERYONE'S YEAR-ROUND FAVORITE GETS A LUXURI-OUS LIFT FROM CHESTNUTS, WHICH TASTE LIKE THE HOLIDAYS THEMSELVES.

8 to 10 servings

crust

- 1 cup whole unblanched almonds (about 5 ounces)
- 2 tablespoons sugar
- 1/8 teaspoon almond extract
- 2 tablespoons (1/4 stick) unsalted butter, room temperature

filling

- 1 10-ounce jar chestnuts (or chestnut pieces) in vanilla syrup*
- 2 8-ounce packages cream cheese, room temperature
- 1/3 cup sugar
- 1 teaspoon vanilla extract
- 2 large eggs

topping

- 1 cup chilled whipping cream

FOR CRUST: Preheat oven to 375°F. Blend whole unblanched almonds, sugar and almond extract in processor until almonds are coarsely chopped. Add unsalted butter and process until almonds are finely chopped. Press almond mixture firmly onto bottom and 1 inch up sides of 8-inch-diameter springform pan with 2½-inch-high sides. Bake crust until light brown, about 13 minutes. Transfer crust in pan to rack and cool. Reduce oven temperature to 300°F.

FOR FILLING: Drain chestnuts thoroughly. Cut enough chestnuts into ¼- to ½-inch pieces to measure 1 cup (reserve remaining chestnuts for topping). Using electric mixer, beat cream cheese, sugar and vanilla in medium bowl until very smooth. Beat in eggs, 1 at a time. Cover bottom of crust with 1 cup chestnut pieces.

Spoon cream cheese mixture over. Place spring-form pan on baking sheet.

Bake cheesecake on baking sheet until center is just set, about 45 minutes. Cool cheesecake 30 minutes. Chill uncovered until cold, about 3 hours, then cover. *(Cheesecake can be made 1 day ahead. Keep refrigerated.)*

FOR TOPPING: Cut around sides of pan to loosen cheesecake; release pan sides. Beat whipping cream in medium bowl until firm peaks form. Spoon cream into pastry bag fitted with medium star tip. Pipe rosettes of cream around top edge of cake. Place 1 reserved chestnut piece on each whipped cream rosette.

*Chestnuts in vanilla syrup are known as marrons glacés. *They are available at specialty foods stores and some supermarkets nationwide.*

Poached Pears in Red Wine Sauce

A FITTING FINALE TO A LOVELY SUPPER, THIS FRUIT DESSERT IS SURPRISINGLY SIMPLE TO MAKE.

8 servings

    3 cups dry red wine
    1 cup orange juice
    ⅔ cup plus 2 tablespoons sugar
    ⅓ cup fresh lemon juice
    2 cinnamon sticks

    8 Bosc pears

    1 cup chilled whipping cream
    2 tablespoons Cognac

Divide wine, orange juice, ⅔ cup sugar, lemon juice and cinnamon sticks equally between 2 heavy large saucepans. Bring to boil over medium heat, stirring until sugar dissolves. Remove from heat.

Peel pears, leaving stems intact. Cut small slice off bottom of each pear so that pear will stand upright. Arrange 4 pears on their sides in each saucepan. Cover and simmer until pears are tender but still hold their shape, turning once, about 30 minutes. Using slotted spoon, transfer pears to upright position in glass baking dish. Boil cooking liquid in each pan until reduced to ½ cup, about 9 minutes. Strain into small bowl. Cover and chill sauce and pears separately until cold, at least 2 hours and up to 2 days.

Beat cream in large bowl until soft peaks form. Add Cognac and 2 tablespoons sugar and beat until stiff peaks form. Spoon whipped cream into pastry bag fitted with medium star tip.

Transfer pears in upright position to plates. Spoon red wine sauce over. Pipe whipped cream around pears and serve.

Warm Pear Shortcakes with Brandied Cream

DO-AHEAD HOMEMADE SHORTCAKES TOP A MIXTURE OF SAUTÉED PEARS, CREAM, BROWN SUGAR AND BRANDY IN THIS APPEALING DESSERT (BELOW).

12 servings

biscuits

1¾ cups all purpose flour

1 cup cake flour

¼ cup sugar

4 teaspoons baking powder

¾ teaspoon salt

½ teaspoon baking soda

10 tablespoons (1¼ sticks) chilled unsalted butter, cut into ½-inch pieces

1 cup buttermilk

1 large egg, beaten to blend

pears

8 firm but ripe Bosc pears, peeled, cored, cut into ½-inch-thick slices

2 tablespoons fresh lemon juice

2 tablespoons unsalted butter

2 cups whipping cream

½ cup (packed) golden brown sugar

5 tablespoons poire Williams (clear pear brandy) or brandy

FOR BISCUITS: Preheat oven to 400°F. Sift both flours, sugar, baking powder, salt and baking soda into large bowl. Add chilled butter pieces. Rub in with fingers until mixture resembles coarse meal. Add buttermilk; stir to blend. Gather dough into ball.

Gently knead dough on floured surface until dough holds together. Roll out dough on lightly floured surface to ½-inch thickness. Using 3-inch-diameter star-shaped cookie cutter, cut out biscuits. Gather dough scraps, reroll and cut out additional biscuits, making total of 24 biscuits. Arrange biscuits on 2 baking sheets, spacing 2 inches apart.

Brush tops of biscuits with egg. Bake until biscuits puff and are light golden, about 12 minutes. *(Can be prepared 8 hours ahead. Cool completely. Wrap in foil. Reheat foil-wrapped biscuits in 350°F oven about 10 minutes before using.)*

FOR PEARS: Toss pears with lemon juice in large bowl. *(Can be prepared 2 hours ahead. Cover and refrigerate.)*

Melt butter in heavy large skillet over medium heat. Add pear mixture and sauté until crisp-tender, about 6 minutes. Remove pear mixture from heat. Add whipping cream and brown sugar, then pear brandy. Bring mixture to boil. Cook until pears are tender and sauce thickens slightly, about 5 minutes.

Divide pear mixture among 12 bowls. Top with warm biscuits and serve.

Chocolate-glazed Croquembouche

TRADITIONALLY, *CROQUEMBOUCHE* IS ASSEMBLED WITH CARAMELIZED SUGAR. HERE A DARK CHOCOLATE GLAZE REPLACES THE TRICKY CARAMEL.

12 to 18 servings

cream puff pastry

1½ cups water
¾ cup (1½ sticks) unsalted butter, cut into ½-inch pieces
1½ cups all purpose flour
¼ teaspoon salt
6 large eggs

vanilla pastry cream

3½ cups half and half
8 large egg yolks
1 cup sugar
⅔ cup all purpose flour
¼ teaspoon salt
1 tablespoon vanilla extract

chocolate glaze

1 cup whipping cream
16 ounces bittersweet (not unsweetened) chocolate, chopped
Fresh mint sprigs (optional)
Candied violets (optional)

FOR CREAM PUFF PASTRY: Bring 1½ cups water and butter to boil in heavy large saucepan. Reduce heat to low. Add flour and salt; stir until mixture is smooth and pulls away from sides of pan to form ball, about 1 minute. Transfer to large bowl. Add eggs 1 at a time, beating with electric mixer until smooth after each addition. Cover loosely; cool completely, about 1 hour. Preheat oven to 425°F. Cut out

8-inch-diameter waxed paper circle. Butter 2 large baking sheets and waxed paper circle; place circle buttered side up on one baking sheet. Spread ⅓ cup pastry over circle; prick all over with fork. Spoon remaining pastry into pastry bag fitted with ½-inch plain tip. Pipe twelve ¾-inch-diameter mounds of pastry around outer edge of circle, spacing apart evenly. Pipe remaining pastry in ¾-inch-diameter mounds on baking sheets, spacing apart. Bake until golden brown, about 20 minutes. Remove from oven and turn off heat. Pierce side of each puff with knife. Return to oven and let stand 10 minutes with door ajar to dry interior. *(Can be made 2 days ahead. Cool completely. Store in airtight containers at room temperature.)*

FOR VANILLA PASTRY CREAM: Bring half and half to simmer in heavy large saucepan over medium heat. Whisk yolks, sugar, flour and salt in large bowl. Gradually add half of hot half and half to yolk mixture, whisking to combine. Return to saucepan and whisk over medium heat until mixture thickens and boils, about 5 minutes. Whisk in vanilla. Transfer to bowl; cover and refrigerate until cold. *(Can be made 2 days ahead; keep chilled.)*

FOR CHOCOLATE GLAZE: Bring cream to simmer in heavy medium saucepan. Add chocolate and whisk over low heat until melted and smooth. Cool to lukewarm, about 30 minutes.

Meanwhile, spoon pastry cream into pastry bag fitted with ¼-inch plain tip. Insert tip into score on each puff and fill. Drizzle 3 tablespoons chocolate glaze over circle of puffs. Fill center of circle with single layer of puffs to form base; drizzle with glaze and refrigerate until set. Spoon 1 teaspoon glaze over top and sides of puff; place atop first layer of puffs. Repeat to form slightly smaller second layer; refrigerate until set. Continue layering puffs, tapering toward top and refrigerating between each layer. Chill until set, at least 2 hours and up to 6 hours. Garnish with mint sprigs and violets.

THE *Guide*

It's the little things as much as the big ones that make Christmas special: the wreath on the front door, the snow stencils on the windows, the candles on the mantel, the crèche that used to be yours when you were a child, the big bow on the dog's collar, the cookie plate for Santa, the tattered copy of *How the Grinch Stole Christmas!* and so on. This section of the book is dedicated to just such pleasures—the small details that can have a big impact on the spirit and sparkle of the season.

Gifts from your kitchen—cookies the kids helped decorate, candies that taste truly homemade—and projects that remind you just how fun it is to decorate and design and craft, these are the things that take the season out of the mall and bring it home. Here, you'll find recipes and ideas for everything from gingerbread (spiced with cinnamon, cloves, cardamom and ginger) to brownies (glazed with white and dark chocolate), fudge (studded with dried cherries) to a topiary (made with pears and kumquats), all sure to lure you into the kitchen, where it's warm and fragrant and Christmasy.

Gifts from the Kitchen

If you want the Christmas gifts you give to be truly memorable, perhaps the best place to "shop" is in the kitchen—your kitchen. A homemade gift, beautifully wrapped and presented, may turn out to be the best of all presents, and on the giver's end, it might be the perfect antidote to that common ailment: too much shopping and spending.

Here are more than a dozen recipes for delicious gifts for everyone on your list, from a favorite teacher to the nice lady next door, the mailman to the soccer coach. There's a fruitcake that turns an unfavorable stereotype on its head, a spiced marmalade that cooks in just five minutes and a citrus-infused vodka that makes for a memorable Martini, among other ideas.

Chocolate-dipped Hazelnut Biscotti

IF YOU SPEND ONE AFTERNOON IN THE KITCHEN, THERE WILL BE COOKIES FOR EVERYONE ON YOUR LIST. YOU'LL NEED AT LEAST A FOUR-QUART BOWL TO MIX THE LARGE AMOUNT OF DOUGH.

makes about 5 dozen

3 cups sugar
1 cup (2 sticks) unsalted butter, room temperature
4 large eggs
4 teaspoons grated orange peel
2 teaspoons baking soda
1 teaspoon salt
6 cups all purpose flour
2½ cups hazelnuts (about 9 ounces), toasted, husked, coarsely chopped
1¾ cups dried tart cherries (about 8½ ounces)

1½ pounds bittersweet (not unsweetened) or semisweet chocolate, chopped
Unsweetened cocoa powder

Position 1 rack in center and 1 rack in top third of oven and preheat to 325°F. Using handheld electric mixer, beat sugar and butter in very large bowl until well blended. Beat in eggs 1 at a time just until blended. Mix in orange peel, baking soda and salt. Add 3 cups flour, hazelnuts and dried cherries; stir until well blended. Add remaining 3 cups flour, 1 cup at a time, stirring until well incorporated.

Transfer dough to floured work surface. Divide into 4 equal pieces. Knead each piece until dough holds together well. Form each piece into 9-inch-long by 3-inch-wide log. Place 2 logs on each of 2 large ungreased baking sheets, spacing about 3 inches apart (logs will spread during baking). Bake until logs are golden and feel firm when tops are gently pressed, switching and rotating baking sheets halfway through baking, about 55 minutes total. Cool logs on baking sheets 15 minutes. Maintain oven temperature.

Using long wide spatula, transfer logs to cutting board. Using serrated knife, cut warm logs crosswise into ½-inch-thick slices. Arrange slices cut side down on 2 baking sheets. Bake biscotti 10 minutes. Turn biscotti over; bake until light golden, about 10 minutes longer. Transfer to racks and cool completely.

Stir chocolate in large bowl set over saucepan of boiling water until melted and smooth. Remove from over water. Dip 1 cut side of each biscotti into melted chocolate to about ¼-inch depth. Gently shake off excess chocolate. Place biscotti, chocolate side up, on baking sheets. Refrigerate until chocolate is firm, about 35 minutes. Dip pastry brush in cocoa, then lightly brush cocoa over chocolate on each biscotti. *(Can be made ahead. Store in airtight containers up to 4 days, or wrap in foil and freeze in resealable plastic bags up to 3 weeks.)*

Chocolate-Almond Sauce

ANY CHOCOLATE LOVERS ON YOUR LIST? THEY'LL APPRECIATE A JAR OF THIS ICE CREAM TOPPING.

**makes about 1³/₄ cups
(enough for two 8-ounce jars)**

¼ cup sugar
¼ cup water
½ cup whipping cream
7 ounces bittersweet (not unsweetened) or semisweet chocolate, chopped
¼ teaspoon almond extract
Generous pinch of salt
½ cup whole almonds (about 2½ ounces), toasted, chopped

Stir sugar and ¼ cup water in heavy small saucepan over low heat until sugar dissolves. Add cream; bring to boil. Remove from heat; add chocolate and whisk until melted and smooth. Whisk in almond extract and salt. Stir in almonds. Divide sauce between two 8-ounce canning jars; seal with lids. *(Can be made 2 weeks ahead; refrigerate. Rewarm sauce over medium-low heat, stirring constantly.)*

Golden Fruitcake

THIS VERSION OF THE MUCH-MALIGNED CHRISTMAS
CLASSIC IS DELICIOUSLY LACKING IN CANDIED CHER-
RIES, GIANT MIXED NUTS AND CITRON, BUT IT IS
FILLED WITH BITS OF MARZIPAN AND LOTS OF
APPEALING DRIED FRUIT. BAKING THE CAKES IN DIS-
POSABLE ALUMINUM LOAF PANS (AVAILABLE AT
SUPERMARKETS) OR IN DECORATIVE CARDBOARD
LOAF PANS (AVAILABLE AT SOME COOKWARE STORES
OR BY MAIL ORDER) MAKES GIFT GIVING EASY; JUST
WRAP EACH CAKE IN ITS PAN IN CELLOPHANE, AND
ADD A COLORFUL RIBBON.

makes 4 loaves

  1 7-ounce package marzipan, cut into
    ½-inch pieces
1¼ cups chopped dried Calimyrna figs
    (about 6 ounces)

3 cups combined chopped dried pears,
  dried apricots and pitted dates
  (about 15 ounces total)
1 cup golden raisins (about 5 ounces)
½ cup brandy

4 8 x 3¾ x 2½-inch disposable aluminum loaf
  pans, 8½ x 3½ x 2-inch corrugated paper
  baking loaf forms or 8¼ x 4¼ x 2½-inch
  metal loaf pans
1½ cups (3 sticks) unsalted butter,
  room temperature
1½ cups sugar
1 cup (packed) golden brown sugar
8 large eggs
1 tablespoon vanilla extract
1 teaspoon ground cardamom
1 teaspoon ground nutmeg
½ teaspoon salt
3 cups all purpose flour
1½ cups pine nuts (about 6 ounces), toasted

Place marzipan on plate; cover with plastic
wrap. Freeze overnight. Combine dried figs
and next 3 ingredients in large bowl. Cover
dried fruit mixture and let stand at room temperature overnight, stirring occasionally.

Preheat oven to 325°F. Butter baking pans or
forms. Beat 1½ cups butter, sugar and brown
sugar in large bowl until light. Beat in eggs 1 at
a time, then vanilla, cardamom, nutmeg and
salt. Stir in flour in 4 additions. Stir in pine
nuts, dried fruit mixture and any soaking liquid from bowl. Gently stir in marzipan.

Divide batter among prepared pans. Place pans
on baking sheet. Bake until tester inserted into
center of cakes comes out clean, about 1 hour
15 minutes. Cool cakes completely in pans on
racks. Wrap in plastic. Let stand at least 1 day
and up to 3 days at room temperature or chill
up to 2 weeks. Serve at room temperature.

LEFT TO RIGHT: CHOCOLATE-DIPPED HAZELNUT
BISCOTTI; CHOCOLATE-ALMOND SAUCE; COFFEE-
CARAMEL SAUCE; AND GOLDEN FRUITCAKE.

Coffee-Caramel Sauce

FOR A GIFT, SIMPLY DECORATE THE JARS WITH GOLD RIBBON, AND ATTACH TAGS THAT INCLUDE THE REWARMING INSTRUCTIONS. OR PACK A BASKET WITH A JAR OF THIS SAUCE, THE CHOCOLATE-ALMOND SAUCE (ON PAGE 151), AN ICE CREAM SCOOP AND FOUR OR SIX SUNDAE GOBLETS.

**makes about 1 3/4 cups
(enough for two 8-ounce jars)**

  8 tablespoons water
  4 teaspoons instant coffee powder
1⅓ cups sugar
⅔ cup whipping cream
  5 tablespoons unsalted butter, diced
    Pinch of salt

Stir 2 tablespoons water and 4 teaspoons coffee powder in small bowl until coffee powder dissolves. Stir remaining 6 tablespoons water and 1⅓ cups sugar in heavy medium saucepan over low heat until sugar dissolves. Increase heat and boil without stirring until syrup turns deep amber, occasionally brushing down sides of pan with pastry brush dipped into water and swirling pan, about 8 minutes. Remove saucepan from heat. Add whipping cream, butter and coffee mixture (mixture will bubble vigorously). Return to heat and bring to boil, whisking constantly until smooth. Whisk in salt. Divide sauce between two 8-ounce canning jars; seal jars tightly with lids. *(Sauce can be prepared 2 weeks ahead; refrigerate. Rewarm over medium-low heat, stirring constantly.)*

Boysenberry and Grapefruit Preserves

PRESENT THIS DELIGHTFUL TART-SWEET SPREAD IN A GLASS JAR TIED WITH A RIBBON. FOR A NICE TOUCH, TIE A SPOON INTO THE BOW.

**makes about 4 generous cups
(enough for four 8-ounce jars)**

  2 pink or ruby red grapefruit, halved
1½ cups sugar
  6 cups frozen unsweetened boysenberries
    (about 1½ pounds), unthawed
  1 12-ounce bag fresh or frozen cranberries

    Canning jars

Squeeze juice from grapefruit. Measure 1 cup juice, discarding seeds; place juice in heavy large saucepan. Add sugar to juice. Mix in 4 cups boysenberries and all cranberries. Spoon 2 cups boysenberries into medium bowl; let thaw at room temperature. Let berry mixture stand until berries thaw and sugar dissolves, stirring occasionally, about 1 hour.

Bring mixture to boil in heavy medium saucepan over high heat. Reduce heat to medium. Boil gently until mixture thickens and liquid drops thickly off end of spoon, stirring often, about 25 minutes. Mix in 2 cups thawed boysenberries with any juices; bring to boil. Spoon preserves into hot canning jar, filling only to ¼ inch from top. Wipe rim, using towel dipped into hot water. Place lid on jar; seal tightly. Repeat with remaining jars and preserves.

Place jars on rack in large pot. Add boiling water to pot so that at least 1 inch of water covers tops of jars. Cover pot; boil rapidly 15 minutes. Remove jars. Cool completely. Press center of each lid. If lid stays down, jar is sealed. (If lid pops up, store preserves in refrigerator.) Store in cool dry place up to 1 year. Refrigerate preserves up to 1 month after opening.

Nuts to you

FULL OF FLAVOR and loaded with natural oils, nuts add taste, texture and richness to cookies, candies and cakes. And of course, these nutrient-packed morsels are delicious on their own. You can buy them either in the shell or already shelled, and while nuts in the shell stay fresh longer, shelling them takes time. If that's something you're short on, opt for packaged, shelled nuts instead and store them in the freezer until ready to use. Toasting enhances the flavor of nuts. And when they're cooked with spices like red pepper and cumin or sweetened with sugar and cinnamon, they make both a welcome gift and a delicious holiday snack.

HELPFUL HINTS

TO CHOP NUTS: Place a dish towel under the cutting board to keep it steady, then chop nuts using a heavy chopping knife.

TO GRIND NUTS IN A FOOD PROCESSOR OR BLENDER: Watch carefully; do not over-process or the nuts may turn into a smooth paste. It helps to add sugar or salt (if the recipe calls for either of them) to the nuts; both ingredients act as a kind of "pumice."

TO TOAST NUTS: Spread nuts in a single layer in an ungreased shallow roasting pan and toast in a 350°F oven until light golden brown, 8 to 20 minutes (timing will depend on the type of nuts). Shake or stir every few minutes, and watch carefully, as they can burn easily. Nuts will continue to cook as they cool.

TO SKIN HAZELNUTS: The thin, dark brown skin is easier to remove once the hazelnuts have been toasted. Toast the hazelnuts as instructed above, then cool to room temperature. Transfer the nuts to a clean, dry kitchen towel. Gather the towel around them and rub the nuts against one another for a few minutes until the skins have loosened.

Sweet and Spicy Candied Nuts

SUGAR MAKES THESE SWEET, BLACK PEPPER AND CAYENNE MAKE THEM SPICY. A SIMPLE GIFT, THEY TAKE LESS THAN 20 MINUTES TO MAKE.

makes 4 1/2 cups

Nonstick vegetable oil spray
1/2 cup light corn syrup
5 tablespoons sugar
2 1/2 teaspoons salt
3/4 teaspoon (generous) freshly ground black pepper
1/2 teaspoon (scant) cayenne pepper
4 1/2 cups mixed whole almonds, raw cashews and pecans

Preheat oven to 325°F. Spray large baking sheet with nonstick spray. Combine corn syrup and next 4 ingredients in large bowl. Stir to blend. Add nuts; stir gently to coat. Transfer to prepared baking sheet.

Place large piece of foil on work surface. Bake nuts 5 minutes. Using fork, stir nuts to coat with melted spice mixture. Continue baking until nuts are golden and coating bubbles, about 10 minutes. Transfer to foil. Working quickly, separate nuts with fork. Cool. *(Can be made 3 days ahead. Divide nuts among decorative tins or jars. Store airtight at room temperature.)*

Five-Minute Spiced Orange Marmalade

HONEY, BRANDY AND SPICES ENHANCE PURCHASED MARMALADE FOR A SIMPLE-TO-MAKE GIFT. THIS RECIPE DOUBLES EASILY IF YOU HAVE A LOT OF PEOPLE ON YOUR GIFT-GIVING LIST.

makes about 3 cups (enough for three 8-ounce jars)

½ cup honey
½ cup brandy
3 cinnamon sticks
3 whole star anise*
1 vanilla bean, cut crosswise into 3 pieces
3 3 x 1-inch strips orange peel (orange part only)
12 whole cloves
2 14- to 16-ounce jars orange marmalade

Combine first 5 ingredients in large saucepan. Pierce each orange peel strip with 4 cloves, spacing apart; add to pan. Simmer until mixture is reduced to ½ cup, about 5 minutes. Add marmalade; bring to simmer, stirring often. Remove marmalade from heat.

Using tongs, transfer 1 star anise, 1 cinnamon stick, 1 vanilla piece and 1 orange-clove strip to each of three 8-ounce canning jars. Fill each jar with hot marmalade and seal with lids. (Can be prepared 4 weeks ahead. Refrigerate.)

Brown star-shaped seed pods sold at Asian markets and specialty foods stores and in the spice section of some supermarkets.

Citrus Vodka

YOU CAN SELECT ANY TYPE OF BOTTLE YOU LIKE FOR THIS CITRUS-SCENTED SPIRIT, BUT CHOOSING A WIDE-NECKED ONE MAKES IT A SNAP TO PLACE THE CITRUS PEEL INTO THE VODKA. SUGGEST THAT THE RECIPIENT USE THE VODKA IN ORANGE JUICE OR LEMONADE, OR IN A MARTINI. IT'S ALSO GOOD ICE-COLD AND STRAIGHT UP.

makes enough to fill one 750-milliliter bottle

6 2 x ½-inch strips orange peel (orange part only)
1 8-inch wooden skewer
6 2 x ½-inch strips lemon peel (yellow part only)
6 2 x ½-inch strips lime peel (green part only)
1 750-ml clean clear wine bottle with cork
1 750-ml bottle vodka

Fold 1 orange peel strip crosswise in half without breaking. Thread onto skewer. Repeat with 1 lemon peel strip, then 1 lime peel strip. Repeat, alternating remaining orange, lemon and lime peel strips on same skewer. Using chopstick as aid, if necessary, guide citrus peel skewer through neck of empty bottle, pushing gently but being careful not to break any peel. Fill bottle with vodka and cork. Refrigerate at least 1 week and up to 3 weeks. Serve chilled.

Four-Spice Gingerbread

CARDAMOM IS DISTANTLY RELATED TO GINGER; IN THIS MOIST DESSERT (OPPOSITE), THE TWO USED TOGETHER ENHANCE EACH OTHER DELICIOUSLY. CINNAMON AND CLOVES ROUND OUT THE QUARTET OF SPICES. WRAP THE CAKES IN THEIR PANS IN CELLOPHANE TO GIVE AS GIFTS.

makes two 9-inch cakes

2 9-inch-square foil cake pans with
   2-inch-high sides
3½ cups unbleached all purpose flour
4 teaspoons ground ginger
2½ teaspoons ground cardamom
2 teaspoons baking soda
½ teaspoon ground cinnamon
½ teaspoon ground cloves
½ teaspoon salt

1 cup (2 sticks) unsalted butter,
   room temperature
1 cup (packed) golden brown sugar
2 large eggs
2 cups mild flavored (light) molasses
1 cup boiling water

Preheat oven to 350°F. Butter cake pans. Sift next 7 ingredients into medium bowl.

Using electric mixer, beat butter in large bowl until creamy. Add brown sugar and eggs and beat until fluffy. Gradually mix in molasses. Add dry ingredients and mix just until combined. Gradually mix in boiling water.

Pour batter into prepared pans, dividing equally. Bake until cakes begin to pull away from sides of pan and tester inserted into center comes out clean, about 50 minutes. Cool in pan on rack (gingerbread may fall slightly in center). Wrap cakes in pans with plastic wrap. *(Can be made 2 days ahead. Store at cool room temperature.)*

Winter Fruit Chutney

THIS CINNAMON- AND CORIANDER-SPICED CHUTNEY COMBINES WINE, RAISINS AND CITRUS. TIE RIBBON AROUND THE NECKS OF THE CANNING JARS, ATTACHING A NOTE ABOUT SERVING THE CHUTNEY WITH MEAT OR POULTRY, OR AS AN APPETIZER WITH GOAT CHEESE AND CRUSTY BREAD.

makes about 6 cups
(enough for three 16-ounce jars)

1 orange, peel and white pith removed
3 cups dry white wine
⅔ cup sugar
2 tablespoons fresh lemon juice
2 cinnamon sticks
2 bay leaves
1 tablespoon coriander seeds
1 tablespoon whole black peppercorns

1 cup dried cranberries
⅔ cup coarsely chopped dried pears
⅔ cup coarsely chopped dried figs
½ cup raisins
3 tablespoons minced crystallized ginger
4 small apples (about 1 pound total), peeled,
   cored, cut into ½-inch pieces

Using small sharp knife, cut between membranes of orange to release segments.

Combine white wine and next 6 ingredients in large nonreactive* saucepan. Cover and simmer 15 minutes. Strain mixture; discard solids.

Return liquid to saucepan. Add cranberries, pears, figs, raisins and ginger. Cover and simmer until fruit is tender, about 10 minutes. Add apples. Simmer until apples are just tender, about 15 minutes. Cool to lukewarm. Stir in reserved orange segments. Transfer to jars; seal and refrigerate. *(Can be prepared 1 week ahead.)*

Nonreactive cookware interiors include the following: stainless steel, anodized aluminum, enamel linings and nonstick surfaces.

Red Pepper and Corn Relish

LUCKY (AND INDUSTRIOUS) HOME CANNERS MAY ALREADY HAVE A PANTRY FULL OF SUMMERTIME CORN RELISH TO OPEN UP OVER THE HOLIDAYS. THE REST OF US CAN CONCOCT THIS SIMPLE-TO-MAKE SUBSTITUTE (BELOW) TO GIVE AS A GIFT.

**makes about 8 cups
(enough for eight 8-ounce jars)**

1 large red bell pepper

¼ cup cider vinegar

3 tablespoons pure maple syrup

2½ teaspoons hot pepper sauce

2 teaspoons ground turmeric

1 teaspoon salt

⅓ cup vegetable oil

3 10-ounce packages frozen corn kernels, thawed, drained

½ cup sliced green onions

Roast pepper over gas flame or under broiler until blackened on all sides. Seal pepper in paper bag and let stand 10 minutes. Peel, seed and chop pepper. Set aside.

Combine vinegar, syrup, hot pepper sauce, turmeric and salt in large bowl. Gradually whisk in oil. Add red pepper, corn and green onions and toss to coat. Cover and refrigerate overnight, stirring occasionally. Divide mixture among jars. *(Can be made 3 days ahead.)*

Let relish stand at room temperature 30 minutes before serving.

Peppercorn, Mustard and Dill Vinegar

THIS EASY CONDIMENT WOULD BE WONDERFUL INCORPORATED INTO A VINAIGRETTE FOR COLD POACHED SALMON. IN FACT, YOU MIGHT MAKE A GIFT BASKET WITH THIS AND OTHER VINAIGRETTE INGREDIENTS, PLUS A FAVORITE RECIPE.

**makes about 3½ cups
(enough for two 375-milliliter bottles)**

3¼ cups white wine vinegar

3 tablespoons yellow mustard seeds

1 tablespoon whole allspice

1 tablespoon white peppercorns

1 teaspoon dill seeds

3 bay leaves

2 lemon slices, halved

1 medium bunch fresh dill sprigs

Place first 5 ingredients in large bowl. Mix in bay leaves, lemon slices and dill sprigs. Divide mixture between bottles. Seal. Store in cool dry place at least 1 week and up to 6 weeks.

Olive Oil Infused with Porcini and Rosemary

THIS ALL-PURPOSE OIL TAKES ITS CUE FROM COOKS IN THE NORTHERN ITALIAN CITY OF MILAN, WHERE ROSEMARY AND PORCINI MUSHROOMS ARE KITCHEN BASICS. ON THE NOTE CARD YOU ATTACH TO THE BOTTLES, TELL THE RECIPIENT TO BE SURE TO REFRIGERATE THE OIL, AND TO USE IT WITHIN THREE WEEKS OF THE DATE IT WAS MADE.

makes about 3 1/2 cups
(enough for two 375-milliliter bottles)

1½ ounces dried porcini mushrooms*
 3 cups olive oil
1½ tablespoons dried rosemary

Place mushrooms in strainer. Rinse under hot water. Drain well. Pat mushrooms dry. Combine mushrooms, oil and rosemary in heavy medium saucepan. Cook over low heat until thermometer inserted into oil registers 180°F, about 8 minutes. Remove from heat. Cover; cool to room temperature, 2 hours.

Divide mixture between bottles. Seal. Refrigerate up to 3 weeks.

Available at Italian markets, specialty foods stores and many supermarkets.

Wrap it up

INNOVATIVE GIFT WRAP doesn't have to be costly or time-consuming, and you don't have to be a whiz with a glue gun. For fresh ideas, think different: Look around the house, and peruse the shelves of hardware stores, cookware shops and fabric stores.

INSTEAD OF TRADITIONAL PAPER, TRY...

FABRIC: felt, tulle, taffeta, silk, wool, flannel or a crisp, new dish towel.

KITCHEN PAPERS: baker's parchment paper, butcher paper or brown paper lunch bags.

NEWSPAPERS AND MAGAZINES: the Sunday comics, foreign-language newspapers or pages from glossy magazines.

INSTEAD OF TRADITIONAL RIBBON, TRY...

- Rickrack
- Twine, cotton string, or gold or copper wire
- Braid or trim from an upholstery shop
- Long strands of dime-store pearls
- Pipe cleaners (for small packages)
- Raffia

INSTEAD OF TRADITIONAL TAGS, TRY...

CUT-OUT IMAGES FROM LAST YEAR'S CHRIST-MAS CARDS: Make a hole in the corner with a hole punch, then slip a piece of ribbon through to tie onto the package. Write your greeting on the back of the tag.

BAKER'S CLAY STARS OR GINGERBREAD MEN: Using a straw, punch a hole in the dough before baking. When cool and dry, paint the recipient's name on the tag with acrylic paint. Slip a ribbon through the hole to tie onto the gift.

Christmas Cookies

It just isn't Christmas without them: Frosted, decorated and brightly colored cookies shaped liked Santas, reindeer, stars and bells are a symbol of the season. And an afternoon in the kitchen, up to your elbows in flour, sugar and butter, is as much a part of the expected seasonal festivities as a Champagne toast on New Year's Eve.

Traditionalists will find a favorite among the ten recipes here, perhaps the Christmas-tree-shaped shortbread; chocolate lovers will head straight for the nutty fudge brownies; and adventurous bakers may find themselves leaning toward the lace cookies. Recipes drawn from other cultures and cuisines remind us that the language of Christmas is one spoken around the world.

Chocolate-glazed Mocha Fans

FOR AN ELEGANT TOUCH, DECORATE THE SHORT-BREAD WITH GOLD LEAF AND PLACE THE COOKIES ON A TRAY LINED WITH GOLD TISSUE PAPER.

makes 16

    Nonstick vegetable oil spray
1½ cups all purpose flour
 ½ cup unsweetened cocoa powder
  2 teaspoons instant espresso powder
 ½ teaspoon salt
  1 cup (2 sticks) unsalted butter,
    room temperature
  1 cup (packed) golden brown sugar

 ¾ cup whipping cream
  8 ounces bittersweet (not unsweetened) or
    semisweet chocolate, chopped

  2 3¾-inch square sheets edible gold leaf
    (optional)*

Preheat oven to 325°F. Spray 10-inch-diameter tart pan with removable bottom with nonstick spray. Sift flour, cocoa, espresso powder and salt into medium bowl. Using electric mixer, beat butter and brown sugar in large bowl until well blended. Add dry ingredients; beat just until dough clumps together. Using fingertips, press dough evenly onto bottom of pan.

Bake shortbread until firm around edges and baked through but slightly soft in center, about 35 minutes. Cool 10 minutes. Gently remove pan sides. Using large sharp knife, cut warm shortbread into 16 wedges. Cool completely on pan bottom on rack.

Bring cream to simmer in medium saucepan. Remove from heat. Add chocolate; stir until melted and smooth. Let stand until glaze begins to thicken but is still pourable, about 10 minutes. Place wedges on rack set over large baking sheet. Spoon glaze over wedges, allowing some of glaze to run down sides and spreading around sides with small spatula. Refrigerate just until chocolate glaze is firm, about 45 minutes.

If desired, press tip of small sharp knife into gold leaf; peel off ½-inch freeform pieces. Using knife as aid, carefully press gold leaf pieces onto cookies. *(Can be made 5 days ahead. Store airtight in single layer at room temperature.)*

*Gold leaf sheets can be found at some cookware stores and at specialty art-supply stores.

Spiced Snowflakes

A WONDERFUL COOKIE TO BAKE WITH KIDS. HAVE THEM CUT OUT THEIR OWN SNOWFLAKE STENCILS, THEN LET THE POWDERED SUGAR FLY. LACE DOILIES WORK WELL AS STENCILS.

makes about 2 dozen

1½ cups sifted all purpose flour
1½ teaspoons baking powder
1¼ teaspoons ground cinnamon
 1 teaspoon ground ginger
 ½ teaspoon ground nutmeg
 ¼ teaspoon ground cloves
 ¼ teaspoon salt
 ½ cup (1 stick) unsalted butter, room temperature
 ¾ cup sugar
 1 large egg
 2 teaspoons vanilla extract

 Powdered sugar

Sift flour, baking powder, spices and salt into medium bowl. Using electric mixer, beat butter in large bowl until light. Gradually beat in ¾ cup sugar. Beat in egg and vanilla extract. Gradually beat in dry ingredients. If dough is too soft to mold, refrigerate until firm enough.

Spoon dough onto large sheet of plastic wrap. Roll into 7-inch-long, 2¼-inch-diameter log. Wrap tightly and refrigerate overnight. *(Can be made 2 weeks ahead and frozen. Let stand 1 hour at room temperature before continuing.)*

Preheat oven to 350°F. Grease 2 large baking sheets. Unwrap dough and cut into ¼-inch-thick slices. Place on baking sheets, spacing slices 1 inch apart. Bake until light golden brown, about 12 minutes. Transfer cookies to rack and cool. *(Can be made 1 week ahead. Store in airtight container at room temperature.)*

Place doilies or stencils atop cookies. Sift powdered sugar over. Carefully remove doilies or stencils and serve cookies.

Christmas Tree Shortbread

makes 3 dozen

1½ cups (3 sticks) unsalted butter,
    room temperature
¾ cup powdered sugar
2 teaspoons vanilla extract
2 teaspoons almond extract
3¾ cups all purpose flour
1¼ teaspoons salt

¾ cup (about) raspberry jam

Maple Icing (see recipe at right)
Green food coloring

Using electric mixer, beat butter in large bowl until light. Gradually beat in powdered sugar. Beat in extracts. Add flour and salt and stir just until combined. Gather dough into ball; divide in half. Flatten each half into disk. Wrap in plastic and refrigerate until firm, about 1 hour. *(Can be prepared ahead. Keep chilled up to 3 days or freeze up to 2 weeks. Let dough soften slightly at room temperature before continuing.)*

Preheat oven to 325°F. Line 3 heavy large baking sheets with parchment paper. Roll out 1 dough disk on lightly floured surface to ⅛-inch thickness, frequently lifting and turning dough to prevent sticking. Cut out cookies, using 3-inch-long Christmas-tree cookie cutter. Gather scraps, reroll and cut out total of 36 cookies, placing 12 cookies on each prepared sheet. Spread 1 teaspoon jam in center of each cookie.

Roll out remaining dough disk and cut out more cookies. Cut out center of each cookie, using 1-inch triangle cookie cutter. Using metal spatula, lift cookie frames onto jam-topped cookies. Gather scraps, reroll and cut additional cookie frames, making total of 36. Place on jam-topped cookies. Bake cookies until slightly golden brown around edges, about 25 minutes. Transfer to racks and cool.

Place half of icing in resealable plastic bag. Mix enough food coloring into remaining icing to make desired green color. Transfer green icing to another resealable plastic bag. Cut very tip off 1 corner of each bag. Pipe white icing along edges of trees. Pipe green icing in dots on trees. *(Can be made 2 days ahead. Store in airtight container at room temperature.)*

Maple Icing

makes about 1 cup

3 tablespoons hot water
1½ teaspoons maple extract
1 teaspoon vanilla extract
¼ teaspoon salt
2¾ cups (about) powdered sugar

Mix 3 tablespoons hot water, extracts and salt in small bowl. Whisk in enough powdered sugar to form icing thick enough to pipe.

Coconut-Macadamia Crescents

TROPICAL FLAVORS GIVE A NEW SPIN TO THESE TRADITIONAL HOLIDAY COOKIES.

makes about 5 dozen

  1 cup (2 sticks) unsalted butter, room temperature
  ¾ cup powdered sugar, sifted
  2 teaspoons vanilla extract
  2 teaspoons coconut extract
2¼ cups sifted all purpose flour
  1 teaspoon salt
  1 cup chopped roasted salted macadamia nuts

  1 egg white, beaten to blend
  1 cup sweetened shredded coconut
    Additional powdered sugar

Using electric mixer, beat butter in medium bowl until light. Gradually beat in ¾ cup powdered sugar. Beat in extracts. Stir in flour and salt, then nuts. Refrigerate dough 30 minutes.

Preheat oven to 325°F. Line 3 large baking sheets with parchment paper. Pinch off 1 tablespoon dough; shape into 2-inch-long, ½-inch-thick crescent. Repeat with remaining dough. Brush crescents with egg white, then dip tops into coconut. Place crescents, coconut side up, on parchment-lined sheets, spacing cookies 1 inch apart. Bake until just barely golden brown, about 20 minutes. Cool cookies on sheets on rack. Sift additional powdered sugar over cookies. *(Can be prepared 1 week ahead. Transfer cookies to airtight container and freeze. Bring to room temperature before serving.)*

Bake like a pro

EXPERIENCED COOKIE BAKERS know all kinds of tips and shortcuts, like how to use a resealable plastic bag with the tip cut off instead of a hard-to-clean pastry bag for icing cookies. Here are more tricks of the trade.

HELPFUL HINTS

✻ When preparing rolled cookies, make sure there's space in the refrigerator for chilling the dough, and always chill the dough as the recipe directs. (Chilled dough is easier to handle.)

✻ Use butter at the temperature the recipe specifies. Melted butter produces different results from chilled or softened butter.

✻ To avoid burning, use heavy-gauge baking sheets with low edges so air can circulate.

✻ Check the oven temperature regularly with a reliable oven thermometer.

✻ To help them keep their shape, let cut-out cookies rest on the baking sheet for about one minute before removing with a spatula. (Hot-from-the-oven cookies are more pliable and apt to bend and lose their shape if moved.)

✻ Cool baking sheets between batches of cookies. A fast way to do this is to run cool water over the bottom of the baking sheet, then dry it with a kitchen towel.

✻ Have plenty of cooling racks handy; arrange cookies in a single layer on racks to cool.

✻ When making cookies with children, put the decorations (colored sugar, dragées, sprinkles, etc.) in bowls that won't easily tip over.

✻ When chopping dried fruit, which can be sticky, chill the fruit first and spray the knife with nonstick cooking spray.

Chewy Pecan Diamonds

THIS IS A TERRIFIC COMBINATION OF COOKIE AND
CANDY, WITH THE CRUMBLY CRUST SERVING AS
COUNTERPOINT TO THE CHEWY CARAMEL TOPPING.
FOR A PRETTY PRESENTATION, PLACE THE COOKIES
IN PAPER CANDY CUPS, AND SET THE CUPS IN A
BASKET; WRAP CLEAR CELLOPHANE AROUND THE
BASKET AND TIE IT UP WITH RAFFIA.

makes about 32

crust

1¾ cups all purpose flour
⅔ cup powdered sugar
¼ cup cornstarch
½ teaspoon salt
¾ cup (1½ sticks) chilled unsalted butter,
cut into ½-inch pieces

topping

1¼ cups (packed) golden brown sugar
½ cup light corn syrup
¼ cup (½ stick) unsalted butter
4 cups coarsely chopped pecans
½ cup whipping cream
2 teaspoons vanilla extract

FOR CRUST: Preheat oven to 350°F. Line
13 x 9 x 2-inch baking pan with foil, leaving
1-inch overhang on all sides. Butter foil. Blend
flour, powdered sugar, cornstarch and salt in
processor. Add butter and process until mixture
begins to clump together. Press dough evenly
onto bottom of foil-lined pan. Bake crust until
set and light golden, about 25 minutes. Remove
from oven. Let stand while preparing topping.
Reduce oven temperature to 325°F.

FOR TOPPING: Stir brown sugar, corn syrup
and butter in heavy medium saucepan over
medium-high heat until sugar dissolves and
mixture boils; boil 1 minute. Add pecans and

cream; boil until mixture thickens slightly,
about 3 minutes. Stir in vanilla. Pour hot topping over warm crust.

Bake nut-topped crust until caramel is darker
and bubbles thickly, about 20 minutes. Transfer
pan to rack. Cool in pan (topping will harden).

Lift foil out of pan onto cutting board. Using
heavy sharp knife, cut crust with nut topping
into 1½ x 1-inch diamonds. *(Can be prepared
1 week ahead. Store airtight between sheets of
waxed paper at room temperature.)*

Cocoa Meringue Kisses

IF YOU WANT CRISP COOKIES, SERVE THESE ON THE
SAME DAY THEY'RE MADE; THEY SOFTEN OVER TIME
EVEN WHEN STORED IN AN AIRTIGHT CONTAINER.

makes about 40

½ cup sugar
¼ cup unsweetened cocoa powder
Pinch of salt
3 large egg whites
⅛ teaspoon cream of tartar

1 tablespoon powdered sugar

Preheat oven to 300°F. Line 2 heavy large baking sheets with foil or parchment paper. Sift
¼ cup sugar, cocoa and salt into small bowl.
Beat egg whites and cream of tartar in large
bowl until soft peaks begin to form. Add
remaining ¼ cup sugar ½ tablespoon at a time
and beat until medium-firm peaks form. Add
cocoa mixture 1 tablespoon at a time and beat
until meringue is stiff and glossy.

Drop meringue onto prepared baking sheets by
rounded teaspoonfuls, spacing 1 inch apart. For
chewy soft cookies, bake meringues 25 minutes.
For drier, crisper cookies, bake meringues
40 minutes. Cool cookies on baking sheets. Sift
powdered sugar over cookies.

Linzer Macaroon Sandwiches

HERE'S A VARIATION ON THE CLASSIC RASPBERRY-JAM-FILLED VIENNESE SPECIALTY, LINZERTORTE.

makes about 25

1⅔ cups blanched slivered almonds
1⅓ cups sugar
 2 large egg whites
 1 teaspoon almond extract

⅓ cup sliced almonds

½ cup raspberry preserves
 2 tablespoons water

   Powdered sugar

Preheat oven to 375°F. Line 2 large baking sheets with parchment paper. Finely grind 1⅔ cups slivered almonds and 1⅓ cups sugar in processor. Add egg whites and almond extract; process until well blended (dough will be sticky).

Using slightly rounded teaspoonful for each cookie, roll dough between damp palms of hands into balls. Place on prepared baking sheets, spacing 1 inch apart. Flatten each ball slightly to 1¼-inch-diameter round. Gently press a few sliced almonds into each cookie.

Bake until light golden, about 18 minutes. Slide parchment with cookies onto racks; cool.

Stir preserves and 2 tablespoons water in heavy small saucepan over medium-high heat until mixture boils. Reduce heat and simmer until mixture thickens slightly, about 4 minutes.

Spoon ½ teaspoon raspberry preserves onto flat side of 1 cookie. Top with second cookie, flat side down. Press to adhere. Repeat with remaining cookies and preserves. *(Can be prepared ahead. Store airtight at room temperature up to 1 week, or freeze up to 1 month.)* Sift powdered sugar over cookies.

Orange-Pistachio Lace Cookies

CRISP, THIN AND LACY, THESE DELICATE COOKIES (ABOVE) ARE FLAVORED WITH ORANGE PEEL AND PISTACHIOS. ALMONDS COULD BE SUBSTITUTED.

makes about 24

¾ cup (1½ sticks) unsalted butter
1½ cups finely chopped shelled pistachios
¾ cup sugar
 1 tablespoon all purpose flour
 2 teaspoons grated orange peel
½ teaspoon salt
 1 large egg, beaten to blend

Preheat oven to 325°F. Line large baking sheet with parchment paper. Stir butter in heavy medium saucepan over medium-low heat until melted. Remove from heat. Stir in pistachios, sugar, flour, orange peel and salt, then stir in egg. Drop some batter by generous tablespoonfuls onto prepared baking sheet, spacing 3 inches apart (cookies will spread).

Bake cookies until lacy and golden brown, about 15 minutes. Gently slide parchment paper with cookies onto rack; cool completely. Transfer cookies to paper towels. Repeat with remaining batter, lining cooled baking sheet with new parchment for each batch. *(Can be made ahead. Store between sheets of waxed paper in airtight container at room temperature up to 1 week, or freeze up to 1 month.)*

A do-ahead guide

A COOKIE-BAKING MARATHON can begin weeks before Christmas, giving you more time to relax with family and friends during the holidays. Early baking also frees up the oven, a real plus if holiday parties are in the plans.

HELPFUL HINTS

❉ Most cookie doughs can be made ahead and stored in the refrigerator for at least three days; rolled doughs can be frozen for several weeks.

❉ If the dough has been refrigerated for more than four hours, it can crack when rolled. To remedy this problem, let the dough stand at room temperature until it has softened and is easier to roll, 10 to 15 minutes.

❉ Always cool just-baked cookies to room temperature before storing.

❉ Once cookies are baked, store them in an airtight container for two to three days.

❉ Baked, cooled cookies can be frozen in freezer bags or airtight containers up to one month.

TO PACK COOKIES

A box of homemade cookies sent through the mail can make a much-appreciated gift. Here are some tips to keep in mind if you want them to get there in one piece.

❉ Pack cookies in airtight containers with crumpled wax paper to fill in the gaps so the cookies won't move around in the container.

❉ Pack the container of cookies in a heavy corrugated cardboard shipping box, and fill in with styrofoam "peanuts," crumpled newspaper or other packing material.

Chocolate Chip, Cherry and Walnut Rugelach

FREEZING THE *RUGELACH* BEFORE BAKING HELPS THE COOKIES (BELOW) MAINTAIN THEIR SHAPE. FOR GIFT GIVING, LAYER THEM BETWEEN SHEETS OF WAXED PAPER AND ARRANGE IN TINS LINED WITH COLORFUL CELLOPHANE OR TISSUE PAPER.

makes 32

dough

    2 cups all purpose flour
    2 tablespoons sugar
    ¼ teaspoon salt
    1 cup (2 sticks) chilled unsalted butter,
      cut into ½-inch pieces
    6 ounces chilled cream cheese,
      cut into ½-inch pieces

filling

    ½ cup sugar
    1 teaspoon ground cinnamon
   12 tablespoons cherry preserves
    8 tablespoons dried tart cherries
    8 tablespoons miniature semisweet
      chocolate chips
    8 tablespoons finely chopped walnuts

    ⅓ cup (about) whipping cream

FOR DOUGH: Blend first 3 ingredients in processor. Add butter and cream cheese and cut in using on/off turns until dough begins to clump together. Gather dough into ball. Divide dough into 4 equal pieces; flatten into disks. Wrap each in plastic and refrigerate 2 hours. *(Can be prepared 2 days ahead. Keep refrigerated. Let dough disks soften slightly at room temperature before rolling out.)*

FOR FILLING: Line large baking sheet with parchment paper. Mix sugar and cinnamon in small bowl. Roll out 1 dough disk on floured surface to 9-inch round. Spread 3 tablespoons cherry preserves over dough, leaving 1-inch border. Sprinkle with 2 tablespoons dried cherries, then 2 tablespoons chocolate chips, 2 tablespoons cinnamon-sugar and 2 tablespoons walnuts. Press filling firmly to adhere to dough.

Cut dough round into 8 equal wedges. Starting at wide end of each wedge, roll up tightly. Arrange cookies, tip side down, on prepared baking sheet, spacing 1½ inches apart and bending slightly to form crescents. Repeat 3 more times with remaining dough disks, preserves, dried cherries, chocolate chips, cinnamon-sugar and walnuts. Place baking sheet with cookies in freezer for 30 minutes.

Position rack in center of oven and preheat to 375°F. Brush cookies lightly with whipping cream. Bake frozen cookies until golden brown, about 40 minutes. Transfer cookies to racks and cool completely. *(Can be made ahead. Store in airtight container at room temperature up to 1 week, or freeze up to 1 month.)*

Fudgy Hazelnut Brownies

makes about 6 dozen

brownie

2½ cups semisweet chocolate chips
 1 cup (2 sticks) unsalted butter
 1 cup sugar
 4 large eggs
 ¼ teaspoon salt
 2 teaspoons vanilla extract
 ¾ cup all purpose flour
 1 cup coarsely chopped toasted hazelnuts

topping

12 ounces semisweet chocolate, chopped
 3 ounces good-quality white chocolate, chopped

FOR BROWNIE: Preheat oven to 350°F. Butter and flour 15 x 10 x 1-inch jelly-roll pan. Stir chocolate and butter in heavy medium saucepan over medium-low heat until melted and smooth. Remove from heat. Combine sugar, eggs and salt in heavy large saucepan. Whisk constantly over low heat just until sugar dissolves, about 5 minutes (do not boil). Remove from heat. Whisk in chocolate mixture and vanilla. Whisk in flour and nuts. Spread batter in pan. Bake until tester inserted into center comes out with some moist crumbs still attached, 30 minutes. Cool in pan on rack.

FOR TOPPING: Stir semisweet chocolate in top of double boiler over barely simmering water until smooth. Spread over brownie.

Stir white chocolate in top of double boiler over barely simmering water until smooth. Spoon into resealable plastic bag. Cut very tip off 1 corner of bag. Pipe lines of white chocolate crosswise atop brownie, spacing lines 1 inch apart. Draw a toothpick lengthwise across lines, alternating direction from left to right and right to left, to create marbled pattern. Chill just until firm enough to cut, about 30 minutes. Cut into small squares.

Christmas Candies

For many, the urge to craft something sweet, pretty and sinfully rich, in our own kitchens, on our own time, comes but once a year—like the jolly old elf himself. What is it about the Christmas season that makes us want to melt chocolate for a crunchy peppermint bark; top two dozen coffee-flavored truffles with miniature candied violets; or spoon a buttery sugar syrup into little candy molds for the Butterscotch Stars? There's no explaining it.

The trick is to give in, pick a favored treat from the eight recipes here, and indulge your candy-making inner self. Enjoy the wrapping part too, the ribbons and cellophane and decorations, the boxes and tins and jars that show off your treasured sweets. And treasure them your friends and family will.

Layered Peppermint Crunch Bark

PACKED IN JARS THAT ARE DECORATED WITH RED RIBBON AND CANDY CANES, THIS SWEET MAKES A FESTIVE GIFT. TO CRUSH THE PEPPERMINTS COARSELY, TAP THE WRAPPED CANDIES FIRMLY WITH THE BOTTOM EDGE OF ANY UNOPENED CAN.

makes 36 pieces

17 ounces good-quality white chocolate (such as Lindt or Baker's), finely chopped
30 red-and-white-striped hard peppermint candies, coarsely crushed (about 6 ounces)

7 ounces bittersweet (not unsweetened) or semisweet chocolate, chopped
6 tablespoons whipping cream
¾ teaspoon peppermint extract

Turn large baking sheet bottom side up. Cover securely with foil. Mark 12 x 9-inch rectangle on foil. Stir white chocolate in metal bowl set over saucepan of barely simmering water (do not allow bottom of bowl to touch water) until chocolate is melted and smooth and candy thermometer registers 110°F (chocolate will feel warm to touch). Remove from over water. Pour ⅔ cup melted white chocolate onto rectangle on foil. Using icing spatula, spread chocolate to fill rectangle. Sprinkle with ¼ cup crushed peppermints. Chill until set, about 15 minutes.

Stir bittersweet chocolate, cream and peppermint extract in heavy medium saucepan over medium-low heat until just melted and smooth. Cool to barely lukewarm, about 5 minutes. Pour bittersweet chocolate mixture in long lines over white chocolate rectangle. Using icing spatula, spread bittersweet chocolate in even layer. Refrigerate chocolate until very cold and firm, about 25 minutes.

Rewarm remaining white chocolate in bowl set over barely simmering water to 110°F. Working quickly, pour white chocolate over firm bittersweet chocolate layer; spread to cover. Immediately sprinkle with remaining crushed peppermints. Refrigerate just until firm, about 20 minutes.

Lift foil with bark onto work surface; trim edges. Cut bark crosswise into 2-inch-wide strips. Using metal spatula, slide bark off foil and onto work surface. Cut each strip crosswise into 3 sections and each section diagonally into 2 triangles. *(Can be made 2 weeks ahead. Chill in airtight container.)* Let stand 15 minutes at room temperature before serving.

Black Forest Fudge

THIS CANDY GETS ITS NAME FROM THE POPULAR GERMAN CAKE FLAVORED WITH CHOCOLATE AND CHERRIES. PLACE THE FUDGE IN PAPER CANDY CUPS, IN PRETTY BOXES TIED WITH SILK RIBBON.

makes 24 pieces

- 6 ounces bittersweet (not unsweetened) or semisweet chocolate, chopped
- ½ cup marshmallow creme
- 1 ounce unsweetened chocolate, chopped
- 1 teaspoon vanilla extract
- 1¼ cups sugar
- ½ cup sweetened condensed milk
- ½ cup cherry preserves
- ⅓ cup whipping cream
- ⅓ cup water
- ¼ cup (½ stick) unsalted butter
- ⅔ cup dried tart cherries (about 3 ounces)
- ¼ cup semisweet chocolate chips

Line 9 x 5 x 3-inch loaf pan with foil. Place first 4 ingredients in medium metal bowl. Mix sugar, condensed milk, cherry preserves, whipping cream, ⅓ cup water and butter in heavy medium saucepan. Stir over medium-low heat until butter melts and sugar dissolves, occasionally brushing down sides of pan with wet pastry brush to dissolve sugar crystals. Add dried cherries. Attach candy thermometer to side of pan. Increase heat to medium-high. Boil until thermometer registers 230°F, stirring constantly but slowly, about 17 minutes.

Immediately pour hot syrup over chocolate mixture in bowl (do not scrape pan). Using wooden spoon, stir vigorously until chocolate melts and fudge thickens slightly but still remains glossy, about 3 minutes. Transfer fudge to prepared pan; smooth top. Sprinkle with chocolate chips. Chill until firm, about 3 hours.

Lift fudge from pan, using foil as aid. Fold down foil. Trim edges of fudge. Cut fudge into 24 pieces. *(Can be made 2 weeks ahead; chill.)*

Gianduia Gold Cups

GIANDUIA IS A CLASSIC ITALIAN COMBINATION OF CHOCOLATE AND HAZELNUTS. IF YOU CAN'T FIND FOIL CANDY CUPS, BUY TWICE AS MANY PAPER ONES AND USE TWO (ONE INSIDE THE OTHER) PER CANDY. (DOUBLING THE PAPER CUPS MAKES A STURDIER FORM.) ARRANGE THE CONFECTIONS IN HOLIDAY TINS, OR PLACE ON DECORATIVE TRAYS, WRAP IN CELLOPHANE AND TIE WITH RIBBONS.

makes 32

  4 ounces good-quality milk chocolate (such as Lindt or Ghirardelli), chopped
  1 cup Nutella (chocolate-hazelnut spread)*
  6 tablespoons coarsely chopped toasted hazelnuts

 18 ounces bittersweet (not unsweetened) or semisweet chocolate, chopped
 32 1-inch-diameter gold foil candy cups

 32 whole hazelnuts, toasted, husked

Stir milk chocolate in medium metal bowl set over saucepan of barely simmering water (do not allow bottom of bowl to touch water) until melted and smooth. Remove from over water. Whisk in Nutella and chopped hazelnuts.

Stir bittersweet chocolate in another medium metal bowl set over saucepan of barely simmering water (do not allow bottom of bowl to touch water) until chocolate melts and candy thermometer registers 110°F (chocolate will feel warm to touch). Remove from over water. Using 1-inch-wide pastry brush, coat insides of candy cups with just enough chocolate to cover. Rewarm chocolate as necessary to maintain temperature. Place cups on baking sheet. Chill until chocolate is firm, about 15 minutes.

Spoon enough hazelnut mixture into center of each chocolate cup to fill to within ⅛ inch of top (about 1 heaping teaspoonful in each cup). Refrigerate until filling sets, about 15 minutes.

Rewarm remaining melted bittersweet chocolate in bowl set over barely simmering water to 110°F. Spoon enough chocolate over filling to cover and to fill cups completely. Immediately top each with whole nut. Refrigerate cups until firm, about 20 minutes. *(Can be made 2 weeks ahead; refrigerate in single layer in airtight container.)* Let candy stand 15 minutes at room temperature before serving.

Nutella is usually found in the jelly and preserves section of the supermarket.

CLOCKWISE FROM TOP: LAYERED PEPPERMINT CRUNCH BARK; COFFEE-SPICE WHITE CHOCOLATE TRUFFLES; BLACK FOREST FUDGE; AND (CENTER) GIANDUIA GOLD CUPS.

Coffee-Spice White Chocolate Truffles

SET THE TRUFFLES IN PAPER OR SILVER-FOIL CANDY CUPS, AND OFFER THEM IN BASKETS WRAPPED IN CLEAR CELLOPHANE AND TIED WITH RAFFIA AND PINECONES. IF YOU PREFER, COAT THE TRUFFLES IN 12 OUNCES OF MELTED BITTERSWEET CHOCOLATE INSTEAD OF WHITE CHOCOLATE.

makes about 24

24 ounces good-quality white chocolate (such as Lindt or Baker's), finely chopped

5 teaspoons instant espresso powder

1 tablespoon ground espresso beans

¾ teaspoon ground nutmeg

¾ teaspoon ground cinnamon

¼ cup crème fraîche or sour cream

1 tablespoon whipping cream

1 tablespoon coffee liqueur

½ teaspoon vanilla extract

24 candied violets or whole espresso beans

Stir 12 ounces white chocolate in medium metal bowl set over saucepan of barely simmering water (do not allow bottom of bowl to touch water) until melted and smooth and candy thermometer registers 110°F (chocolate will feel warm to touch). Remove from over water. Mix in espresso powder, ground espresso beans and spices. Add crème fraîche, whipping cream, liqueur and vanilla; whisk until blended (mixture may appear curdled). Freeze until firm enough to hold shape, whisking occasionally, about 25 minutes.

Line 2 baking sheets with foil. Using about 1 tablespoon espresso mixture for each truffle, spoon mixture in mounds onto 1 sheet. Freeze truffles until just firm but still malleable, about 15 minutes. Quickly press or roll each mound into irregular ball. Return to freezer on sheet.

Stir remaining 12 ounces white chocolate in medium metal bowl set over saucepan of barely simmering water (do not allow bottom of bowl to touch water) until melted and smooth and candy thermometer registers 110°F. Remove from over water. Drop 1 truffle into chocolate. Using fork, turn to coat. Lift truffle from chocolate on fork tines, allowing excess to drip back into bowl. Using knife as aid, slide truffle off fork onto second foil-lined sheet, being careful to keep truffle upright. Top with 1 candied violet or 1 espresso bean. Repeat with remaining truffles and chocolate, rewarming chocolate as necessary to maintain temperature of 110°F. Chill truffles until coating is firm, about 30 minutes. (Can be made 2 weeks ahead. Chill in airtight container.) Let stand 20 minutes at room temperature before serving.

Tricks of the trade

CHOCOLATE CAN BE persnickety if it's not used correctly in candy recipes. Here are some tips you'll want to remember.

HELPFUL HINTS

❋ Chocolate scorches easily, so when melting, it's best to use a double boiler. Partially fill the bottom of a double boiler with water and bring to a low simmer. Put the chocolate in the top pan and stir gently over the heat until the chocolate is fluid. Be careful that the pan does not touch the water.

❋ When melting chocolate, do not let any water—not even a drop or a mist of steam from a double boiler—touch the chocolate, or it will "seize" and become stiff and hard to work with.

❋ To chop chocolate, break into small chunks, then chop into smaller pieces with a heavy knife on a clean, dry work surface.

DECORATING TIPS

TO MAKE CHOCOLATE CURLS: Warm the wrapped chocolate bar with your hands to soften it slightly. Unwrap, then use a vegetable peeler to make curls. Or drag a sharp knife across the surface of the chocolate.

TO MAKE CHOCOLATE CUTOUTS: Melt six ounces of semisweet chocolate, then blend in one teaspoon of vegetable shortening. Spread the melted chocolate evenly on a parchment-lined baking sheet; refrigerate until it begins to harden. Cut into shapes with cookie cutters, or cut into squares, triangles or rectangles. Return to the refrigerator and chill until hardened, 30 minutes.

TO "WRITE" WITH CHOCOLATE: Melt semi-sweet chocolate with a few drops of light corn syrup until slightly thickened. Drizzle off the end of a teaspoon, push through a pastry bag or squeeze through a plastic squeeze bottle.

Pecan Toffee

IDEAL FOR GIFT-GIVING, THIS RICH AND CRUNCHY CANDY (OPPOSITE) TAKES ONLY ABOUT 15 MINUTES TO MAKE AND CAN BE WHIPPED UP SEVERAL DAYS AHEAD OF WHEN YOU MIGHT NEED IT.

makes about 1 1/2 pounds

1 cup (2 sticks) butter
1½ cups sugar
¼ teaspoon cream of tartar

6 ounces bittersweet (not unsweetened) or semisweet chocolate, finely chopped
1 cup coarsely chopped pecans (about 5 ounces)

Line 9-inch square baking pan with foil, over-lapping sides. Butter foil. Melt butter in heavy medium saucepan over medium heat. Add sugar and cream of tartar and stir until sugar dissolves. Increase heat to medium-high. Brush down sides of pan with wet pastry brush. Cook until mixture registers 310°F on candy ther-mometer, stirring occasionally, about 11 minutes.

Immediately pour toffee into prepared pan. Let stand 1 minute. Sprinkle with chocolate. Let stand 2 minutes to soften. Spread chocolate with back of spoon over toffee until melted and smooth. Sprinkle with pecans. Refrigerate until firm. Remove toffee from pan, using foil as aid. Break into 3-inch pieces. *(Can be prepared 4 days ahead. Chill in airtight container.)*

Peanut Butter and Chocolate Balls

A FAVORITE FLAVOR COMBINATION HIGHLIGHTS THESE SIMPLE CANDIES.

makes about 50

½ cup (1 stick) unsalted butter
2 cups cornflakes cereal
2 cups creamy peanut butter (do not use old-fashioned style or freshly ground)
2 cups dry milk powder
2 cups powdered sugar

15 ounces semisweet chocolate, chopped

Line baking sheet with foil. Melt butter in heavy small saucepan over low heat. Combine cereal, peanut butter, dry milk powder and powdered sugar in large bowl. Mix in butter. Moisten hands and roll 1 tablespoon mixture into ball. Place on prepared sheet. Repeat with remaining mixture. Chill overnight.

Line baking sheets with foil. Melt chocolate in double boiler over low heat, stirring occasionally. Remove chocolate from over water. Using fork, dip peanut butter balls 1 at a time into chocolate and transfer to prepared sheets. Refrigerate until chocolate is firm. *(Can be prepared ahead. Refrigerate in airtight container up to 1 week or freeze up to 1 month. Soften slightly at room temperature before serving.)*

Pine Nut and Orange Fudge

makes 24 pieces

2¼ cups sugar
¾ cup whipping cream
⅔ cup sweetened condensed milk
½ cup sour cream
⅓ cup water
2 tablespoons (¼ stick) unsalted butter, cut into pieces, room temperature
2 tablespoons light corn syrup
1 tablespoon grated orange peel

¾ cup pine nuts (about 4 ounces), toasted

Line 9 x 5-inch loaf pan with foil, overlapping sides. Combine all ingredients except pine nuts in heavy 3-quart saucepan. Stir over medium-low heat until sugar dissolves, about 15 minutes. Brush down sugar crystals from sides of pan using wet pastry brush. Increase heat to high and bring to boil. Reduce heat to medium-high and cook until clip-on candy thermometer registers 234°F, stirring frequently, about 12 minutes. Pour onto rimmed baking sheet; do not scrape pan. Let cool 15 minutes.

Scrape mixture into medium metal bowl using rubber spatula. Using electric mixer, beat until fudge is thick and creamy and no longer glossy, about 5 minutes. (To test for proper consistency, mound fudge mixture on spoon; turn upside down. If mixture falls off spoon, beat fudge again and repeat test.) Mix in pine nuts and immediately transfer fudge to prepared pan. Cover with plastic and press to flatten fudge into even layer. Refrigerate fudge until firm enough to cut, about 1 hour.

Lift fudge from pan using foil as aid. Fold down foil sides. Trim ends of fudge. Cut into 24 pieces. *(Can be prepared 1 week ahead. Refrigerate in airtight container.)*

Butterscotch Stars

HERE, STAR CANDY MOLDS ARE USED FOR A FESTIVE TOUCH. WRAP EACH OF THESE SWEETS (BELOW) IN WAXED PAPER AND RED OR GREEN CELLOPHANE. FOR A LOVELY HOLIDAY GIFT, PLACE THE STARS IN AN ANTIQUE GLASS JAR TIED WITH A BOW.

makes about 100

    5 trays of bite-size star candy molds*
      Nonstick vegetable oil spray
 1½ cups sugar
    6 tablespoons light corn syrup
 4½ teaspoons water
 1½ teaspoons fresh lemon juice
  ¾ teaspoon cream of tartar
    6 tablespoons (¾ stick) unsalted butter,
      cut into pieces
  ¾ teaspoon vanilla extract

100 (about) 4¼ x 5½-inch white confectionery
      waxed papers*
      Colored cellophane, cut into one hundred
      4¼ x 5½-inch pieces

Spray molds with vegetable oil spray. Combine sugar, corn syrup, 4½ teaspoons water, lemon juice and cream of tartar in heavy deep medium saucepan over medium heat, stirring until sugar dissolves. Bring to boil, brushing down sides of pan occasionally with pastry brush dipped into water. Increase heat to high and bring to boil. Gradually add butter and stir until melted. Boil without stirring until syrup is golden brown and candy thermometer registers 295°F. Remove from heat. Add vanilla (mixture will bubble) and stir vigorously until smooth.

Meanwhile, pour water into heavy large pot to depth of 1 inch. Set steamer rack in pot. Bring water to rolling boil.

Set saucepan with syrup on steamer rack in boiling water (steam will help keep syrup in liquid state). Using teaspoon and working quickly, carefully spoon syrup into prepared molds. Cool completely.

Turn out candies onto work surface, twisting mold gently if necessary. Set 1 piece waxed paper atop 1 piece cellophane. Place 1 candy in center of waxed paper. Twist waxed paper and cellophane around candy. Repeat with remaining waxed paper, cellophane and candy. Store candies in airtight containers. *(Can be prepared 1 week ahead. Store at room temperature.)*

Molds and white confectionery waxed papers are available at some cake and candy supply stores.

Christmas Projects

At least half the fun of Christmas is in the preparations—trimming the tree, wrapping the presents and decorating the house. In fact, once you get going, it can be hard to stop: Before you know it, you're applying gumdrops to the roof of a gingerbread house. Christmas brings out the clever, crafty homemaker in all of us.

With that in mind, here's a collection of recipes and ideas for projects ranging from a fresh fruit topiary to cookie ornaments. There are place cards, caramel apples, a gorgeous centerpiece and a gingerbread house that's perfectly possible, since it starts with a bakery-bought, ready-made structure. Because it's the decorating—with candy, crackers, seeds and frosting—that everybody loves.

Caramel-dipped Apples

THE PROJECT PART OF THIS RECIPE COMES INTO PLAY IN THE DECORATING.

makes 12

1 1-pound box dark brown sugar
1 cup (2 sticks) unsalted butter, room temperature
1 14-ounce can sweetened condensed milk
⅔ cup dark corn syrup
⅓ cup pure maple syrup
1½ teaspoons vanilla extract
1 teaspoon robust-flavored (dark) molasses
¼ teaspoon salt

12 wooden chopsticks
12 medium Granny Smith apples
    Assorted decorations (such as chopped nuts, dried apricots and dried cranberries, toffee bits, mini M&M's and candy sprinkles)
    Melted dark, milk and/or white chocolates

    Whipping cream (if necessary)

Combine first 8 ingredients in heavy 2½-quart saucepan (about 3 inches deep). Stir with wooden spatula or spoon over medium-low heat until sugar dissolves (no crystals are felt when caramel is rubbed between fingers), occasionally brushing down sides of pan with wet pastry brush, about 15 minutes.

Attach clip-on candy thermometer to side of pan. Increase heat to medium-high; cook caramel at rolling boil until thermometer registers 236°F, stirring constantly but slowly with clean wooden spatula and occasionally brushing down sides of pan with wet pastry brush, about 12 minutes. Pour caramel into metal bowl (do not scrape pan). Submerge thermometer bulb in caramel; cool, without stirring, to 200°F, about 20 minutes.

While caramel cools, line 2 large baking sheets with foil; butter foil. Push 1 chopstick into stem end of each apple. Set up assorted decorations and melted chocolates.

Holding chopstick, dip 1 apple into 200°F caramel, submerging all but very top of apple. Lift apple out, allowing excess caramel to drip back into bowl. Turn apple caramel side up and hold for several seconds to help set caramel around apple. Place coated apple on prepared foil. Repeat with remaining apples and caramel, spacing apples apart (caramel will pool on foil). If caramel becomes too thick to dip into, add 1 to 2 tablespoons whipping cream and briefly whisk caramel in bowl over low heat to thin to desired consistency.

Chill apples on sheets until caramel is partially set, 15 minutes. Lift 1 apple from foil. Using hand, press pooled caramel around apple; return to foil. Repeat with remaining apples.

Firmly press decorations into caramel; return each apple to foil. Or dip caramel-coated apples into melted chocolate, allowing excess to drip off, then roll in nuts or candy. Or drizzle melted chocolate over caramel-coated apples and sprinkle with decorations. Refrigerate until decorations are set, about 1 hour. Cover and refrigerate up to 1 week.

Pomanders

THIS SIMPLE PROJECT TAKES HARDLY ANY TIME AT ALL, AND THE PAYOFF IS BIG: SWEET-SMELLING ORANGES TO HANG ON THE TREE, PLACE IN A BOWL OR BASKET AS A CENTERPIECE, OR HANG IN A CLOSET, FILLING IT WITH A FRESH, SPICY AROMA. OTHER CITRUS FRUITS, LIKE LEMONS, LIMES, TANGERINES AND KUMQUATS, CAN ALSO BE USED.

Push pin or darning needle
Medium-size navel or thin-skinned oranges
Good-quality whole cloves (about 3 ounces per orange)
Ribbon
Heavy-duty paper clips

Use a push pin or darning needle to make holes in rind of orange. Insert a whole clove into each hole. Cover the entire fruit with cloves or make a spiral, stripe, diamond or checkerboard pattern. Tie a ribbon around the pomander and knot it securely; then tie a bow. Or to hang the pomander on a tree, use a heavy-duty paper clip and open one end enough to pull a knotted ribbon through. Use the paper clip to hang the pomander over a branch. (*Can be made ahead; the more cloves used, the longer the pomander will keep.*)

Winter Fruit Place Cards

A CLEVER ALTERNATIVE TO TRADITIONAL PLACE CARDS.

Gold- or silver-ink pen*
Red pears or assorted fruits, including
Red Delicious apples, McIntosh apples and
pomegranates
Star-shaped sequins
Gold wire or gold wire with stars

Using a gold or silver pen, write guests' names directly on fruit. Thread sequins on the gold wire (or use wire with stars) and wrap it decoratively around the top of the fruit.

Available at art-supply and photo stores.

Fresh Herb Place Cards

POTTED HERBS (BELOW) MAKE USEFUL PLACE CARDS AND MUCH-APPRECIATED PARTY FAVORS.

Small terra-cotta pots
Assorted fresh herbs in 3-inch plastic pots
Potting soil
Wired ribbon
Heavy paper
Gold cord

Using the terra-cotta pots, repot the herbs in fresh potting soil. Tie a bow around each pot with wired ribbon. Select a sophisticated typeface and print out guests' names on heavy paper. Cut out each card, punch holes in them, and tie onto the ribbon using gold cord.

Leaves under Glass Place Cards

THESE LOVELY PLACE CARDS (RIGHT) MAKE NICE KEEPSAKES FOR YOUR GUESTS.

> Gold-ink pen*
> Assorted leaves
> Small panes of glass (2 per place card)**
> Double-sided tape
> Straw or ribbon

Using a gold pen, write guests' names directly on leaves. Press each leaf between 2 panes of glass. Wrap double-sided tape around the edges of the panes. Cover tape with straw or riboon.

*Available at art-supply and photo stores.

**Available from a glazier.

Photo Place Cards

YOUNG CHILDREN WILL ENJOY HELPING OUT WITH THESE PLAYFUL PLACE CARDS, WHICH ARE REMINISCENT OF A FAVORITE PRESCHOOL PROJECT. SCRABBLE TILES, TWIGS OR SMALL CANDIES CAN BE USED INSTEAD OF THE PASTA OR BEANS.

> Pasta or beans
> Camera with film
> Glue
> Heavy paper

Spell out guests' names with pasta or beans, then photograph the names. Paste the photos onto pieces of heavy paper and fold in half.

Winter Garden Place Cards

THESE PLACE CARDS TAKE THEIR INSPIRATION FROM ITEMS FOUND IN THE GARDEN; FEEL FREE TO USE ANY VARIETY OF FRUITS, VEGETABLES AND FLOWERS OR GRASSES.

> Small tags
> Ribbon, gold cord or raffia
> Assorted baby vegetables (such as yellow squash or zucchini), wheat stalks* or kumquats
> Netting (optional)

Write guests' names on tags. Using ribbon, cord or raffia, tie tags onto vegetables or slim bunches of wheat stalks. Or wrap kumquats in netting, secure top with ribbon and tie on tag.

*Available at florist's shops.

Christmas Centerpiece

SEASONAL FRUITS AND VEGETABLES, FLOWERS AND GREENERY COMBINE IN THIS ELEGANT ARRANGEMENT (OPPOSITE).

> Florist's foam
> Shallow container
> Wooden picks*
> Assorted fruits and vegetables, such as Gala apples, small pears, crab apples, red table grapes, Champagne grapes, baby cauliflower and broccoli, chilies, artichokes and kumquats
> Assorted flowers, such as Leonidas roses, calla lilies, orchids and alstroemeria
> Greenery, such as geranium and magnolia leaves, ivy, pittosporum and hypericum

Soak florist's foam in water and place in shallow container. Using wooden picks, attach fruits and vegetables to foam. Arrange them at various angles to create an unstructured effect, checking for stability as you work. You may need to use several wooden picks per item. Using flowers in colors that work with the fruits and vegetables you've chosen, arrange them in groups of four to six blooms. Keep tallest flowers low in the arrangement so that the finished centerpiece is no more than 12 inches tall. Fill in with greenery.

Available at florist's shops.

Child-size fun

THE WEEKS BEFORE Christmas are heady with anticipation and filled with activities that children look forward to all year. In addition to the visits with Santa, holiday parties and school performances, they also like all of the preparations that go into decorating and gift-giving. For those who want their own project, here are a couple of ideas. (You could also set up an ornament-making table at your tree-trimming party to keep the kids entertained.)

DRIED FRUIT ORNAMENTS

Using a ten-inch length of thin wire, string dried cranberries, dried cherries or dried golden raisins (or mix all three) so they fill all but one inch of wire at each end. Tie the ends of the wire together securely to form a circle. Cover the tied wire ends by wrapping with narrow ribbon or raffia and tying a bow.

STRAW SNOWFLAKE ORNAMENTS

Using pinking shears, cut four strips of flat straw (available at craft shops) into three-inch lengths. (Or substitute thin twigs, and use pruning shears to cut into three-inch lengths.) Lay the straw pieces across one another at angles to make a snowflake shape. Glue the pieces together at the center where they cross, using a glue gun (the younger kids will need some help here). Using very thin wire, secure the pieces together by weaving the wire over and under the straw. Make a loop with the wire at the back, which can be used to hang the ornament on the tree. Tie a thin satin ribbon around the center of the snowflake to camouflage the glue and wire.

Easy Gingerbread House

PURCHASE AN UNDECORATED GINGERBREAD HOUSE FROM YOUR LOCAL BAKERY OR MAKE A BASIC GINGERBREAD HOUSE USING MOLDS FROM A CAKE OR CANDY SUPPLY STORE. PUT THE PIECES TOGETHER WITH THE ROYAL ICING (SEE RECIPE), ALLOW IT TO SET, THEN GET CREATIVE WITH SOME OF THESE DECORATING IDEAS.

> Royal Icing (see recipe at right)
> Purchased or homemade plain gingerbread house
> Blue and yellow food colorings
>
> Red licorice vines
> Peppermint candies
> Unshelled sunflower seeds
> Cotton batting
> Chocolate-covered graham crackers
> Pine cones
> Powdered sugar

Spread icing over roof of house. For rooftop icicles, allow icing to drip down eaves of house, using tines of fork as aid. Spread more icing around the house to create a snowy landscape. To make a door, tint some icing blue and spread in rectangle shape on one side of house. To make windows, tint some icing yellow and spread in smaller rectangles on sides of house; allow icing to harden. For lattice windows, spoon some white icing into pastry bag fitted with small plain tip; pipe diagonal lines over yellow rectangles. Repeat in opposite direction to form lattice pattern.

Use white icing as glue to attach other decorations to house. Red licorice vines make festive columns. A peppermint candy above the door looks like a stained-glass window. Press sunflower seeds into icing on the chimney and around the peppermint candy as flagstones. Arrange cotton batting in chimney as smoke. Place chocolate-covered graham crackers in icing on ground for walkway. Pine cones make good trees, especially when snow-tipped with white icing. A dusting of powdered sugar over the whole scene looks like a fresh snowfall.

Royal Icing

ONE BATCH OF THIS ICING IS ENOUGH TO ASSEMBLE AND DECORATE ONE HOUSE. DON'T EAT THE ICING BECAUSE IT CONTAINS RAW EGG WHITES.

> 4 large egg whites
> 7 cups powdered sugar

Using electric mixer, beat whites in medium bowl until foamy, about 1 minute. Add ½ cup sugar and beat until blended. Add remaining sugar, ½ cup at a time, beating well after each addition and scraping down sides of bowl occasionally. Beat icing at high speed until very thick and stiff, about 5 minutes.

Stained-Glass Cookie Ornaments

ANY HOLIDAY-MOTIF COOKIE CUTTER CAN BE USED
TO MAKE THESE. IF YOU DON'T HAVE SMALL COOKIE
CUTTERS (ABOUT ONE INCH IN DIAMETER) TO CUT
OUT THE CENTERS, USE THE WIDE END OF A
SMALL PASTRY-BAG TIP INSTEAD.

makes about 30

1 cup (2 sticks) unsalted butter,
   room temperature

¾ cup sugar

1 large egg yolk

2 teaspoons grated lemon peel

1 teaspoon vanilla extract

2¼ cups all purpose flour

½ teaspoon salt

6 ounces (about) red and/or green
   hard candies

   Additional sugar

   Ribbon

Using electric mixer, beat butter and ¾ cup
sugar in large bowl until well blended. Beat in
yolk, lemon peel and vanilla extract. Add flour
and salt and beat until mixture begins to clump
together. Divide dough into 3 equal pieces.
Flatten each into disk; wrap each in plastic and
refrigerate at least 2 hours. *(Dough can be prepared 2 days ahead. Soften dough slightly at room
temperature before rolling out.)*

Finely grind red and/or green hard candies separately in processor. Transfer each color to separate small bowl; cover and set aside.

Position 1 rack in center and 1 rack in top third
of oven and preheat to 375°F. Line 2 large baking sheets with parchment paper. Roll out

1 dough disk on floured surface to ¼-inch
thickness. Using 2½- to 2¾-inch-diameter cookie cutter or biscuit cutter, cut out cookies. Using
small cookie cutter (about 1 inch in diameter),
make cutout in center of each cookie.

Transfer cookies to prepared baking sheets.
Carefully spoon ground candies into cookie
cutouts, filling cutouts completely to same
thickness as cookies. Sprinkle cookies lightly
with additional sugar. Using straw, cut out hole
in top of each cookie. Repeat with remaining
dough disks, ground candies and additional
sugar. Reroll dough scraps and cut out additional cookies. Place on sheets; fill cutouts with
ground candies and sprinkle with sugar.

Bake cookies until firm and light golden and
ground candies look translucent, about 8 minutes. Cool cookies completely on baking sheets.
*(Can be made ahead. Store in airtight container at
room temperature up to 1 week, or freeze up to
1 month.)* Thread ribbon through holes in
cookies to use for hanging.

Pear and Kumquat Topiary Tree

A LOVELY HOLIDAY ARRANGEMENT (OPPOSITE) THAT IS ALSO A FUN FAMILY PROJECT. FEEL FREE TO USE NATURAL GREEN LEAVES IN YOUR TOPIARY, BUT THE FABRIC ONES HOLD UP LONGER. (ACTUALLY, YOU SHOULD FEEL FREE TO IMPROVISE AS YOU LIKE WHILE CREATING THE TREE, USING THE DIFFERENT ELEMENTS AS THEY WORK AND FIT BEST.) ALSO, TO ADD A SCENTED TOUCH TO YOUR TREE, TRY INSERTING A FEW WHOLE CLOVES INTO THE KUMQUATS FOR MINI POMANDERS.

1   6- to 7-inch-diameter terra-cotta pot
    Florist's foam
    Hot glue gun
3   12-inch bamboo skewers
1   18-inch-tall, 5-inch-diameter (at base) green
    styrofoam cone* (or spray white cone with
    green spray paint)

42 (about) firm Seckel pears, ranging in size
    from 2 to 3 inches
    Flat toothpicks

50 (about) kumquats

30 (about) 1-inch pine cones with wire bases*
48 2½-inch cloth and/or velvet single
    green leaves*
    Wired ribbon (optional)

Fill terra-cotta pot snugly with foam, leaving 1-inch space at top of pot. Secure foam with hot glue gun. Insert bamboo skewers halfway into bottom (base) end of styrofoam cone, spacing evenly. Place some hot glue atop foam in pot. Working quickly, insert skewers into foam, attaching cone to pot.

Begin attaching pears to cone. Insert wide end of 3 toothpicks into one side of larger pear. Firmly but gently press pear into cone, positioning bottom of pear just even with top rim of pot. Repeat, forming 1 row of larger pears (about 9 pears). Using same technique, form another row of pears atop first with larger pears (about 9). Form two more concentric rows of pears using medium pears (1 row of 8, 1 row of 7). Form 1 row using small pears. Using small serrated knife, trim top of styrofoam cone even with tops of small pears. Insert 3 toothpicks into bottom of one 3-inch pear and push onto top of cone.

Begin attaching kumquats to cone. Insert flat end of toothpicks into stem ends of kumquats. Insert kumquats into spaces between pears.

Trim wire slightly at ends of pine cones and leaves. Place pine cones around base of topiary and into any empty spaces. Insert leaves into spaces, arranging evenly. Tie ribbon around pot (securing with glue gun if necessary), if desired. Tie bow atop topiary, if desired. *(Can be made 1 to 2 weeks ahead, depending on ripeness of fruit.)*

*Available at art-supply stores.

Index

Page numbers in *italics* indicate photographs.

ALMONDS
Chestnut Cheesecake, 144
Chocolate-Almond Sauce, 151, *152*
Dark Chocolate Honey-Almond Fondue, 74, *75*
Linzer Macaroon Sandwiches, 165
Skewered Lamb with Almond-Mint Pesto, 103

APPETIZERS
Baked Goat Cheese with Roasted Garlic and Caramelized Onion, 106
Broiled Oysters with Hazelnut Pesto, 108
Caviar Stars, 22, *23*
Cheddar Cheese Tartlets, 107
Chicken, Wild Rice and Pecan Salad in Romaine Spears, 20, *24*
Cornmeal Blini with Sour Cream and Caviar, 72
Crab Cakes with Chive and Caper Sauce, 105
Lemon-Parmesan Artichoke Bottoms, 46
Mushrooms Stuffed with Herbed Breadcrumbs, *107*, 109
Prosciutto Rolls with Arugula and Figs, 54
Prosciutto-wrapped Asparagus, 24
Shiitake Scrambled Eggs and Caviar on Toasts, 109
Skewered Lamb with Almond-Mint Pesto, 103
Smoked Bluefish Dip, 27
Smoked Chicken Salad on Corn Bread Triangles, 80
Smoked Salmon and Goat Cheese Crostini, 104
Snappy Red Bell Pepper Dip with Shrimp, 81
Spiced Moroccan-Style Shrimp, 102
Spiced Pecans, 54
Sweet and Spicy Candied Nuts, 154
Sweet and Spicy Olives, *21*, 22
Wild Mushroom and Crab Cheesecake, 25
Winter Crudités with Walnut-Garlic Dip, 106

APPLES
Apple Stuffing, *90*, 91

Butternut Squash Soup with Cider Cream, 114, *115*
Caramel-dipped Apples, 176
Potato and Apple Galette with Sage, 125
Roast Goose with Caramelized Apples, 99

ARTICHOKES
Goat Cheese, Artichoke and Ham Strata, *71*, 73
Lemon-Parmesan Artichoke Bottoms, 46

ARUGULA
Chicken, Wild Rice and Pecan Salad in Romaine Spears, *20*, 24
Prosciutto Rolls with Arugula and Figs, 54
Smoked-Turkey Sandwiches with Arugula Mayonnaise, *12*, 14

BACON
Beef Tenderloin with Roasted Shallots, Bacon and Port, 56
Buttermilk Corn Bread with Bacon, 130, *131*
Corn and Winter Squash with Spinach, 119
Creamy Leek Soup with Bacon and Shallots, 112
Curly Endive Salad with Radishes, Coriander and Bacon, 117
Leek, Mushroom and Bacon Dressing, 120
Baked Goat Cheese with Roasted Garlic and Caramelized Onion, 106
Baked Pasta with Ham, Tomatoes and Cheese, 47

BEANS
Buttered Green Beans and Carrots, 56
Layered Rice Salad with Red and Green Salsas, *38*, 40
Marinated Green Beans and Red Peppers, *79*, 81

BEEF
Beef Tenderloin with Roasted Shallots, Bacon and Port, 56
Beef Wellington with Madeira Sauce, 96
Herb-crusted Beef Tenderloin with Bell Pepper Relish, 92
Spicy Beef and Sausage Tacos, *37*, 39

Belgian Endive with Egg Salad, 82
BELL PEPPERS. *See* Peppers
BEVERAGES
Candy Cane White Hot Chocolate, 63
Citrus Vodka, 155
cocktail basics, 26
Holiday Eggnog, 27
Mulled Cider with Winter Spices, 42
serving for brunch, 72
tea, serving, 16
Black Forest Fudge, 169, *170*
Boysenberry and Grapefruit Preserves, 153
BREADS. *See also* Stuffings & Dressings
Buttermilk Corn Bread with Bacon, 130, *131*
Cheddar Cheese Biscuits with Dill and Chives, 127
Chili Cornmeal Muffins, 128, *129*
Cinnamon French Toast, *62*, 63
Cranberry-Walnut Braid, *132*, 133
Crusty Rosemary Breadsticks, 48, *49*
Goat Cheese, Artichoke and Ham Strata, *71*, 73
Green Chili Corn Bread, 80
making ahead, 128
Mashed Potato Bread, 129
Orange-Currant Scones, 16, *17*
Poppy Seed Dinner Rolls, 126
Sesame-Onion Crescent Rolls, 131
Shiitake Scrambled Eggs and Caviar on Toasts, 109
Smoked Chicken Salad on Corn Bread Triangles, 80
Smoked Salmon and Goat Cheese Crostini, 104
Steamed Pumpkin Bread with Walnuts and Dates, 130, *131*
Wild-Mushroom Bread Pudding, 123
Broccoli and Cauliflower with Chive Butter, 125
Broiled Oysters with Hazelnut Pesto, 108
Broiled Tomato Sauce with Roasted Garlic, 101
Brown Sugar-glazed Sweet Potatoes with Marshmallows, 123
Buttered Green Beans and Carrots, 56

Buttermilk Corn Bread with
    Bacon, 130, *131*
BUTTERNUT SQUASH
    Butternut Squash Soup with Cider
        Cream, 114, *115*
    Corn and Winter Squash with
        Spinach, 119
Butterscotch Stars, 175
Caesar Salad, 46
CAKES
    Chestnut Cheesecake, 144
    Chocolate-Cranberry Poinsettia
        Cake, 140
    Chocolate-Orange Bûche de
        Noël, 30, *31*
    Four-Spice Gingerbread, *156,* 157
    fruitcake, about, 137
    Gingerbread Cake with Maple
        Whipped Cream, 139
    Golden Fruitcake, 152
    Holiday Fruitcake, *29,* 34
    Individual Frozen Cake "Presents"
        with Strawberry Sauce, 58
    Molten Chocolate Cakes, 69
    Warm Pear Shortcakes with
        Brandied Cream, 146
CANDIES
    Black Forest Fudge, 169, *170*
    Butterscotch Stars, 175
    Chocolate-Walnut Rum
        Balls, *13,* 19
    Christmas Turtles, *29,* 33
    Coffee-Spice White Chocolate
        Truffles, *170,* 171
    Gianduia Gold Cups, 170
    Layered Peppermint Crunch
        Bark, 168, *170*
    Peanut Butter and Chocolate
        Balls, 174
    Pecan Toffee, 172, *173*
    Pine Nut and Orange Fudge, 174
candles, about, 66
Candy Cane White Hot Chocolate, 63
Caramel-dipped Apples, 176
CARROTS
    Buttered Green Beans and
        Carrots, 56
    Carrot Puree with Ginger and
        Orange, 124
CAVIAR
    Caviar Stars, 22, *23*
    Cornmeal Blini with Sour Cream
        and Caviar, 72
    Shiitake Scrambled Eggs and
        Caviar on Toasts, 109
CHEESE
    Baked Goat Cheese with Roasted
        Garlic and Caramelized
        Onion, 106

Baked Pasta with Ham, Tomatoes
    and Cheese, 47
Cheddar Cheese Biscuits with Dill
    and Chives, 127
Cheddar Cheese Pastry, 107
Cheddar Cheese Tartlets, 107
Chicken and Corn
    Enchiladas, *38,* 39
Goat Cheese, Artichoke and Ham
    Strata, *71,* 73
Green Chili Corn Bread, 80
Layered Potato, Onion and Celery
    Root Casserole, 82
Lemon-Parmesan Artichoke
    Bottoms, 46
Peas with Caraway and Parmesan
    Butter, 118
Potato and Shiitake Mushroom
    Gratin, 57
Prosciutto Rolls with Arugula and
    Figs, 54
Prosciutto-wrapped Asparagus, 24
Roasted Eggplant Lasagna with
    Broiled Tomato Sauce, 101
Smoked Salmon and Goat Cheese
    Crostini, 104
Smoked-Salmon Sandwiches with
    Red Onion Relish, *12,* 14
Snappy Red Bell Pepper Dip with
    Shrimp, 81
Wild Mushroom and Crab
    Cheesecake, 25
CHERRIES
    Black Forest Fudge, 169, *170*
    Chocolate Chip, Cherry and
        Walnut Rugelach, 166
    Honey-roasted Ham and Turkey
        with Dried Cherry Relish, 78, *79*
    Wild Rice Dressing with Pearl
        Onions, Dried Cherries and
        Apricots, 120, *121*
CHESTNUTS
    about, 144, 145
    Chestnut Cheesecake, 144
    Rice Pilaf with Chestnuts, 119
Chewy Pecan Diamonds, 164
CHICKEN
    Chicken and Corn
        Enchiladas, *38,* 39
    Chicken, Wild Rice and Pecan
        Salad in Romaine Spears, *20,* 24
    Smoked Chicken Salad on Corn
        Bread Triangles, 80
Chili Cornmeal Muffins, 128, *129*
Chive and Caper Sauce, 105
CHOCOLATE
    Black Forest Fudge, 169, *170*
    Candy Cane White Hot
        Chocolate, 63

Chocolate-Almond Sauce, 151, *152*
Chocolate-Caramel Tart, 142, *143*
Chocolate Chip, Cherry and
    Walnut Rugelach, 166
Chocolate-Cranberry Poinsettia
    Cake, 140
Chocolate-dipped Hazelnut
    Biscotti, 150, *152*
Chocolate-glazed
    Croquembouche, 147
Chocolate-glazed Mocha Fans, 160
Chocolate-Orange Bûche de
    Noël, 30, *31*
Chocolate-Walnut Rum
    Balls, *13,* 19
Christmas Turtles, *29,* 33
Cocoa Meringue Kisses, 164
Coffee-Spice White Chocolate
    Truffles, *170,* 171
Dark Chocolate Honey-Almond
    Fondue, 74, *75*
Double Chocolate-Mint Chip Ice
    Cream Sundaes, 51
Fudgy Hazelnut Brownies, 167
Gianduia Gold Cups, 170
Individual Frozen Cake "Presents"
    with Strawberry Sauce, 58
Layered Peppermint Crunch
    Bark, 168, *170*
Marbleized White Chocolate
    Leaves, 141
Mocha and Raspberry
    Trifle, 134, *135*
Mocha Mousse Torte, 41
Molten Chocolate Cakes, 69
Peanut Butter and Chocolate
    Balls, 174
Pecan Toffee, 172, *173*
Raspberry Linzer Tart, 32
tips, 172
Christmas centerpiece, *180,* 181
Christmas Pudding with Brandy
    Butter, 136
Christmas Tree Shortbread, 162
Christmas Turtles, *29,* 33
Cinnamon French Toast, *62,* 63
Cinnamon-Sugar Biscotti, 74
Citrus Vodka, 155
cleaning up, helpful hints, 59
cocktail basics, 26
Cocoa Meringue Kisses, 164
Coconut-Macadamia Crescents, 163
COFFEE
    Chocolate-glazed Mocha Fans, 160
    Coffee-Caramel Sauce, *152,* 153
    Coffee-Spice White Chocolate
        Truffles, *170,* 171
    Mocha and Raspberry Trifle, 134, *135*
    Mocha Mousse Torte, 41

CONDIMENTS & RELISHES
Bell Pepper Relish, 92
Boysenberry and Grapefruit
Preserves, 153
Five-Minute Spiced Orange
Marmalade, 155
Honey-roasted Ham and Turkey
with Dried Cherry Relish, 78, 79
Olive Oil Infused with Porcini and
Rosemary, 159
Peppercorn, Mustard and Dill
Vinegar, 158
Pineapple Relish, 89
Piquant Cranberry Sauce, 122
Red Pepper and Corn Relish, 158
Winter Fruit Chutney, 157
COOKIES
baking tips, 163
Chewy Pecan Diamonds, 164
Chocolate Chip, Cherry and
Walnut Rugelach, 166
Chocolate-dipped Hazelnut
Biscotti, 150, 152
Chocolate-glazed Mocha Fans, 160
Christmas Tree Shortbread, 162
Cinnamon-Sugar Biscotti, 74
Cocoa Meringue Kisses, 164
Coconut-Macadamia
Crescents, 163
Double-Lemon Bars, 18, 19
Fudgy Hazelnut Brownies, 167
Ginger and Spice Shortbread
Diamonds, 34
Linzer Macaroon Sandwiches, 165
making ahead, 166
Orange-Pistachio Lace Cookies, 165
Pumpkin Spice Cookies, 42
Spiced Snowflakes, 161
Stained-Glass Cookie
Ornaments, 183
CORN
Buttermilk Corn Bread with
Bacon, 130, 131
Chicken and Corn
Enchiladas, 38, 39
Chili Cornmeal Muffins, 128, 129
Corn and Winter Squash with
Spinach, 119
Cornmeal Blini with Sour Cream
and Caviar, 72
Green Chili Corn Bread, 80
Red Pepper and Corn Relish, 158
Smoked Chicken Salad on Corn
Bread Triangles, 80
CRAB
Crab Cakes with Chive and Caper
Sauce, 105
Wild Mushroom and Crab
Cheesecake, 25

CRANBERRIES
about, 122
Boysenberry and Grapefruit
Preserves, 153
Chocolate-Cranberry Poinsettia
Cake, 140
Cranberry, Tangerine and
Blueberry Sauce, 100
Cranberry-Walnut Braid, 132, 133
Mixed Green Salad with Oranges,
Dried Cranberries and
Pecans, 114, 115
Orange- and Balsamic-glazed
Roast Duck, 100
Piquant Cranberry Sauce, 122
Sliced Oranges with Dried
Cranberries, 71, 73
Cream of Zucchini and Anise
Soup, 66, 67
Creamy Leek Soup with Bacon and
Shallots, 112
Creamy Scrambled Eggs with
Herbs, 61, 62
Crown Roast of Pork with Apple
Stuffing and Cider Gravy, 90
Crusty Rosemary Breadsticks, 48, 49
Curly Endive Salad with Radishes,
Coriander and Bacon, 117
CUSTARDS & PUDDINGS
Chocolate-glazed
Croquembouche, 147
Christmas Pudding with Brandy
Butter, 136
Eggnog Custards, 136
Mocha and Raspberry
Trifle, 134, 135
Mocha Mousse Torte, 41
plum pudding, about, 137
Wild-Mushroom Bread
Pudding, 123
Dark Chocolate Honey-Almond
Fondue, 74, 75
DECORATIONS. See also Projects
candles, about, 66
centerpieces, 50
Christmas centerpiece, 180, 181
fragrance, creating Christmas, 35
mantels, 43
throughout home, 62
Double Chocolate-Mint Chip Ice
Cream Sundaes, 51
Double-Lemon Bars, 18, 19
DUCK. Orange- and Balsamic-glazed
Roast, 100
Easy Gingerbread House, 182
Easy Pastry Dough, 138
EGGS
Belgian Endive with Egg Salad, 82
Cocoa Meringue Kisses, 164

Creamy Scrambled Eggs with
Herbs, 61, 62
Eggnog Custards, 136
Goat Cheese, Artichoke and Ham
Strata, 71, 73
Holiday Eggnog, 27
Shiitake Scrambled Eggs and
Caviar on Toasts, 109
ENDIVE
Belgian Endive with Egg
Salad, 82
Curly Endive Salad with Radishes,
Coriander and Bacon, 117
Smoked Salmon and Fennel Salad
with Horseradish Dressing, 116
Spinach, Beet and Walnut
Salad, 117
FENNEL
Red Snapper Roasted with Fennel
and Breadcrumbs, 91
Smoked Salmon and Fennel Salad
with Horseradish Dressing, 116
FISH. See also Salmon
Red Snapper Roasted with Fennel
and Breadcrumbs, 91
Smoked Bluefish Dip, 27
smoked, about, 104
Five-Minute Spiced Orange
Marmalade, 155
Four-Spice Gingerbread, 156, 157
fragrance, creating Christmas, 35
Fresh Herb Place Cards, 178
FRUIT. See also individual names
of fruits
Boysenberry and Grapefruit
Preserves, 153
Christmas Pudding with Brandy
Butter, 136
Cranberry, Tangerine and
Blueberry Sauce, 100
Golden Fruitcake, 152
Holiday Fruitcake, 29, 34
Mini Mincemeat Pies, 15
Orange-Currant Scones, 16, 17
Pear and Kumquat Topiary
Tree, 184, 185
Prosciutto Rolls with Arugula and
Figs, 54
Steamed Pumpkin Bread with
Walnuts and Dates, 130, 131
Wild Rice Dressing with Pearl
Onions, Dried Cherries and
Apricots, 120, 121
Winter Fruit Chutney, 157
Winter Fruit Place Cards, 178
Fudgy Hazelnut Brownies, 167
Garlic-studded Racks of Lamb, 93
Gianduia Gold Cups, 170
gift wrap ideas, 159

Ginger and Spice Shortbread
    Diamonds, 34
Gingerbread Cake with Maple
    Whipped Cream, 139
GLAZES & ICINGS
    Maple Icing, 162
    Orange Glaze, 42
    Royal Icing, 182
Goat Cheese, Artichoke and Ham
    Strata, *71, 73*
Golden Fruitcake, 152
Golden Mashed Potatoes with Parsnips
    and Parsley, 124
GOOSE with Caramelized Apples,
    Roast, 99
GRAPEFRUIT
    Boysenberry and Grapefruit
        Preserves, 153
    Orange- and Balsamic-glazed
        Roast Duck, 100
GRAVIES. *See* Sauces & Gravies
Green Chili Corn Bread, 80
HAM. *See also* Bacon; Pork; Prosciutto
    Baked Pasta with Ham, Tomatoes
        and Cheese, 47
    Goat Cheese, Artichoke and Ham
        Strata, *71, 73*
    Honey-roasted Ham and
        Turkey with Dried Cherry
        Relish, 78, *79*
    Marmalade-glazed Ham with
        Pineapple Relish, 88, *89*
HAZELNUTS
    Broiled Oysters with Hazelnut
        Pesto, 108
    Chocolate-dipped Hazelnut
        Biscotti, 150, *152*
    Fudgy Hazelnut Brownies, 167
    Gianduia Gold Cups, 170
    Herb-crusted Beef Tenderloin with
        Bell Pepper Relish, 92
    Herb-stuffed Leg of Lamb with
        Parsnips, Potatoes and
        Pumpkin, *94, 95*
Holiday Eggnog, 27
Holiday Fruitcake, *29,* 34
Honey-brined Turkey with Cream
    Gravy, 98
Honey-Pecan Pumpkin Pie, 138
Honey-roasted Ham and Turkey with
    Dried Cherry Relish, 78, *79*
Hot Cucumber and Watercress
    Soup, 112, *113*
ICE CREAM
    Double Chocolate-Mint Chip Ice
        Cream Sundaes, 51
    Individual Frozen Cake "Presents"
        with Strawberry Sauce, 58
ICINGS. *See* Glazes & Icings

LAMB
    Garlic-studded Racks of Lamb, 93
    Herb-stuffed Leg of Lamb with
        Parsnips, Potatoes and
        Pumpkin, 94, *95*
    Lamb Stock, 93
    Skewered Lamb with Almond-
        Mint Pesto, 103
Layered Peppermint Crunch
    Bark, 168, *170*
Layered Potato, Onion and Celery
    Root Casserole, 82
Layered Rice Salad with Red and
    Green Salsas, *38,* 40
Leaves under Glass Place Cards, 179
LEEKS
    Butternut Squash Soup with Cider
        Cream, 114, *115*
    Creamy Leek Soup with Bacon
        and Shallots, 112
    Hot Cucumber and Watercress
        Soup, 112, *113*
    Leek, Mushroom and Bacon
        Dressing, 120
    Phyllo-wrapped Salmon with
        Leeks and Red Bell Peppers, 68
LEMONS
    Double-Lemon Bars, *18,* 19
    Lemon-Parmesan Artichoke
        Bottoms, 46
Linzer Macaroon Sandwiches, 165
LOBSTER and Orange Crème
    Fraîche, Sweet Potato Soup
    with, 55
Madeira Sauce, 97
Maple Icing, 162
Marbleized White Chocolate
    Leaves, 141
Marinated Green Beans and Red
    Peppers, *79,* 81
Marmalade-glazed Ham with
    Pineapple Relish, 88, *89*
Mashed Potato Bread, 129
Mini Mincemeat Pies, 15
Mixed Green Salad with Oranges,
    Dried Cranberries and
    Pecans, 114, *115*
Mocha and Raspberry Trifle, 134, *135*
Mocha Mousse Torte, 41
Molten Chocolate Cakes, 69
MOUSSES. *See* Custards & Puddings
Mulled Cider with Winter Spices, 42
MUSHROOMS
    Leek, Mushroom and Bacon
        Dressing, 120
    Mushrooms Stuffed with Herbed
        Breadcrumbs, *107,* 109
    Olive Oil Infused with Porcini and
        Rosemary, 159

Potato and Shiitake Mushroom
    Gratin, 57
Shiitake Scrambled Eggs and
    Caviar on Toasts, 109
Wild Mushroom and Crab
    Cheesecake, 25
Wild-Mushroom Bread
    Pudding, 123
Wild Rice and Wild Mushroom
    Soup, 111
nonreactive cookware, about, 157
NUTS. *See also individual names of nuts*
    Coconut-Macadamia Crescents, 163
    Orange-Pistachio Lace Cookies, 165
    preparation, 154
    Sweet and Spicy Candied Nuts, 154
Olive Oil Infused with Porcini and
    Rosemary, 159
ORANGES
    Carrot Puree with Ginger and
        Orange, 124
    Chocolate-Orange Bûche de
        Noël, 30, *31*
    Five-Minute Spiced Orange
        Marmalade, 155
    Mixed Green Salad with Oranges,
        Dried Cranberries and
        Pecans, 114, *115*
    Orange- and Balsamic-glazed
        Roast Duck, 100
    Orange-Currant Scones, 16, *17*
    Orange Glaze, 42
    Orange-Pistachio Lace Cookies, 165
    Pine Nut and Orange Fudge, 174
    Pomanders, 177
    Pumpkin Spice Cookies, 42
    Sliced Oranges with Dried
        Cranberries, *71, 73*
    Sweet Potato Soup with Lobster
        and Orange Crème Fraîche, 55
OYSTERS
    Broiled Oysters with Hazelnut
        Pesto, 108
    oysters, about, 108
Parslied Rice Pilaf, *65, 69*
PARSNIPS
    Golden Mashed Potatoes with
        Parsnips and Parsley, 124
    Herb-stuffed Leg of Lamb with
        Parsnips, Potatoes and
        Pumpkin, 94, *95*
parties, planning, 83
PASTA
    Baked Pasta with Ham, Tomatoes
        and Cheese, 47
    Roasted Eggplant Lasagna with
        Broiled Tomato Sauce, 101
PASTRY. *See also* Pies & Tarts
    Cheddar Cheese Pastry, 107

Easy Pastry Dough, 138
Peanut Butter and Chocolate Balls, 174
PEARS
    Pear and Kumquat Topiary
        Tree, 184, *185*
    Poached Pears in Red Wine
        Sauce, 145
    Warm Pear Shortcakes with
        Brandied Cream, 146
Peas with Caraway and Parmesan
    Butter, 118
PECANS
    Chewy Pecan Diamonds, 164
    Chicken, Wild Rice and Pecan
        Salad in Romaine Spears, 20, 24
    Christmas Turtles, *29, 33*
    Holiday Fruitcake, *29,* 34
    Honey-Pecan Pumpkin Pie, 138
    Honey-roasted Ham and Turkey
        with Dried Cherry Relish, 78, *79*
    Mixed Green Salad with Oranges,
        Dried Cranberries and
        Pecans, 114, *115*
    Pecan Toffee, 172, *173*
    Spiced Pecans, 54
    Wild Rice Dressing with Pearl
        Onions, Dried Cherries and
        Apricots, 120, *121*
Peppercorn, Mustard and Dill
    Vinegar, 158
PEPPERS
    Bell Pepper Relish, 92
    Green Chili Corn Bread, 80
    Marinated Green Beans and Red
        Peppers, *79,* 81
    Phyllo-wrapped Salmon with
        Leeks and Red Bell Peppers, 68
    Red Pepper and Corn Relish, 158
    Shrimp, Zucchini and Red Pepper
        Bisque, 110
    Snappy Red Bell Pepper Dip with
        Shrimp, 81
    Spiced Moroccan-Style Shrimp, 102
Photo Place Cards, 179
Phyllo-wrapped Salmon with Leeks
    and Red Bell Peppers, 68
PIES & TARTS
    Cheddar Cheese Tartlets, 107
    Chocolate-Caramel Tart, 142, *143*
    Honey-Pecan Pumpkin Pie, 138
    Mini Mincemeat Pies, 15
    Raspberry Linzer Tart, 32
PINEAPPLE
    Pineapple Relish, 89
    Spiced Moroccan-Style Shrimp, 102
PINE NUTS
    Golden Fruitcake, 152
    Pine Nut and Orange Fudge, 174
Piquant Cranberry Sauce, 122

Poached Pears in Red Wine Sauce, 145
Pomanders, 177
Poppy Seed Dinner Rolls, 126
PORK. *See also* Bacon; Ham;
        Prosciutto
    Apple Stuffing, *90,* 91
    Crown Roast of Pork with Apple
        Stuffing and Cider Gravy, 90
    Spicy Beef and Sausage
        Tacos, *37,* 39
POTATOES. *See also* Sweet Potatoes
    Golden Mashed Potatoes with
        Parsnips and Parsley, 124
    Herb-stuffed Leg of Lamb with
        Parsnips, Potatoes and
        Pumpkin, 94, *95*
    Layered Potato, Onion and Celery
        Root Casserole, 82
    Mashed Potato Bread, 129
    Potato and Apple Galette with
        Sage, 125
    Potato and Shiitake Mushroom
        Gratin, 57
PROJECTS
    Caramel-dipped Apples, 176
    Christmas centerpiece, *180,* 181
    Easy Gingerbread House, 182
    Fresh Herb Place Cards, 178
    gift wrap ideas, 159
    Leaves under Glass Place
        Cards, 179
    ornaments for children, 181
    Pear and Kumquat Topiary
        Tree, 184, *185*
    Photo Place Cards, 179
    Pomanders, 177
    Stained-Glass Cookie
        Ornaments, 183
    Winter Fruit Place Cards, 178
    Winter Garden Place Cards, 179
PROSCIUTTO
    Prosciutto Rolls with Arugula and
        Figs, 54
    Prosciutto-wrapped Asparagus, 24
PUDDINGS. *See* Custards & Puddings
PUMPKIN
    Herb-stuffed Leg of Lamb with
        Parsnips, Potatoes and
        Pumpkin, 94, *95*
    Honey-Pecan Pumpkin Pie, 138
    Pumpkin Spice Cookies, 42
    Steamed Pumpkin Bread with
        Walnuts and Dates, 130, *131*
RASPBERRIES
    Christmas Tree Shortbread, 162
    Linzer Macaroon Sandwiches, 165
    Mocha and Raspberry
        Trifle, 134, *135*
    Raspberry Linzer Tart, 32

Red Pepper and Corn Relish, 158
Red Snapper Roasted with Fennel and
    Breadcrumbs, 91
RELISHES. *See* Condiments &
    Relishes
RICE
    Chicken, Wild Rice and Pecan
        Salad in Romaine Spears, 20, 24
    Layered Rice Salad with Red and
        Green Salsas, *38,* 40
    Parslied Rice Pilaf, *65,* 69
    Rice Pilaf with Chestnuts, 119
    Wild Rice and Wild Mushroom
        Soup, 111
    Wild Rice Dressing with Pearl
        Onions, Dried Cherries and
        Apricots, 120, *121*
Roasted Eggplant Lasagna with
    Broiled Tomato Sauce, 101
Roast Goose with Caramelized
    Apples, 99
roasting meat and poultry, about, 96
Royal Icing, 182
SALADS
    Belgian Endive with Egg
        Salad, 82
    Caesar Salad, 46
    Chicken, Wild Rice and Pecan
        Salad in Romaine Spears, 20, 24
    Curly Endive Salad with Radishes,
        Coriander and Bacon, 117
    Layered Rice Salad with Red and
        Green Salsas, *38,* 40
    Marinated Green Beans and Red
        Peppers, *79,* 81
    Mixed Green Salad with Oranges,
        Dried Cranberries and
        Pecans, 114, *115*
    serving, 116
    Smoked Chicken Salad on Corn
        Bread Triangles, 80
    Smoked Salmon and Fennel Salad
        with Horseradish Dressing, 116
    Spinach, Beet and Walnut
        Salad, 117
SALMON
    Phyllo-wrapped Salmon with
        Leeks and Red Bell Peppers, 68
    Smoked Salmon and Fennel Salad
        with Horseradish Dressing, 116
    Smoked Salmon and Goat Cheese
        Crostini, 104
    Smoked-Salmon Sandwiches with
        Red Onion Relish, *12,* 14
    Smoked Salmon with Sour Cream-
        Caper Sauce, 78
SANDWICHES
    Smoked-Salmon Sandwiches with
        Red Onion Relish, *12,* 14

Smoked-Turkey Sandwiches with
  Arugula Mayonnaise, *12, 14*
SAUCES & GRAVIES
  Broiled Tomato Sauce with
    Roasted Garlic, 101
  Chive and Caper Sauce, 105
  Cranberry, Tangerine and
    Blueberry Sauce, 100
  Madeira Sauce, 97
  Piquant Cranberry Sauce, 122
SAUCES, DESSERT
  Chocolate-Almond Sauce, 151, *152*
  Coffee-Caramel Sauce, *152,* 153
  Dark Chocolate Honey-Almond
    Fondue, 74, *75*
  Strawberry Sauce, 59
Sesame-Onion Crescent Rolls, 131
Shiitake Scrambled Eggs and Caviar
  on Toasts, 109
SHRIMP
  Shrimp, Zucchini and Red Pepper
    Bisque, 110
  Snappy Red Bell Pepper Dip with
    Shrimp, 81
  Spiced Moroccan-Style
    Shrimp, 102
Skewered Lamb with Almond-Mint
  Pesto, 103
Sliced Oranges with Dried
  Cranberries, *71, 73*
Smoked Bluefish Dip, 27
Smoked Chicken Salad on Corn Bread
  Triangles, 80
Smoked Salmon and Fennel Salad
  with Horseradish Dressing, 116
Smoked Salmon and Goat Cheese
  Crostini, 104
Smoked-Salmon Sandwiches with Red
  Onion Relish, *12, 14*
Smoked Salmon with Sour Cream-
  Caper Sauce, 78
Smoked-Turkey Sandwiches with
  Arugula Mayonnaise, *12, 14*
Snappy Red Bell Pepper Dip with
  Shrimp, 81
SOUPS
  Butternut Squash Soup with Cider
    Cream, 114, *115*
  Cream of Zucchini and Anise
    Soup, 66, *67*
  Creamy Leek Soup with Bacon
    and Shallots, 112
  garnishes for, 113
  Hot Cucumber and Watercress
    Soup, 112, *113*
  Lamb Stock, 93
  preparation of, 113
  Shrimp, Zucchini and Red Pepper
    Bisque, 110

Sweet Potato Soup with Lobster
  and Orange Crème Fraîche, 55
Wild Rice and Wild Mushroom
  Soup, 111
Spiced Moroccan-Style Shrimp, 102
Spiced Pecans, 54
Spiced Snowflakes, 161
Spicy Beef and Sausage Tacos, *37, 39*
SPINACH
  Corn and Winter Squash with
    Spinach, 119
  Spinach, Beet and Walnut Salad, 117
Stained-Glass Cookie Ornaments, 183
star anise, about, 155
Steamed Pumpkin Bread with
  Walnuts and Dates, 130, *131*
STOCKS. *See* Soups
Strawberry Sauce, 59
STUFFINGS & DRESSINGS
  about, 121
  Apple Stuffing, *90,* 91
  Leek, Mushroom and Bacon
    Dressing, 120
  Wild Rice Dressing with Pearl
    Onions, Dried Cherries and
    Apricots, 120, *121*
Sweet and Spicy Candied Nuts, 154
Sweet and Spicy Olives, *21, 22*
SWEET POTATOES
  Brown Sugar-glazed Sweet Potatoes
    with Marshmallows, 123
  Sweet Potato Soup with Lobster
    and Orange Crème Fraîche, 55
TARTS. *See* Pies & Tarts
tea, serving, 16
TOMATILLOS
  about, 40
  Layered Rice Salad with Red and
    Green Salsas, *38,* 40
TOMATOES
  Baked Pasta with Ham, Tomatoes
    and Cheese, 47
  Broiled Tomato Sauce with
    Roasted Garlic, 101
TORTILLAS
  Chicken and Corn
    Enchiladas, *38, 39*
  Spicy Beef and Sausage Tacos, *37, 39*
TURKEY
  Honey-brined Turkey with Cream
    Gravy, 98
  Honey-roasted Ham and Turkey
    with Dried Cherry Relish, 78, *79*
  Smoked-Turkey Sandwiches with
    Arugula Mayonnaise, *12,* 14
VEGETABLES. *See also individual
  names of vegetables*
  Broccoli and Cauliflower with
    Chive Butter, 125

Hot Cucumber and Watercress
  Soup, 112, *113*
Layered Potato, Onion and Celery
  Root Casserole, 82
Peas with Caraway and Parmesan
  Butter, 118
Prosciutto-wrapped Asparagus, 24
Roasted Eggplant Lasagna with
  Broiled Tomato Sauce, 101
Spinach, Beet and Walnut
  Salad, 117
Winter Crudités with Walnut-
  Garlic Dip, 106
WALNUTS
  Chocolate Chip, Cherry and
    Walnut Rugelach, 166
  Chocolate-Walnut Rum
    Balls, *13,* 19
  Cranberry-Walnut Braid, *132,* 133
  Holiday Fruitcake, *29,* 34
  Sliced Oranges with Dried
    Cranberries, *71, 73*
  Spinach, Beet and Walnut
    Salad, 117
  Steamed Pumpkin Bread with
    Walnuts and Dates, 130, *131*
  Winter Crudités with Walnut-
    Garlic Dip, 106
Warm Pear Shortcakes with Brandied
  Cream, 146
Wild Mushroom and Crab
  Cheesecake, 25
Wild-Mushroom Bread Pudding, 123
Wild Rice and Wild Mushroom
  Soup, 111
Wild Rice Dressing with Pearl Onions,
  Dried Cherries and
  Apricots, 120, *121*
Winter Crudités with Walnut-Garlic
  Dip, 106
Winter Fruit Chutney, 157
Winter Fruit Place Cards, 178
Winter Garden Place Cards, 179
ZUCCHINI
  Cream of Zucchini and Anise
    Soup, 66, *67*
  Shrimp, Zucchini and Red Pepper
    Bisque, 110

Acknowledgments

The following people contributed the recipes included in this book: Bruce Aidells; Nicole Aloni; Arman's at Park Lane, Mountain Brook, Alabama; John Ash; Yvonne Askew; Mary Barber; Barrington Country Bistro, Barrington, Illinois; Carrie Beilke; Veronica Betancourt; Lena Cederham Birnbaum; Carole Bloom; Emma and Simon Burns; Lauren Chattman; Lynda Chernek; Janet and Bob Cole; Sara Corpening; Lane Crowther; Robin Davis; Jodi and Jeff DuFresne; Suzanne Dunaway; Sue Ellison; Emeril's, New Orleans, Louisiana; Barbara Pool Fenzl; Janet Fletcher; Gerri Gilliland; Grand View Beach Hotel, St. Vincent and the Grenadines, West Indies; Sophie Grigson; Dahlia and Andy Haas; Ken Haedrich; Mike Hessler; Karen Kaplan; Jacqueline Karamanos; Mollie Katzen; Jeanne Thiel Kelley; Kristine Kidd; La Bastide de Tourtour, Toutour, France; Donata Maggipinto; Michael McLaughlin; Alice Medrich; Jinx and Jefferson Morgan; Selma Brown Morrow; Tootie and Jimmy O'Flaherty; Rochelle Palermo; Caprial Pence; Peter Reinhart; Wendy Remer; Ristorante Araxi, Whistler, British Columbia; Claudia Roden; Rick Rodgers; Betty Rosbottom; Michele Sbrana; Tracy Scott; Lana Sills; Marie Simmons; Hatice Sivrican; Scott Snyder; Kate and Carl Swope; Sarah Tenaglia; Connie Vlasis; Charlotte Walker; Cynthia Wilson; Mike Wilson.

The following people contributed the photographs included in this book: Jack Andersen; Noel Barnhurst; David Bishop; Wyatt Counts; Reed Davis; Julie Dennis; Sandra Johnson; Michael La Riche; Brian Leatart; Paul Moore; Jeff Sarpa; Ellen Silverman; Elizabeth Zeschin.

Original photography, front and back jackets and pages 1-86, 95, 102, 108, 110, 118, 126, 134, 148, 149, 150, 156, 158, 160, 168, 173, 175, 176 and 185 by Quentin Bacon. Food stylist: Rori Spinelli. Prop Stylist: Suzie Smith.

Special thanks to Richard and Ann Sarnoff and Libby Borden for the generous use of their homes.

Shopping Directory

Jacket: "Crosshaven" dessert plate by Waterford Fine China, available at most major department stores or from www.waterford-usa.com.

Page 10: Wreath from Bloom, 212-620-5666. Stockings by Little Souls from Ad Hoc Softwares, 888-748-4852.

Page 11: "Kells" rim soup bowl by Waterford Fine China (see above).

Page 21: Square dinner plate in cream, variegated horn bowl (with olives), tapered bowl in cream and hand-blown glass decanter all from Simon Pearce, 212-334-2393. Stainless tray and cocktail napkins from Pottery Barn, 212-579-8477. Glass ice bucket from Banana Republic, 888-277-8953. "Stack Glasses" by Konstantin Grcic for iittala from Ad Hoc Softwares (see above).

Page 45: "Paloma" flutes from Crate&Barrel, 800-996-9960.

Page 53: "Kells" rim soup bowls and bread-and-butter plates and "Crosshaven" dinner plates, all by Waterford Fine China (see above). "Kells" wineglasses (with wide gold band) and "Golden Lismore Tall" wineglasses, both by Waterford Crystal, available at most major department stores or from www.waterford-usa.com.

Page 65: Linen napkins by Area from Ad Hoc Softwares (see above).

Page 71: "Tivoli Bamboo" napkins by Le Jacquard Français from Ad Hoc Softwares (see above).

Page 84: "Olde Avesbury" china by Royal Crown Derby from Geary's, 310-273-4741.

Page 92: "Tassel" silver-plate carving set by Leeber Limited, 800-533-2372.

Page 98: Pewter platter by Match and horn carving set by Jean Pierre Gerber, both from Geary's (see above).

Page 104: "Sparte Platinum" salad plate by Bernardaud, 800-884-7775.

Page 117: "Nacres Sand" dinner plate by Puiforcat from Geary's (see above).

Page 146: "Aztec" glass plate and bowl by Peter Crisp from Barneys New York, 212-826-8900. "Bernadotte" sterling silver spoon by Georg Jensen, 212-759-6457.

All other items are privately owned.